ENDORSEMENTS

"The Key of David: Loving God and Neighbor is an outstanding book! Angela captures an extraordinary view of David's life through extensive research and brilliant revelation. She articulates a perfect marriage between theological insights and practical application. I highly recommend this book to both individuals and churches who desire to receive a deeper understanding of God's redemptive power through the life of David."

MICHAEL THORNTON
Senior Associate Pastor Global River Church
Founder/Director of Ignite Ministries Inc.
Author of *Fire in the Carolinas* and *Ignite Cities*

"The Key of David series has been a tremendous blessing to edit. It has brought clarity and confirmation to many circumstances that I have walked through in my journey with the Creator. Every time I worked on a new chapter, I found something that I needed to hear—and precisely at that moment in my life. Even more, it encouraged me to continue to master the spiritual lessons I have been learning. I'm very excited to see this book in print, and I plan on adding the set to my bookshelf. I know the content in these books will bless and empower many others."

ELISA EATON
Living Colors & Expressions

"The Key of David was eloquently written, personable, and relatable. I would give this book 5 stars! The writer connected with the reader in a unique way, and it was very clear we all could relate to the characters in the story. To the potential reader, I encourage you to sit

back, kick your feet up, and pray before you open this book! Be ready to encounter some truths, avoid some pitfalls, repent, trust God's timing, walk in your calling, and connect the truth to your life in a way that's transformational! You are in for a special treat, and it's a page worth turning."

PRECIOUS SIMONE
INNERstrength Coach
Founder of INNERgized Coaching & Consulting, LLC
Author of *Confronting the Age-Old Question: Why Me?*

"*The Key of David* is the most thought-provoking and insightful study I have ever read about the life of David. I was amazed at the revelation I received about my own life and the baggage I have hidden behind that has kept me from walking in the fullness of what Yahweh has for me. I had several 'aha' moments that gave me clarity into my own life. If you are looking for more insight into your own life or just want to study more about David, this is the book. The Key of David is a must-have for your personal library and one you are sure to pick up often! I absolutely love it!"

TASHA KELLY
Tasha Kelly Ministries
Author of *Not My Mother's Daughter*

"*The Key of David* is one of the most beautiful literary tapestries of our lifetime on the subject of the true biblical King David. Woven within its pages are a deep academic survey of the events of David's life, a complete Hebraic understanding of the prophetic connections to the life of the Messiah, and a heartfelt thread of practical application that is found on virtually every page. This book is an absolute must-have for every serious student of the Bible."

JIM STALEY
Staley Family Ministries

"*The Key of David* beautifully unlocks the intricate life of David and the prophetic tapestry woven into it like none other. Angela not only illuminates the Scripture beautifully but weaves it all together to show us how to practically apply it to our lives. It is one of the most captivating books I have ever read. I truly believe this book is a must-read for anyone wanting to dig deeper into the life of David and have their eyes opened to many prophetic and symbolic connections."

CHERYL STALEY
Staley Family Ministries

"Angela Dawn chronicles the life of King David with meaty new insights for the modern Bible scholar to chew on. Her comprehensive study of the Davidic narratives will challenge any student of Scripture to grow in their understanding of God's love. I love what *The Key of David* had to teach me that I wouldn't necessarily have known by just reading the biblical account. I believe Angela's work to be divinely inspired. Clearly, she has been seeking the Source, for her book overflows with the fruit of love, joy, peace, patience, kindness, goodness, faithfulness, gentleness, and self-control.

From Genesis to Revelation, she spans the lengths of Scripture, pointing out the importance of King David's life, legacy, and heart. Readers travel with God's beloved king as he manages his dysfunctional family, rules a nation, and seeks pinnacle heights of intimacy with his Creator. What we are to do with the love we've been shown is the question we must answer at the crux of this book."

MALIEA LUQUIN

THE KEY OF DAVID

LOVING GOD AND NEIGHBOR VOL. 1

AN IN-DEPTH LIFE APPLICATION STUDY OF
THE LIFE AND TIMES OF KING DAVID

ANGELA DAWN

DIVINE PURPOSE PUBLISHING
CELEBRATION, FLORIDA

Cover Art and Jacket Design by David Munoz Prophetic Art
www.davidmunozart.com

Editor: Elisa Eaton
Living Colors and Expressions
www.livingcolorsandexpressions.com

DiViNE Purpose Publishing
P.O. Box 471004
Celebration, FL. 34747
www.divinepurposepublishing.com
" Igniting and Promoting Purpose"

Scripture quotations are taken from the following sources:

Unless otherwise indicated, all Scripture quotations are from the King James Version, public domain. Scriptures cited as AMP are from the Amplified® Bible (AMP), Copyright © 2015 by The Lockman Foundation. Used by permission. www.Lockman.org Scriptures cited as AMPC are from the Amplified® Bible (AMPC), Copyright © 1954, 1958, 1962, 1964, 1965, 1987 by The Lockman Foundation Used by permission. www.Lockman.org Scriptures cited as BSB are from The Holy Bible, Berean Study Bible, BSB Copyright ©2016 by Bible Hub. Used by Permission. All Rights Reserved Worldwide. Scriptures cited as NIV are from THE HOLY BIBLE, NEW INTERNATIONAL VERSION®, NIV® Copyright © 1973, 1978, 1984, 2011 by Biblica, Inc.® Used by permission. All rights reserved worldwide. Scriptures cited as NKJV are from the New King James Version®. Copyright © 1982 by Thomas Nelson. Used by permission. All rights reserved. Scriptures cited as YLT are from Young's Literal Translation, public domain.

A portion of net proceeds from the sales of this book, will be sent to the following ministries: Samaritan's Purse, Open Doors International, One For Israel and Operation Underground Railroad. These donations of funds by the author, in no way implies any endorsement of this book by any of the ministries, or their representatives.

ISBN: 978-1-948812-03-0 (paperback)
ISBN: 978-1-948812-04-7 (ePub)

Printed in the United States of America

I dedicate this book to my Creator and King, YHVH,
and to every precious human on earth,
each one a special treasure in the heart of their Creator.

Angela Dawn

MISSION STATEMENT

As the author of The Key of David: Loving God and Neighbor, my mission is to bring glory to the name of the true and living God of Israel - YHVH. Having been called by Him to be an ambassador of the Messiah in this generation, my mission is also to share the amazing love, grace, and mercy of our Creator with every child of God. Through David's life story, I reveal YHVH's eternal plan of redemption through the Messiah, the reality of spiritual warfare against us, and the way to victoriously overcome it.

It is the goal of this study to bring incredible clarity to the Scriptures, thereby eliminating confusion and misunderstandings in YHVH's Word. I also seek to dispel false judgments against YHVH's character and nature, especially in the Old Testament. Many throughout history have judged Him to be a harsh and cruel God of judgment, leading them to discard a large portion of the Holy Scriptures or reject Him altogether. My aim is to help the reader have a greater understanding of God's enduring Fatherly love for them, which has existed since the beginning of time.

Having walked through a tremendous amount of adversity, with God's help to overcome, it is also my earnest heart's desire to bring healing and encouragement to those who may be currently walking through adversity. I hope to show the reader how to practically apply YHVH's Word to empower them in facilitating healing, reconciliation, and restoration in every area of their lives (marriage, family and social relationships, dealing with enemies, etc.). The overarching purpose of The Key of David: Loving God and Neighbor is to facilitate restoration of brotherly love and unity among YHVH's people. Additionally, this study will help every child of God become a more perfect reflection of the Father's love and the Good Shepherd's heart, in every area of their life. This study will facilitate us in our preparation as the beautiful and pleasing bride who is ready for the Bridegroom (the Messiah) at His coming.

TABLE OF CONTENTS

ACKNOWLEDGMENTS

First and foremost I acknowledge my Creator, King, and Heavenly Father (YHVH), His Messiah, and Ruach ha-Kodesh (Holy Spirit) as my head Teacher. Without Him I would have no true understanding of His Word and spiritual matters.

I also acknowledge all the wonderful people YHVH has blessed my life with to support and help guide me to this season. Thank you to my husband, all five of my beautiful children, my parents, grandparents, and all the rest of my dear family and friends. I am grateful for your love and prayers for me throughout the thick and thin of my life journey.

I especially want to thank the many shepherds after YHVH's own heart, whose obedience to preach YHVH's Word and serve our family in prayer and wise counsel has been an immeasurable blessing.

Special thanks are due to Maliea Luquin for her preliminary editing contributions, Felicia Sinclair for her assistance with preliminary marketing and author photography, and the Staley family for financial assistance with publishing expenses.

INTRODUCTION

The prophet Isaiah wrote that the holder of "the key of the house of David" opens what "none shall shut" and shuts what "none shall open" (Isa. 22:22 KJV). In our lives, we have all faced closed doors that we wish would open and have desired some doors we wish had never opened to be shut. Therefore, it behooves us to understand what this key is and how we can get its mechanism to work in our lives.

YHVH[1] said He would set the aforementioned key on the shoulder of His "servant." This is a term used for His chosen ones, anyone who brings His Word to others, brings His Word honor, or carries out His will for His people (Isa. 22:20-22). "My servant" is also a term that is specifically used to refer to King David (2 Sam. 7:8) and to the prophesied Messiah of Israel, the Son of David (Isa. 42:1, Ezek. 37:24).[2] As we embark on an in-depth life application study of King David's life, it will become clear that the key of David is love—love for both YHVH and neighbor.

King David's life is chronicled with more detail than almost any other character of the Bible. We are allowed to follow his life from his teen years to his death in a sweeping narrative. The precision and attention to detail by the writers of the *Tanach* (also known as the Old Testament) is evidence to me that they were inspired by the One who orchestrated the events and wanted us to glean wisdom from the chronicles of David's life. How many of us dove deep into all the accounts of King David in our lives? I will be the first to admit that I spent two decades as a believer having never thoroughly studied the substantial details of King David's life and times.

Surely, almost all of us are familiar with the classic Davidic story elements: his anointing by the hands of Samuel, his musical skills and how he was called upon to play soothing music for Saul, his famous victory over Goliath, his infamous sin with Bathsheba, and his preparations for Solomon's temple. We are all familiar with the psalms he wrote; but have we truly gleaned to the utmost depth all that we can learn from the annals of David's life? Over the course of nearly a few decades of attending various churches, I had yet to experience such an in-depth study of his life in any setting. Though I have read through the entire Bible and the chronicles of David's life several times over the decades of my faith journey, it now seems I was always doing just that: reading through and barely scratching the surface.

However, over these last few years, something happened in my life and in my local community that prompted me to dive deeper into studying David's life. The search began in the midst of a crisis involving significant strife and division in our family's local congregation. It was not my first experience with strife and division in a congregational setting. However, this most recent experience was the most traumatic and deeply wounding experience for my family and many other dear brothers and sisters.

Through fasting and prayer, I sought the Heavenly Father to understand why tremendously painful events were being allowed to unravel inside our congregation. He gave me both a vision and a word of wisdom related to David that has changed me forever. Then, as it happened naturally, my daily devotional through-the-Bible study schedule brought me through a chronological study in the Tree of Life Version (TLV) of the chronicles and psalms of David's life.[3] It was the first time I had ever done a chronological study of his life. Through the study, it became very apparent to me that unless we study the various writings about David, and the psalms that he wrote over the course of his life in chronological order, we can miss an incredible amount of pertinent detail.

As I began to read and study David's saga this time through the Scriptures, the Heavenly Father made known the vision and word He had given me in deeper ways. He gave me so much prophetic revelation and insight into David's saga that each day I leapt out of my seat astounded by the clarity, depth, and richness. Have you ever had one of those "aha" moments with Scripture where you see something that you have never seen, even though you have read the same thing several times before? Yeah, I had so many of those "aha" moments that I felt like a kid in a candy store being allowed to taste every offering by a generous shop owner!

While engaging with David's narrative, I experienced an intensely deep, personal connection to David's own faith journey. I saw numerous parallels to my life and the lives of fellow brothers and sisters in Messiah. I learned many lessons from the Heavenly Father as I traversed my own wilderness and walked side by side with my brothers and sisters in theirs. These lessons deepened my understanding of David's experiences and how YHVH used every one of them to work together for good, just as He was doing for us.

In my own mind, the revelations the Father had downloaded to me the first time through David's narrative were already sufficiently incredible to complete this book. However, in the course of the time of writing my manuscript, I had come full circle to reading through the chronology of David's life a second time, this time using another chronological study in the King James Version (KJV).[4] It was certainly not by accident either, as there were divinely ordered delays that kept me from publishing this book before its time. It became increasingly apparent that the Father wanted to reveal even deeper truths.

Through both studies, the Father continued pulling out principles and truths from both testaments of the Bible, showing how they were connected to David's journey and his family experience. Such revelations, it seems, cannot be contained. They are a fire in my belly, ardently burning for the edification of all who would read.

I invite you to join me on this journey through the garnered revelations of David's life. I guarantee that every reader will personally identify with his human journey, triumphs, and struggles, as well as those of the other people in his life. His life paints the prophetic picture of every person who is chosen by YHVH, heeds His call, and seeks to follow Him with their whole heart. Like our own journey, David's journey was filled with mountaintop experiences and deep wilderness valleys, victories and disappointments, times of worship, and egregious bouts of sinfulness. David's life serves as a treasure trove of lessons for our lives to be enriched with.

We all know David best as the man after YHVH's own heart. And isn't that how most of us earnestly want to be known? But do we really know what made him or what makes us people after YHVH's own heart? Some say David's worship merited him this title. Some even think that the key of David was the distinct sound frequency made only by the special tuning of his *kinnor* (a type of lyre).[5] While some scientific evidence suggests that sound frequencies are powerful enough to effect change in physical properties of some matter,[6] I do not believe a sound frequency is the key of David the Scriptures are referring to. While David truly was an unparalleled worshipper, who wrote about two-thirds of the Psalms and whose music did affect change in the spiritual realm, I do not believe his songwriting, singing, or kinnor playing alone qualifies as the key of David or defined him as a man after YHVH's own heart.

Through the psalms ascribed to David, we see his heart—all of it. They put David's raw human emotions while in the throngs of distress on a public stage, emotions mixed with his faith and hope in YHVH's help in times of trouble. The psalms open for us the door of David's heart to reveal the wrestling of his flesh and spirit in the inner man. They are not unlike our own honest prayers during similar times. Just as it is with us, sometimes what we see pouring out of David's heart through the psalms was not after YHVH's own heart of grace and mercy. At other times, what poured out of David's heart was a pure reflection of YHVH's love.

As we will soon discover, I believe it was ultimately the shepherd's heart that YHVH saw in David from his youth that primarily defined him as a man after YHVH's own heart—a heart continually refined and developed at broader depth through all that David walked through. David was a good shepherd, willing to lay down his own life for his father Jesse's sheep (evidenced by his fighting off a bear, a lion, and his fight against Goliath, to name a few). This was the very quality YHVH looked for in a man who would shepherd and rule over His flock of Israel. As both shepherd and king, David qualifies as both a prophetic archetype and the forefather of the Messiah of Israel who would be sent to shepherd the lost sheep of Israel.

In fact, we are going to explore just how prevalent the message of the Messiah is in the minutest details of David's life. Throughout this first volume and the next, we will see the prophetic foreshadowing of the Messiah in nearly every chapter, even in David's most unexpected and downright ugliest moments. We will see not only the prevalence of the Messianic message and the abundantly clear revelations of the identity of the Messiah, but we will also see a tremendous amount of prophetic revelation and insight into the schemes and plots of *ha-Satan* (Hebrew for the adversary or Satan).[7] The best part of that: we will learn how to overcome the adversary's devices.

This book is designed to be an in-depth, life-application study. Therefore, I encourage you to pray before reading each day that YHVH will enlighten you with His understanding and revelation. I ask you to read every Bible passage and Strong's Hebrew or Greek word that is referenced. Though I have taken great care and diligence for accuracy, do not just take my word for anything; test everything through prayer and personal study as the noble-minded Bereans did (Acts 17:11). I certainly do not claim to have all the right answers or to have reached the bottom depths of revelation's well. Only the *Ruach ha-Kodesh* (Hebrew for the Holy Spirit)[8] can claim that!

As I share the revelations I garnered from the *Ruach ha-Kodesh*, my prayer is for them to act as catalysts, opening up even deeper and more appreciable truths for you. I highly encourage you to take time at the end of each chapter to reflect and journal as you experience His revelation. Therefore, I have provided a journey journal at the end of each chapter to help facilitate deeper reflection and note-taking. Many of these questions are questions that I ask of myself as I engage with the biblical narrative.

This study and the journey journal are intended to act as a mirror to every student of the Bible, to help us see what we might not otherwise be able to see. So, I encourage you to pause at every question and answer it honestly. Any time you feel the prick of YHVH's conviction in your heart as you identify with different characters and situations, I encourage you to take a moment and bring it before Him in prayer and repentance so that you may receive His grace, mercy, and forgiveness. I pray that this study edifies you and builds up your faith in YHVH and His eternal plan of the Messianic redemption of humankind in exponential ways, just as it has mine.

There are simply so many biblical principles that can be found in the annals surrounding David's life. Honestly, more than a kid in a candy store, on first discovery I felt as though I was a traveler on the road to Emmaus, walking alongside *Yeshua* (Hebrew for Jesus), listening to Him proclaim of Himself in the volume of the Davidic chronicles and psalms (Luke 24:13-25). My hope and prayer as you read this book is for you to feel like you are walking this road with us. So, I invite you to strap on your walking sandals and join us for the first leg of our journey, from David's anointing through his carrying the Ark of the Covenant into Jerusalem. As we follow the course of his life, it will become increasingly clear that the key of the house of David is love. Love serves as the key to open the heart of YHVH and the heart of humankind, and love shuts the door on the adversary (*ha-Satan*) and his schemes.

Blessings and Shalom!

*Note to the reader: There are many debates about the names of our Creator, Messiah, and adversary among different denominational and inter-denominational groups. As I have been called to cast my nets wide as far as audience and to avoid as much offense as possible, I was led to use the most neutral, original Hebrew names of our Creator, our Messiah, and our adversary consistently throughout. To help those unfamiliar with these names, I have included a parenthetical reference with the first use and have kept the Hebrew names in italics throughout. Some also include a bibliography reference for further explanation. To maintain

sensitivity for the sacred quality of the Hebrew four-letter name of our Creator, I have employed an English abbreviation of the Hebrew letters yod-heh-vav-heh (YHVH). All quotes of biblical translations that replace the sacred name of YHVH with "LORD" remain in their original form.

1
THE ANOINTING

Some people rise naturally to places of leadership because of their physical stature, family reputation, or disposition. Often those who we would consider natural leaders are poised, educated, skillful, successful, and qualified in the eyes of man. Others rise from the lowest of lows in society into places of leadership solely because they are chosen and anointed by YHVH. They might be rather quirky, uneducated, or may have only done some menial job their whole life, yet YHVH chooses and qualifies them as leaders. We are going to start off our journey by looking at both types of leaders and exploring what truly sets them apart in YHVH's eyes.

The Rise of King Saul

The Davidic saga was chronicled by the prophets Samuel, Nathan, Gad, and an unknown chronicler.[1] The saga opens in 1

Samuel 16 with the fall of Israel's tall, dark, and handsome warrior King Saul. YHVH chose and anointed Saul to lead Israel; however, Saul was disobedient to YHVH's instructions and lost his anointing. A word from Heaven's throne descended to Samuel, "How long wilt thou mourn for Saul, seeing I have rejected him from reigning over Israel?" (1 Sam. 16:1 KJV). YHVH was informing Samuel that the time of Saul's reign had passed, and He was ready to prosper a new king. Before we get to the anointing of Israel's next king, we need to answer a crucial question: what was the cause of Saul's removal from the throne?

It is important for us to start with a little background information. Saul was a descendant of the barely surviving tribe of Benjamin. His tribe was nearly annihilated by the rest of the tribes of Israel. The other tribes were incensed against the Benjamites because they fought to protect the wicked men of Gibeah, who had brutally raped and caused the death of a Levite's concubine. Much like Lot's daughters were given to placate the men of Sodom (Gen. 19:8), the Levite's concubine had been given to the wicked men of Gibeah to placate their initial desire to commit sodomy against the Levite (Jud. 19-21).

Gibeah was actually Saul's hometown (1 Sam. 10:26). The Benjamite men of Gibeah, Saul included, were considered least in the eyes of the rest of the tribes of Israel. Therefore, it is wildly ironic that YHVH's answer to the cries of Israel for a king, other than Him, would be a man of Gibeah.

When Saul first met Samuel and was told he was chosen to be king of Israel, he displayed humility. He did not think higher of himself than he ought to and even wondered how YHVH could have chosen a Benjamite to rule over Israel (1 Sam. 9:21). Saul knew he was considered least by the rest of the tribes. He seemed to believe in the *Elohim* (Hebrew for God)[2] of Israel and even tried to follow Him, yet Saul did not obey *all* His instructions.

Saul's Weaknesses as a King

When Samuel anointed Saul as king of Israel and then went to announce the newly appointed king to the masses, Saul had gone into hiding behind some baggage from which the people had to pull him out. It would appear that Saul was reluctant about stepping into YHVH's calling and anointing upon him. It is very prophetic that he was found hiding behind baggage (1 Sam. 10:1-22). In modern times, we refer to our emotional injuries and weaknesses as our "baggage." As we continue to study David's chronology in later chapters, we will clearly see that Saul had emotional baggage that would keep him from boldly walking in his anointing.

In fact, we shall discover that being driven by his emotions played a substantial role in his downfall. It will prove to be an eye-opening lesson for all of us to glean from. Unfortunately, Saul struggled with impatience, impulse control, and overconfidence to the point of deliberately overriding YHVH's specific instructions in order to carry out his own agenda. He did what was right in his own eyes, walked by his own sight, and leaned on his own understanding instead of being led by YHVH's Spirit and truth.

For example, once Saul grew impatient waiting for Samuel to arrive and perform a burnt offering on an appointed day before Israel was prepared to enter into warfare against the Philistines. Anxious to get on with the battle awaiting him, Saul decided to jump into a role that did not belong to him. He was not a priest or Levite, and yet he performed an offering to YHVH—and just moments before Samuel arrived (1 Sam. 13). It is clear from the record of Saul's very first encounter with Samuel the Prophet that Saul really had no prior experience with the protocols of proper worship of YHVH. It is also clear that he had never taken part in a divinely ordered battle against the Philistines (such as the one recorded in 1 Samuel 7), for he did not even recognize the famous prophet of Israel at first meeting (1 Sam. 9:18).

Despite his ignorance and inexperience, YHVH still expected Saul to be obedient to His commandments spoken through His prophet Samuel. Samuel specifically instructed Saul to wait seven days until he came to the battlefront to give him further direction. Unfortunately, Saul's armies grew afraid and started to scatter in Samuel's absence. Yet these circumstances were a test from YHVH to see if Saul would remain obedient to His Word and the authority that had been placed over him no matter what. Needless to say, Saul failed the test miserably.

Saul's impatience, disobedience, and disregard for authority led to YHVH prophesying the early termination of his kingship. His actions also set in motion the search for a man after YHVH's own heart to replace Saul as king (1 Sam. 13:13-14). Have you ever been impatient waiting on someone else to carry out their appointed task, jumped into a role that did not belong to you, or usurped the authority placed over you because you thought the circumstances demanded it? I surely have, in more times and ways than I would like to admit or could possibly contain in this chapter!

The Amalekite Blunder

Another example of Saul's disobedience was when he had been specifically instructed to utterly destroy the Amalekites, including their king, every last man, woman, child, and all of their livestock (1 Sam. 15). Why did YHVH deem this necessary, by the way? Well, one must know the history of the Amalekites and the spiritual root of Amalek to truly understand why YHVH judged them so. Amalek was the grandson of Jacob's brother Esau (Gen. 36:12), and the Amalekites were his descendants. The biblical record testifies that the anger, rage, vengeance, bitterness, jealousy, and murderous spirit that Esau had toward his brother Jacob for supposedly stealing the birthright and blessing (Gen. 27:36) was passed down to his grandson Amalek and continued to live on in his descendants.

The Amalekites wanted the birthright and all the blessings of Jacob because they believed they were rightfully theirs. This proved itself out after the exodus from Egypt. The Amalekites heard about the descendants of Jacob (Israel) coming out of the land with the wealth of the Egyptians. They warred against Israel in an effort to take the possessions for themselves. YHVH spoke to Moses at that time saying that He would continually wage war against Amalek (Exod. 17:8-16). The Amalekites continued to plunder Israel for their possessions and wealth after Saul's failure to wipe them out, forcing David to deal with this generationally vengeful remnant, as we will see in future chapters.

Sixteen generations later in 474 BC, a descendant of the Amalekite King Agag, Haman the Agagite,[3] rose up against Jacob's descendants in Persia. Haman attempted to lead the Persians in a murderous mass plunder of all of Jacob's wealth. Thankfully, Haman's efforts were thwarted by Queen Esther, a courageous Jewish woman who was willing to lay down her own life to save her people. Without this historical context, it may be difficult for modern Bible readers to understand just what YHVH's heart was behind His rejection of the Amalekites.

Jacob and the people of Israel have been targeted by this same Amalekite spirit throughout history, as recent as this past century. Although any genetic link to Amalek cannot be proven, one can clearly argue that Adolf Hitler's agenda against the Jews of Europe was frighteningly similar to Haman's agenda against the Jews of Persia. And it appears that each enemy of Israel shares the same motive: just as the Amalekites aimed to decimate and pillage, the Nazi machine plundered an incredible amount of the wealth from Jacob's descendants and sought to destroy every last one of them.

Is it possible YHVH saw this iniquity growing in Amalek's descendants? Did He foresee the destruction the Amalekites would reap upon His chosen people if they were allowed to survive and continue fostering this sin inside themselves? Is it possible that YHVH's instructions to Saul were an effort to prevent future heartache and destruction for His people? Unfortunately, instead of obeying YHVH's commandment, Saul decided it would be best to show his power over the Amalekites by parading the captured Amalekite King Agag. This act was Saul's pride which went before his destruction (Prov. 16:18). Moreover, this act proliferated Israel's future tribulations; Agag's impregnated maidservant[4] somehow also escaped, and the seed of the murderous spirit of Amalek lived on in those like Haman.

In addition to leaving Agag alive, Saul also allowed the choicest of the livestock to be retained. Could it have been that Saul thought he would somehow earn kudos from YHVH if his slaughter of the Amalekite livestock came in the form of a big sacrificial burnt offering, displaying his extraordinary devotion? Was it this thought that held him back from killing the livestock as instructed? The Amalekites' livestock was not set apart for worship of the true and living *Elohim* YHVH.

The Amalekites were part of the Edomites who were idolaters and worshippers of Quas, and possibly Baal and Ashteroth.[5] Livestock raised for sacrifices to a foreign idol would be considered "unclean" and unfit for sacrifice to the true and living *Elohim* of Israel. Therefore, by using something formerly dedicated for pagan idolatry—which is strictly forbidden by YHVH's Torah (Deut. 12:4, 30-31)—Saul's sacrifice and worship would have been performed on his own terms.

Saul's Fall from the Throne

Saul seemed to have all kinds of good intentions and often used human reasoning to justify doing things his way, but YHVH was clearly displeased with Saul's good intentions. In 1 Samuel 15, He said (via Samuel the prophet), "Hath the LORD as great delight in burnt offerings and sacrifices, as in obeying the voice of the LORD? Behold, to obey is better than sacrifice, and to hearken than the fat of rams. For rebellion is as the sin of witchcraft, and stubbornness is as iniquity and idolatry. Because thou hast rejected the word of the LORD, he hath also rejected thee from being king" (1 Sam. 15:22-23). His flagrant disobedience, even after having been rebuked by YHVH once before, now sealed the judgment that YHVH had spoken in 1 Sam. 13:13-14.

Saul thought he was pretty much following YHVH's instructions and adding bonuses on top, and he truly did not see anything wrong with what he was doing. Perhaps he had never heard the Torah's record of Achan who took what was under the ban, caused Israel to run in defeat from the battle of Ai by his sin, and was ultimately stoned to death for it (Joshua 7). Maybe Saul questioned the old chronicles and figured they were just children's tales. Whatever the case may be, Saul did not seem to have enough reverence or fear of YHVH to be obedient to His Word. His willingness to let what he considered small details slide cost him his throne.

As a result of YHVH's rebuke from Samuel, Saul admitted his sin and that he feared man more than he feared YHVH. He acknowledged that he was a people pleaser and therefore not a God pleaser (Gal. 1:10). He implored YHVH for pardon so as to continue in his position as king and continue to worship YHVH, but YHVH answered that there was no pardon for what he had done. YHVH said he would not return to Saul because of his rejection of His word (1 Sam. 15:17-30). Mind you, Saul did not reject the whole word of YHVH, but just the parts that he deemed unnecessary, irrelevant, or not important to obey. In essence, Saul was exercising a pick-and-choose faith.

The worst part of Saul's discipline for this was not his loss of position as king (though he seemed to think so). The worst part was that YHVH removed His Spirit from Saul, which is equivalent to spiritual death. Some might wonder how this could be a fair and just punishment when Saul acknowledged his sin, repented, and asked for pardon. Why wasn't it granted? I believe Saul's repentance is disingenuous for a few key reasons.

First, his primary concern was maintaining his position as king. The loss of the throne was an adequate and just consequence, which he rightfully deserved but did not want to accept. This is very much like a child who gets caught and says, "I'm sorry, I'm sorry! I was wrong and I will never do that again. Please, just do not take my screen time away from me!" They are not usually sorry, nor do they feel remorse for having broken the rule. They are merely concerned about whatever consequence they have earned, and they will say or do anything to avoid that consequence.

Secondly, if Saul's repentance was genuine and he had wanted to worship YHVH, he would have continued to worship Him regardless of what happened with his position as king. We will later see that Saul may have had idols in his palace and his children, namely his daughter Michal, had household idols (1 Sam. 19:13). Saul also became consumed with bitterness and anger and did not respect or honor the sovereignty of YHVH in His judgment to make another king succeed after him. We watch his life unravel in Scripture as he spends it all trying to hang on to his kingdom and kill YHVH's next anointed, who he sees as a threat to his throne. Bitterness and anger towards YHVH's judgment is a sure sign of insincere repentance.

Lastly, I believe Saul's repentance was not genuine because YHVH did not accept it. YHVH is the only one who can see into a person's heart and know its contents. He "is the same yesterday, today, and forever" (Heb. 13:8 BSB) and in Him is "no variableness, neither shadow of turning" (James 1:17). Had Saul's repentance been genuine, YHVH would have accepted it, just as He accepted David's sincere repentance after committing adultery with Bathsheba and attempting to cover it up. The most glaring difference between Saul and David was the latter's foremost concern with losing his spiritual position in relationship to the *Ruach Ha-Kodesh*. David cared about his standing with YHVH; Saul cared about his standing with men. Saul was preoccupied with losing his worldly position as king and could not care less about his spiritual position in relationship with the *Ruach ha-Kodesh*.

Acts 10:34 and Romans 2:11 tell us YHVH does not show partiality or favoritism. In Old and New Testament alike, we learn that YHVH does not "have any pleasure in the death of the wicked" (Ezek. 18:23 BSB), but desires that all come to repentance (John 3:16). However, when we do not repent with true sincerity, at some point, His Spirit will no longer strive with us; He is a perfect gentleman who lets us walk the way we want to and never forces us into anything. This is why Saul was left to his own devices. YHVH looks for those who will "worship Him in spirit and in truth" (John 4:22-24); since Saul did not want to do that, YHVH let him live out his choice. He was honoring Saul's free will.

The Gift of Free Will

For all believers in *Yeshua,* Saul's discipline should cause us to pause and consider. In Revelation 1:6 and 5:10, John the apostle tells us we have all been made to be "kings and priests" in YHVH's kingdom. We should carefully avoid treating YHVH's instructions with the same nonchalant attitude as Saul, one where we pick and choose which instructions we want to follow, do what is right in our own eyes, or justify our actions with our human reason. Instead, we should strive to perfectly obey Him. We need to check our hearts to ensure that we are sincerely repentant before Him and not just concerned about our position, the consequences of our sin, or whatever else we prize. Rather, our earnest desire should be to please Him only.

As stated before, YHVH is always the same. He still desires obedience rather than sacrifice. Our Heavenly Father has given us the gift of free will and He will always honor that, just as He did with Saul. But He did not give us this gift of free will so that we would bow down to it and serve it. He gave it to us so that we might choose to lay it down on His altar as a freewill offering unto Him. Obedience to His will instead of ours is what being a living sacrifice is all about, and living sacrifices are acceptable and pleasing to Him (Rom. 12:1). Saul disqualified himself from being king of Israel by not being a willing, living sacrifice.

The Parade of Jesse's Sons

YHVH was ready to identify to Samuel who the planned successor and next anointed king of Israel would be. He told Samuel to load up his horn with anointing oil and go down to Jesse's house, where he would find the chosen one among Jesse's sons. Samuel was afraid of what Saul might do if he heard of this planned anointing. After all, this was just another nail driven into the coffin of Saul's imminent termination from the throne.

YHVH authorized Samuel to take a heifer and tell Saul that he was going to make a sacrifice to Him. He instructed Samuel to invite Jesse and his sons to the sacrifice (1 Sam. 16:1-3). On a side note, only when YHVH specifically authorizes such covert operations—ones which might otherwise give the appearance of being deceitful—are we permitted to carry them out. It was permitted in this circumstance specifically to save a life.

Before they could attend the sacrifice, Samuel consecrated Jesse and his sons—at least the sons that Jesse deemed worthy attending. Samuel looked upon the eldest son, Eliab, and probably thought, "Surely, this tall, dark, and handsome one must be the next king." Eliab must have looked a lot like Saul did when he was chosen as king. But YHVH said to Samuel, "Look not on his countenance, or on the height of his stature; because I have refused him: for the LORD seeth not as man seeth; for man looketh on the outward appearance, but the LORD looketh on the heart" (1 Sam. 16:5-7).

In the next chapter, we will discuss Eliab's pride and mean spirit towards his youngest brother, David. Eliab mocked, belittled, made speculations, and falsely accused his brother concerning David's simple curiosity about Israel's enemy Goliath (1 Sam. 17:28). Who else do we know that has pride, a mean spirit, and has an arsenal that includes weapons like mocking, belittling, and falsely accusing? These are the calling cards of our adversary (ha-Satan), and YHVH was not about to make anyone comfortably walking in these characteristics an anointed leader of His people. Had Eliab struggled against these characteristics and allowed himself to be refined into a greater reflection of YHVH's heart, it might have been a different story. As we read several paragraphs back, YHVH had indicated that He was looking for a replacement for Saul who was after His own heart (1 Sam. 13:13-14).

One by one Samuel looked upon Jesse's sons, and yet none were YHVH's choice for the next king of Israel. Samuel must have discerned something, for he asked Jesse if there were any more sons among Jesse's house that he had not yet seen. Jesse responded that the youngest boy was out in the field tending sheep. David had been rendered insignificant by his father and brothers; clearly, they deemed him unqualified and unworthy of consideration for an invitation from Samuel the prophet to attend this sacrifice. In their eyes, David was nothing more than a baby brother and family ranch hand. They must have thought, "David certainly is not a potential king!" However, Samuel insisted that he be brought before him right away (1 Sam. 16:8-11).

Behold the Good Shepherd King

When the prophet Samuel laid eyes upon this ruddy, handsome, young shepherd with beautiful eyes, YHVH commanded, "Arise, anoint him: for this is he" (1 Sam. 16:12). Perhaps David was bright-eyed and his countenance lightened by YHVH because he had been worshipping YHVH in the field with songs of praise on his lyre and had been filled with the joy of YHVH. Though he was considered least by his entire family—and quite apparently treated so—David took joy in knowing YHVH and being in relationship with Him. This is what faith-filled belief looks like in action!

The young shepherd David obviously drew upon YHVH's strength and had impressive faith in YHVH's protection, especially as we later learn he had taken on both a lion and a bear to protect his father's sheep (1 Sam. 17:37). David was a man after YHVH's own heart because he was courageous and loved his father's sheep more than he loved his own life. He was willing to fight wild beasts to protect the sheep, even if it meant dying. His heart was conformed into the image of *Yeshua*, the Good Shepherd, who loves His Father's sheep more than His own life (John 10:11). This made David a perfect candidate for king of YHVH's chosen people and the forefather of the Messiah of Israel.

For anyone who is called to be a shepherd or leader over YHVH's sheep—whether pastor, mother, father, husband, wife, king, teacher, etc.—YHVH is looking for the same quality of love and care that David had for his father's sheep. He is looking for shepherds and leaders who live out the image of *Yeshua*, willing to be totally selfless and lay down their life for the sheep placed under their authority and care. He is looking for a bold and courageous shepherd, willing to pursue any predator or enemy threatening the flock, even if it costs his or her life.

YHVH saw these qualities in David, which led Samuel to anoint this littlest brother in front of his whole family. "The Spirit of the LORD came upon David from that day forward," though David did not immediately enter into his leadership role upon anointing (1 Sam. 16:13). This was David's baptism in the Spirit. Before he could become Israel's leader, he had to go through a season of extensive leadership training, physical and spiritual warfare, and a wilderness wandering. Like every other significant leader in the Bible (including Moses, Elijah, *Yeshua*, and Paul the Apostle), YHVH allows his followers to traverse the wilds of literal wastelands and the depths of their own hearts. In the wilderness, His future leaders must face trials from the enemy before they can start their ministries. David was no exception.

We will find out in future chapters that the heart is prone to sin and weakness, and even in this David's heart is the same. During our study, we will learn what specific pursuits, struggles, and urges David's heart would need to avoid and be purged of through literal and spiritual wilderness wanderings before he could take up the throne and walk in his anointing. Each of us are called and anointed for a variety of glorious purposes in YHVH's kingdom, but we too must be purged of our weaknesses and sins of the heart before He can truly put us in positions of effective leadership and transformation. Sometimes that wait is agonizing, but believe me, it is better, in the long run, to wait on YHVH and let him finish the good work He began in preparing us (Phil. 1:6).

If we run ahead of YHVH and try to jump into our calling too soon, we could make a huge mess of things. I have seen it and done it. It's not fun for us or for Him who has to do all the clean-up. Besides, He is still using and refining our various skills through the process, just as He used David to train up a mighty team of valiant warriors. We must trust YHVH's training process, wait on His time, and be content with wherever He has us. Our time *will* come, and it *will* be more than worth the wait!

Saul's Descent into Spiritual Torment

Now, as David was receiving his calling and anointing in YHVH's Spirit, Saul was losing his anointing. When YHVH's Spirit left, all of Saul's prideful, stubborn, willful disobedience left the door wide open for an evil spirit to torment him. As long as the *Ruach ha-Kodesh* remained in Saul, the evil spirit could not torment him. The evil spirit was already working in his heart yet was restrained by the *Ruach ha-Kodesh* from completely overtaking him. This principle is evident in 2 Thessalonians 2, which speaks of how lawlessness ("the mystery of iniquity") is already operating—though temporarily held back—until the restraining force is removed and the lawless one ("the Wicked") is revealed (2 Thes. 2:7-9). What truly opened the door for the evil spirit to overtake Saul was his inability to love YHVH with *all* his heart, mind, soul, and strength. Saul broke the first and greatest commandment. And technically, by failing to lead Israel in obedience to YHVH, he was also breaking the second greatest commandment— to love your neighbor as yourself.

Sadly, I have personally seen this same kind of evil overtake people who once called upon the name of YHVH, just as it had happened to Saul. I once worked as an outside consultant to two inpatient psychiatric facilities where I reviewed hundreds of patient charts for over a year. My heart broke often as I read how many of these patients believed in the *Elohim* of the Bible, called *Yeshua* their savior, even knew many Bible verses, but had fallen into a pattern of willful disobedience to YHVH's Word and had become entrenched in sins of fornication, witchcraft, idolatry, so much so that they lived in a state of hell on earth, severely tormented by evil spirits.

These poor souls lived in a state of literal weeping, wailing, and gnashing of teeth. Their anguish from the torment drove them to violence. Many were medicated to the hilt and required physical restraints for their own safety and that of their caregivers. Their stories crushed me, and their subsequent lives of terror reminded me of the demoniac with the legion of demons in Luke 8:26-38. When medicated and in their right mind, they talked as lovingly about *Yeshua* as any Christian. All I could do as my heart broke was pray that they might somehow have an encounter with *Yeshua's* loving and healing touch. My employer's contract certainly did not permit me to be anywhere near these patients. From a distance, I read and prayed, read and prayed.

The experience working in these mental institutions made me all the more grateful for the radical way that YHVH encountered me in my own rebellious, prodigal teenage years.[6] I once started dabbling in many of the things these poor patients deeply entrenched themselves in. Then, one night I had a horrific recurring dream, one which played through seven times before I awoke in a pool of sweat with my heart pounding out of my chest. Through this dream, YHVH gave me a very clear message that I was walking a path to certain destruction; there would be incredible torment in store if I did not turn around quickly and pursue Him with everything inside of me.

Let me just say, the experience literally scared the hell right out of me, and I came to understand what it means to "work out our salvation with fear and trembling" (Phil. 2:12). I also came to understand the intensity of the Heavenly Father's love for me, that He would intervene in my life, and call me to repent and receive His grace, mercy, and forgiveness after all that I had done in rebellion. My life radically changed after that night. All this is to say, there appears to be a line that can be crossed: if we give the enemy an inch, he will take a mile. We simply cannot walk in lawlessness or we risk falling into torment here on earth as Saul did, as the patients I witnessed did, and as I would have had I ignored the word and vision of YHVH on that night of destiny.

The Hebrew word for the "evil" spirit which tormented Saul in 1 Samuel 16:14-16 is 'ra (H7451). It has the following meanings according to Brown-Driver-Briggs Hebrew Lexicon (BDB) and Strong's Exhaustive Concordance (SEC): "adversity, evil, pain, unhappiness, misery, displeasing, sad, vicious, injury, wrong, evil deeds, distress, affliction, vexation, sorrow, trouble, calamity, grief, heaviness, hurt, mischief, and wretchedness."[7] Experiencing any of these things in your life? I have experienced all of these feelings at one time or another and have known many righteous believers who have also. Experiencing them in a season is one thing while being overtaken by it for the remainder of your life, like Saul, is another. We can avoid the latter by learning from Saul's mistakes and applying those lessons to our lives.

In my experience, observation, and Scripture study over the past two decades, I have learned that such adverse feelings described above can be an indication for spiritual weaknesses or impurities in our lives that we are unaware of. They often lurk beneath the surface undetected until we are put through the fires of refinement (adversity), which brings the impurities (dross) to the surface to be sloughed off and discarded. As was the case with Job, his adversity allowed all of the weaknesses or impurities in his faith that were lying dormant in his heart during the good times to rise to the surface. Once YHVH could help him see them, he could repent for them and receive His grace, mercy, and forgiveness (Job 38-42). We will see the same process happen with David throughout his life.

In addition to drawing out our impurities of heart, such adverse feelings can indicate unclean spirit activity in and against our lives. Therefore, it is important to take it in prayer and supplication before the Father to root out the source (generational curses, traumatic experiences, personal sin, etc.). He will give us the strategy to overcome through the blood of *Yeshua* and the power of the *Ruach ha-Kodesh*. In some cases, His wisdom may call us to enlist the assistance of our spiritual authority or intercessors to assist us in the spiritual battle.

Music Soothes the Soul

Because of Saul's torment by the evil spirit, his advisors recommended he find someone in the land who could play soothing music for him. As it would happen, our young David had quite the reputation in Israel for being an exceptional lyre player. Saul's advisors, not knowing of David's antecedent anointing and future replacement, recommended the shepherd. They described him as "a mighty valiant man, and a man of war, and prudent in matters, and a comely [handsome] person, and the LORD is with him" (1 Sam. 16:18).

Saul missed the peace that came from having YHVH with him. Ever since YHVH's Spirit left him, Saul had no peace, only torment. Saul longed to experience that peace once again and thought maybe YHVH's presence with David would be enough to bring him that peace. After agreeing with their recommendation, David was summoned to the palace (1 Sam. 16:14-19).

We do not know which psalms David may have sung to Saul during these visits, as scholars are not certain about the psalms that had been penned at this time in David's life. Some timelines suggest Psalms 8 and 19 may have already been written at this point.[8] Certainly, Psalm 8 seems written from the perspective of a young shepherd. The psalm reads as if its author spent many nights gazing into the sky at the glory of the heavens, learning dominion over the sheep and the wild beasts alike, and yet feels tremendously humbled by the honor of his new chosen, anointed crown of glory.

Psalm 19 also opens with the declaration, "The heavens declare the glory of God; and the firmament sheweth his handywork. There is no speech or language where their voice is not heard" (Ps. 19:1, 3). As he spent long hours gazing into the night sky while watching over his father's sheep, I wonder if David had any knowledge of the ancient Hebrew understanding of the constellations, otherwise known as the Mazzaroth.[9] Did David understand the eternal plan of redemption that was written in the heavens? Were these declarations of Psalms 8 and 19 the new song of David's heart at the time he was summoned to the palace? And is it possible that they were sung for Saul? David is like the rest of us who cannot help but share the new song of our heart with others, hoping to bless them.

As we see David minister to Saul, we get a glimpse of a piteous king, once described exactly as David: a mighty man of valor, a warrior, a handsome man, and YHVH was with him (1 Sam. 9:2). However, that identity in Saul was lost after he started following his own set of rules instead of following YHVH's rules. If those who ascribe Psalm 19 to this time in David's life are correct, would David have actually recited it all in Saul's presence? Or would David have kept some of the psalm to himself, as a reminder of what YHVH was looking for in a king? YHVH was looking for a king whose heart was to obey Him out of love (1 John 5:3). He rejected the king who said in his heart, "Well, I will just make a sacrifice offering after deliberately breaking YHVH's instructions. YHVH will accept me."

Based on the words of Psalm 19, David's heart desired to follow YHVH's commandments out of love. His perception of

YHVH's Torah was all positive. He declared, "The law of the LORD is perfect, converting the soul: the testimony of the LORD is sure, making wise the simple. The statutes of the LORD are right, rejoicing the heart: the commandment of the LORD is pure, enlightening the eyes. The fear of the LORD is clean, enduring for ever: the judgments of the LORD are true and righteous altogether. More to be desired are they than gold, yea, than much fine gold: sweeter also than honey and the honeycomb. Moreover by them is thy servant warned: and in keeping of them there is great reward" (Ps. 19:7-11).

Furthermore, as David ministered to and witnessed the sad shell of a tormented man Saul had become, because of his presumptuous sins, this wise youth was learning what he never wanted to become. He cried out to his Heavenly Father, saying, "Cleanse thou me from secret faults. Keep back thy servant also from presumptuous sins; let them not have dominion over me: then shall I be upright, and I shall be innocent from the great transgression. Let the words of my mouth, and the meditation of my heart, be acceptable in thy sight, O LORD, my strength, and my redeemer" (Ps. 19:12-14, *condensed*). David did not want to follow in his predecessor's foolish footsteps, and, instead, desired to be a righteous and honorable king before YHVH.

Calling All Kings, Priests, and Shepherds

What kind of kings, priests, and shepherds in YHVH's kingdom are we going to be? That is the question of the day. I do not know about you, but I want to be a king, priest, and shepherd after YHVH's own heart, conformed into the image of *Yeshua*, who was "obedient unto death" (Phil. 2:8-9); death of the will, the flesh, and of self. This was what YHVH called and anointed David for, but this is also what He has called all His children for. Let us walk in it, my brothers and sisters.

"And from Jesus Christ, who is the faithful witness, and the first begotten of the dead, and the prince of the kings of the earth. Unto him that loved us, and washed us from our sins in his own blood, And hath made us kings and priests unto God and his Father; to him be glory and dominion for ever and ever. Amen." (Rev. 1:5-6)

JOURNEY JOURNAL

1. Do you personally identify with any of Saul's characteristics or experiences? If so, which one(s)?

2. Do you personally identify with any of David's characteristics or experiences? If so, which one(s)?

3. How has this chapter's study affected your perspective of YHVH's judgment against Saul concerning the Amalekites, or YHVH's judgment to annihilate the Amalekites?

4. How has this chapter's study affected your perspective on the importance of obedience to the whole Word of YHVH?

5. How has this chapter's study affected your perspective on what it means to be made kings and priests in YHVH's kingdom? What kind of king and priest are you compelled to be?

6. Did you experience any personal conviction as you read this chapter and answered the questions presented? What were you convicted about? (Conviction is meant to lead us to prayers of repentance, wherein we receive YHVH's grace, mercy, and forgiveness.)

7. How has this chapter's study encouraged you to greater love for YHVH and your neighbor?

2
THE STONE

Outstanding leaders are not just born into leadership or ready to start leading the moment they are chosen. Superior leaders are often developed through the school of tremendous adversity. We humans have been created with the innate capacity to become better, stronger, and wiser through some of the most perplexing experiences. How we weather our challenges determines whether we make the cut of leadership or not. In 1 Samuel 17, we are going to look at the account of a colossal battle, one which initiated the preparatory training for David's newly anointed leadership.

The Enemy Encampment

Almost immediately after David was anointed future king of Israel, he was detained at home tending his father's sheep. Meanwhile, his three oldest brothers proudly joined Saul's army to battle against the formidable Philistines. I wonder how this made David initially feel. Did he wonder how long it would be before he would take up the throne? Did he have even the slightest shred of doubt in Samuel's prophetic word over him or that his kingly anointing was really true? Several close friends and I have questioned prophetic words spoken over us when initial circumstances did not seem to line up with how we expected the prophetic words to play out. This is often how our faith is tested when we receive a promise from YHVH.

David's brothers marched off to the battlefront. The Philistines (Israel's arch-enemy) encamped against Israel "between Shochoh and Azekah in Ephesdammim" (1 Samuel 17:1 KJV). *Ephesdammim* means "boundary/brink of blood drops" (H658),[1] *Shochoh* means "bough or branch" (H7754),[2] and *Azekah* has a root meaning of "tilled or digging" (H5825).[3] Prophetically speaking, Israel's enemy camped between two places known for bearing fruit (branches and tilled soil), purposing to bring Israel to the brink of death by shedding their blood. Likewise, our adversary (*ha-Satan*) sets up battlefronts against the fruitful places of our lives and seeks to steal, kill, and destroy. It reminds me of *Yeshua's* parables of the sower and the weeds in Matthew 13, wherein our hearts are the fruit-bearing soil where YHVH sows the seed of His Word and the enemy tries to either snatch it away and/or sow his tares to choke it out.

In opposition to the enemy's encampment, Israel encamped "by the valley of Elah" (1 Sam. 17:2). *Elah* (H425)[4] is the Hebrew word for terebinth (oak)[5] trees. Israel was being tested and tried for forty days in the valley of the terebinth trees, taunted and mocked by the massive Philistine giant Goliath from Gath. Forty is the number of testing in the Bible.[6] Moses, Elijah, *Yeshua*, and Paul all spent forty days in a wilderness being tested. Israel spent forty years in the wilderness being tested and purged before entering their promised inheritance. Likewise, everyone chosen and anointed by YHVH for magnificent purposes will be tested.

Failing the Faith Test of Fear

Unfortunately, Israel was not passing their faith test with flying colors. Jesse had not heard from his sons, so he decided to send David with some food for his brothers and their captain and to bring a report of their welfare back to him. When David arrived at Israel's encampment, he witnessed Israel's army rushing out to the battle line with enthusiastic shouting and war cries, acting all macho and eager to wage war. However, the moment Goliath came out and started taunting, Israel turned tail in substantial fear and ran back to camp to hide. They had been repeating this pattern every day for forty days already (1 Sam. 17:11, 24-25).

When the enemy (*ha-Satan* working through the Philistine army) taunted and mocked them and their *Elohim*, "they were dismayed, and greatly afraid" (1 Sam. 17:11), instead of having a "sound mind" (2 Tim. 1:7). Israel's army lacked faith in YHVH's promises to protect and keep them. They were filled with doubt, unbelief, and paralyzing fear. They hid from any and all confrontation with the enemy.

They were content to sit in the comfort of camp and avoid warfare, lacking faith, courage, and already accepting defeat because of their understanding of Goliath's sheer size. From their limited human perspective, which often only looks into the seen physical realm, the size of the feared object mattered. However, YHVH sees behind-the-scenes into the spiritual realm; from His perspective, Goliath was nothing more than a gnat. Sadly, I have been there, done that, and seen many other believers do the same. We go out eager for battle against the enemy, thinking we are so tough and ready to kick his tail, but the moment he shows up and starts to taunt us, we turn tail and shrink back in fear.

When David saw his brothers and the rest of Israel cowering in fear, he did not prejudge them as faithless wimps, but rather he dropped his baggage and inquired after their welfare (1 Sam. 17:22). I suggest there is a prophetic spiritual principle for us to consider. When we see our brothers and sisters in Messiah cowering in fear over their circumstances, we need to drop our baggage (our emotional offense, judgments, etc.) and check on their welfare. Too many of us are so wrapped up in our own emotional baggage or judgments of our brother or sister's behavior to show that we are truly concerned about assisting or ministering to them.

We can also see another major difference between David and Saul in David's action here. If you recall from the previous chapter, after Samuel declared to Saul that he would be made king of Israel and used to deliver them from the oppression of the Philistines, Saul went and hid behind some baggage, revealing some reluctance to step into His ordained role (1 Sam. 10:22). Yet, here was David in a similar situation, just after Samuel declared to him that he would be made king of Israel, facing fellow countrymen who were oppressed by the Philistines. However, instead of hiding behind the baggage, David set it aside, having more care and concern for the state of his fellow countrymen than he did for himself.

As David stood with Israel's army, he was in proximity to hear Goliath defy the *Elohim* of Israel. David was far more perturbed that YHVH had been blasphemed than he was with his brothers' fear. *David's only judgment was against the original source of his brothers' fear.* He demanded to know who was going to put an end to this blasphemous giant. Saul heard about David's desire to see Goliath defeated and summoned him to his royal tent. He attempted to convince David not to fight the giant, but he ultimately conceded to David's staunch determination to fight the one no other soldier was willing to.

What are we going to do the next time we see a brother or sister being taunted, threatened, and oppressed by the enemy? Will we stand in the gap to defend them in the face of the giant who stands against them, no matter what the potential cost to us? It takes a special heart like David's to do so. Despite the great potential cost to me and my family, I have personally stood in the gap for a few brothers and sisters in Messiah to defend them against their giant.

Armor Fit for a King

Saul endeavored to give young David his own garments of warfare and weaponry to fight with. However, David recognized they were ill-fitted and would only hinder him in battle, so he respectfully declined. Here is another prophetic spiritual principle for us to consider. We are not meant to face our battles against the adversary (*ha-Satan*) with what someone else has fought their battles with, but rather our weapons are whatever YHVH has specifically trained and gifted us with.

We can be guilty of looking at the armor, training, and gifts of others and covet their garments of warfare. However, it would only hinder us to do so because YHVH most often uses our own life experiences to train us for battle against the enemy. Additionally, we should use extreme caution in attempting to give our garments of warfare to others, unless YHVH specifically instructs us to. How we have overcome a similar battle may not be appropriate for their situation. In a future chapter, we will see how YHVH provided different strategies for two nearly identical battles between David and the Philistines. We need to encourage each other to seek YHVH for how to fight with our own spiritual training and gifts, relying on YHVH to empower us through them, just as David did.

David prepared to face off with Goliath in the Valley of Elah (terebinth trees). Genesis 18:1-15 comes to mind because YHVH appeared to Abraham by the terebinth trees of Mamre when He delivered the promise of Isaac's birth to Abraham and Sarah. I wonder if David pondered this legendary testimony as he approached his epic battle with Goliath. Is it possible David remembered how YHVH manifested Himself amidst the terebinth trees for his forefather Abraham and wondered if He would likewise manifest Himself to Israel amongst the terebinth trees of Elah? Is it possible such thoughts could have lent him courage?

The Battle Behind the Scenes

Before we delve into the nitty gritty details of this epic battle between David and Goliath, it is imperative that we understand David's childhood experience and why his victory in this battle was such a crucial preparation for his position as king of Israel. This battle ultimately primed David to overcome many future battles. Every battle in life prepares us for future ones.

As the youngest son, David was often overlooked by his father and the rest of his brothers. In the first chapter, we reviewed how his father, Jesse, initially deemed him unworthy to attend Samuel's sacrifice with his brothers. In 1 Samuel 17, when David inquired about Goliath, his brother Eliab got very angry with him. Eliab belittled David by asking who was attending to the family sheep as if he assessed that was all David was useful for. Eliab did not seem to recognize or affirm David's anointing. Furthermore, Eliab falsely accused David of "pride," "naughtiness" in his heart, and ulterior motives and motioned for him to return home (1 Sam. 17:28).

From the record of these family interactions, is it possible David might have struggled with feeling like an exile in his own family? Did YHVH know David would have to first overcome any emotional issues that may have stemmed from his family's ill-treatment, such as rejection, fear of intimacy, lack of trust in relationships, or insecurity, before properly assuming the throne? Interestingly, Goliath's name has its root in the word *galah*, which means "uncover, remove, banish, betray, exile, take away into captivity" (H1540).[7] Is it possible that YHVH brought David to this battlefield to defeat the spiritual giant who embodied all of his emotional response to feeling uncovered, removed, banished, betrayed, and exiled by his family?

How many of us have had to face this same spiritual giant? Many of us have had family members or other influential people in our lives who have treated us in the same fashion as David was treated or worse. The good news is that we can defeat this giant as successfully as David did. We will learn the strategy to overcome in just a moment.

Goliath "disdained" David when he saw him coming out to the battle line against him (1 Sam. 17:42). Likewise, our enemy always looks upon Holy Spirit-anointed, faith-filled believers with disdain; he sees the countenance of his arch-enemy, the *Elohim* of Israel, upon us and it really gets his goat. Regardless, David stared Goliath down and proclaimed his victory over him, shouting, "I come to thee in the name of the LORD of hosts, the God of the armies of Israel, whom thou hast defied. This day will the LORD deliver thee into mine hand; ...for the battle is the LORD's, and he will give you into our hands" (1 Sam. 17:45-47, *condensed*).

Like us, David was made in the image of YHVH, and his faith-filled proclamation carried tremendous creative power. He effectually spoke his victory over Goliath into existence. Our words likewise carry tremendous creative power over our ultimate destiny. Therefore, we need to remain mindful of what we speak over our life circumstances. Our very life or death can hinge on our words (Prov. 18:21).

David was not like the rest of Israel, merely a man full of shouting and enthusiastic war cry without resolve. He was surely a man of faith in action, not fear and retreat. After he took a total of five stones with him in his bag (there were a total of five giants among the Philistines), David rushed toward Goliath with unmatched courage and faith to overcome in YHVH's strength, and hurled the first stone at him.

It only took a single stone square between the eyes of Goliath to topple him. Symbolically, a stone in Scripture points to *Yeshua*: "This [Yeshua] is the stone, which was set at nought of you builders, which is become the head of the corner." (Acts 4:11) *Yeshua*—and our acceptance to our Heavenly Father through the atoning blood of His sacrifice—is all we need to defeat this spiritual giant of feeling uncovered, removed, banished, betrayed, and exiled.

When we fully know who we are in YHVH, our identity is rooted one hundred percent in Him and His splendid love, acceptance, and inclusion of us as His children and heirs (Rom. 8:16-17). From this place of sonship and daughtership, we are empowered to overcome rejection, fear of intimacy, lack of trust in relationships, and insecurity. These emotional struggles arise only when our identity has been misplaced in who our family or other people say we are or how they treat us. It has been my personal experience and observation, spending much of my life in and around highly dysfunctional family units like David's, that these emotional struggles hinder us from reaching our full potential. We cannot be the parents, spouses, teachers, friends, pastors, or leaders that YHVH has created us to be when we allow ourselves to be defined by another's opinion(s) of us. Only when we understand our identity solely through the context of our Heavenly Father, can we reach our fullest potential to lead others into their kingdom identity.

Yeshua, the stone that was rejected by His people and the religious leaders, understood His identity solely through the context of His Father. This is why He did not fall into offense over all the false accusations, mockery, beatings, or murderous plots perpetrated mostly by his own Jewish "family." He never took upon Himself the victim identity that we so commonly see in our modern culture today. Instead, He was fully secure in who He was in the eyes of the Heavenly Father, so all other opinions could not offend Him. Like it is for us, it was crucial for David to rise up in the same identity of knowing who he was in YHVH in order to be the extraordinary shepherd and king of Israel he had been anointed to be.

Having our identity rooted in YHVH is the basic spiritual principle of Ephesians 6:10-18. David was donning the invisible full armor of YHVH. He had buckled on the belt of truth by knowing, believing, and speaking out YHVH's promises to deliver Israel from their enemies. His willingness to do the righteous act of standing up for YHVH's holy name proved that David wore the breastplate of righteousness. His feet were shod with the gospel of peace through proclaiming YHVH's salvation from the enemy. The shield of David's faith was waved in Goliath's face as he proclaimed victory over him. His knowledge of who he was in YHVH protected his head with the helmet of salvation. Finally, he wielded the stone (*Yeshua*), who is the living word of YHVH and the sword of the Spirit. I would be willing to bet he was praying in the Spirit through the whole experience as well.

The Enemy Has Been Defeated

While barreling like a freight train towards Goliath, David

hurled the stone from his shepherd's slingshot, nailing Goliath square between the eyes. The giant toppled over dead, leveled like a telephone pole by a hundred mile per hour wind (1 Sam. 17:50). David did not have to use a literal sword to defeat his enemy, just the *stone*. David only used a sword after Goliath was defeated by the stone. There was "no sword in David's hand," so David literally grabbed Goliath's gargantuan sword and decapitated him (1 Sam. 17:51). By severing the giant's head, the Philistine army could have no doubt that their champion was dead, just in case they doubted a single stone was really enough to kill him.

David's action also serves as another prophetic pointer to *Yeshua* and the actions we must take once we become believers in Messiah. *Yeshua's* death and resurrection have already defeated the enemy (*ha-Satan*). Biblically, a head represents authority. Once we receive the salvation from sin's death penalty through acceptance of *Yeshua's* atoning sacrifice of the cross, we still have to take up the sword (YHVH's Word). In order to completely sever the authority that the enemy has over us through sin, we must also wield the sword of YHVH properly by submitting to its authority.

Furthermore, I want to point out another beautiful prophetic message in the root meaning of Goliath's name, *galah*. In the Garden of Eden, Adam and Eve's betrayal against YHVH's instructions led to all mankind becoming uncovered and exposed in sin, which entered all humanity from that moment onward. The punishment for sin is death, which is eternal banishment or exile from YHVH's presence. *Yeshua's* atoning sacrifice effectively stripped death's authority over us, forever ending our exile from YHVH's presence. It is absolutely amazing how deeply David's victory foreshadows our victory in Messiah!

As soon as David decapitated Goliath, the Philistine army turned tail and fled (1 Sam. 17:51). This gives a whole new understanding to "resist the devil, and he will flee" (James 4:7).

Resisting means to take up the sword of the Spirit (the Word of YHVH) and take the seat of the enemy's authority (his head) off with it. When we submit to YHVH's Word, that is exactly what we are doing. That is precisely what *Yeshua* did as He was tempted in the wilderness. Three times, he wielded the sword and cut off the enemy's attempt to take authority over him through sin. He set the example for us to follow.

Not only did the Philistine army flee like a bunch of puny little fleas after seeing their champion headless, but when the men of Israel who had been cowering in fear saw it, they were inspired with faith and courage to pursue the enemy army as they fled. It was no half-hearted pursuit either. Israel's army pursued the Philistines "to the gates of Ekron," "by the way to Shaarim," and "even unto Gath" (1 Sam. 17:52). Ekron's root meaning is "eradication" (H6138),[8] Shaarim means "double gates" (H8189),[9] and Gath means "winepress" (H1661).[10] The children of Israel were going for no small victory here. They were out to totally eradicate the enemy, to chase them all the way to the double gates and the winepress of YHVH's wrath (Rev. 14:19).

Covered in YHVH's Glory

When David returned from his exploits against the Philistines, carrying the head of Goliath, Saul asked him whose son he was, because he nor Abner could recognize him as the son of Jesse (1 Sam. 17:55-58). Why couldn't they recognize David who had been playing the lyre for Saul and was Saul's armor-bearer for some time before the war (1 Samuel 16:19-23)? Is it possible that David's countenance was so changed by the presence of the *Ruach ha-Kodesh* that was upon him in this miraculous battle, that he was unrecognizable to those who had been well acquainted with him under ordinary circumstances?

I believe YHVH's countenance shined upon David brightly because of his perfect faith, much like it did when Moses was in His presence. David was fully engaged in his spirit man with the *Ruach ha-Kodesh*. Perhaps because Saul and Abner were seeing YHVH's countenance instead of the flesh and blood man David, they did not recognize the young man who had been by their side many times before. Have you ever been so engaged in the *Ruach ha-Kodesh* that people who know you very well barely recognize you and remark about how much your countenance has changed? I have, so I know this is an entirely possible explanation for Saul and Abner's unfamiliarity.

While we do not know for certain when David wrote many of his psalms, some scholars have suggested the possibility that Psalm 9 may have been written soon after this monumental victory over Goliath and the Philistine army.[11] Reading the words of this psalm, it would certainly seem fitting to this particular victory: "When mine enemies are turned back, they shall perish at thy presence" (Ps. 9:3). "O thou enemy, destructions are come to a perpetual end: and thou hast destroyed cities; their memorial is perished with them" (Ps. 9:6). "Put them in fear, O LORD: that the nations may know themselves to be but men" (Ps. 9:20).

Whether Psalm 9 was written at this time or not, its words and David's example serve as an excellent reminder for all of us. As believers in *Yeshua*, we have seen the enemy of our souls defeated by the stone (which the builders rejected), *Yeshua*. We are to rise up like David as faith-filled warriors, one hundred percent secure in our identity in Messiah. We are to remove all authority the enemy has over our thoughts, feelings, and actions by the word of YHVH, the sword of the Spirit. We ought to be the kind of warriors for Him that inspire our brothers and sisters to rise up as faith-filled warriors, and together, we should be chasing the enemy army right to the wine-press of YHVH's wrath. Are we ready to live with the kind of radical faith that accepts nothing less than the total eradication of every aspect of the enemy out of our lives and our land? That is my question for us dear brothers and sisters.

"Be it known unto you all, and to all the people of Israel, that by the name of Jesus Christ of Nazareth, whom ye crucified, whom God raised from the dead, even by him doth this man stand here before you whole. This is the stone which was set at nought of you builders, which is become the head of the corner. Neither is there salvation in any other: for there is none other name under heaven given among men, whereby we must be saved." (Acts 4:10-12)

"To whom coming, as unto a living stone, disallowed indeed of men, but chosen of God, and precious, Ye also, as lively stones, are built up a spiritual house, an holy priesthood, to offer up spiritual sacrifices, acceptable to God by Jesus Christ. Wherefore also it is contained in the scripture, Behold, I lay in Sion a chief corner stone, elect, precious: and he that believeth on him shall not be confounded. Unto you therefore which believe he is precious: but unto them which be disobedient, the stone which the builders disallowed, the same is made the head of the corner, And a stone of stumbling, and a rock of offence, even to them which stumble at the word, being disobedient: whereunto also they were appointed. But ye are a chosen generation, a royal priesthood, an holy nation, a peculiar people; that ye should shew forth the praises of him who hath called you out of darkness into his marvellous light;" (1 Pet. 2:4-9)

JOURNEY JOURNAL

1. Do you personally identify with any of David's characteristics or experiences? If so, which one(s)?

2. Do you personally identify with any of the characteristics or experiences of Israel's army? If so, which one(s)?

3. How do you relate to brothers and sisters in Messiah when it comes to their fears and spiritual weaknesses?

4. What unique weapons and strategies has the Heavenly Father trained you up with over the course of your life to help you successfully engage in battle against the adversary?

5. How much of your identity and security rests in who the Heavenly Father says you are? How much of your identity and security rests in who other people (including family) say you are?

6. Did you experience any personal conviction as you read this chapter and answered the questions presented? What were you convicted about? (Conviction is meant to lead us to prayers of repentance, wherein we receive YHVH's grace, mercy, and forgiveness.)

7. How has this chapter's study encouraged you to greater love for YHVH and your neighbor?

3
A COVENANT FRIEND

We never know the depth of our faith or who our real friends are until life throws a curve ball at us and everything in our life is shaken. Like David's recent victory over Goliath, awe-inspiring victories and mountaintop experiences are often followed by catastrophic times in our lives. These trials will not only test the depths of our faith but also call out the best or the worst in those who call themselves our friends. There are friends who will stick closer than a brother and love us through any circumstance. They will love us no matter what we are accused of or what we are actually guilty of doing. These friends are covenant friends. One covenant friend is more valuable than many so-called "friends" who desert us when things get rough. Jonathan, son of King Saul of Israel, was one such valuable covenant friend to the anointed and future King David.

The Gift of Extraordinary Friendship

Jonathan would have naturally been David's bitter rival in the ancient Middle Eastern culture. As a son of the reigning king, Jonathan would have wanted to kill anyone threatening his future throne. However, YHVH can make those who would naturally be our "enemies to be at peace with" us (Prov. 16:7 KJV), and such was the case with David and Jonathan.

Jonathan was never the least bit threatened by David but loved David more than a brother. The Bible says, "Jonathan and David made a covenant, because he loved him as his own soul." Jonathan actually "stripped himself of the robe that was upon him," including all his weapons of warfare, "and gave it to David" (1 Sam. 18:3-4).

Jonathan's actions were a beautiful prophetic foreshadow of what Messiah has done for every disciple. *Yeshua*, Son of the Most High King of the Universe, loved us more than a brother, willing "to lay down his life for" us (John 15:13). He stripped Himself of His royal robe of righteousness and gifted it to us (Rev. 7:9-14, Isa. 61:10). He has also given us His spiritual armor and garments of warfare (Eph. 6:10-18, Isa. 59:17). And even though He is King of kings, He has called us to be "kings and priests," willing to share the reign of His Kingdom with us (Rev. 1:6, 5:10 NKJV). Even *Jonathan's* name meaning "YHVH has given" (H3083)[1] indicates that YHVH was actually giving something prophetically through Jonathan to David.

I wonder if David understood the significance of what was happening in the spiritual realm through this physical realm action. He had just received his calling and anointing of the *Ruach ha-Kodesh* from YHVH, seen the enemy defeated by the *stone,* and now he was being given a royal robe and garments of warfare by the king's own son. This is precisely what happens in the life of every disciple of Messiah *Yeshua*. We are chosen by the Heavenly

Father to receive a calling and anointing in His *Ruach ha-Kodesh*, we come to the cross of Calvary to understand that the enemy of our souls has been defeated through His atoning sacrifice, and then the Son of the King of the Universe (*Yeshua*) clothes us in His righteous robe and puts His spiritual armor upon us. Isn't that awesome?

Jealousy Rears its Ugly Head

After receiving such tremendous honor from Jonathan, David was given authority over all of Israel's men of war. He had such outstanding success at everything he put his hands to that he gained the unanimous favor of the people of Israel. The women sang songs commemorating David's unmatched victories, far more glorious than the mighty warrior-King Saul's. As a result, Saul became intensely jealous of David's success in warfare and his popularity with the people (1 Sam. 18:5-9). Saul feared that he would lose the hearts of Israel to David, and this fear drove him to anger against David. He allowed his anger to fester overnight, giving the devil a foothold to turn his jealousy, fear, and anger into full-blown sin (Eph. 4:26-27, James 3:14-16).

Because Saul did not capture his thoughts (2 Cor. 10:5), and he no longer had the *Ruach ha-Kodesh* to rule his heart and mind, he opened the door wide to a tormenting evil spirit. As we saw in the first chapter, the word used in 1 Samuel 18:10 to describe the evil spirit in Saul is *'ra* and its meaning is: "adversity, evil, pain, unhappiness, misery, displeasure, sad, vicious, injury, wrong, evil deeds, distress, affliction, vexation, sorrow, trouble, calamity, grief, heaviness, hurt, mischief, and wretchedness" (H7451).[2] This Hebrew word captures the whole essence of who our adversary (*ha-Satan*) is and how he operates in our lives. He seeks "to steal, and to kill, and to destroy" the life, joy, and peace of every believer (John 10:10) and he often does it through affliction, adversity, injury, trouble, and distress by manipulating our emotional responses to our life circumstances.

We should see the prophetic similarities between Saul and our adversary. *Ha-Satan* is jealous and angry because he has been rejected by YHVH for his rebellion, cast away from His presence, and has no pardon or way back to his former position, just like Saul.[3] Mankind gave *ha-Satan* a position of dominion over the earth by choosing his word over YHVH's in the Garden of Eden; but *Yeshua's* atoning sacrifice on the cross redeemed us from *ha-Satan's* dominion. *Yeshua* is the anointed King to take dominion of the earth over from *ha-Satan.* Every true disciple of the Messiah *Yeshua* (who are reflections of Him) is a reminder of that fact. *Ha-Satan* is very jealous of our position through Messiah *Yeshua* as children and heirs (Gal. 4:1-7), "kings and priests" (Rev. 1:6, 5:10 NKJV), and the fact that man has been made a little "lower than the angels" (Heb. 2:6-7). But he is also jealous that man was given the opportunity to repent for the sin of rebellion and now has YHVH's Spirit and everlasting life in Heaven (Acts 2:38, Acts 3:19-20, John 3:16).

Just like Saul wanted to destroy David, *ha-Satan* wants to destroy us. He is jealous of our eternal position and angered over his ultimate destiny. *Ha-Satan* often attempts to destroy us by using the same emotions that he used in Saul to attempt David's destruction. *Ha-Satan* earnestly desires to destroy every disciple of *Yeshua* and end our calling and anointing as future kings and priests in YHVH's kingdom. He works through adversity, affliction, trouble, distress, and the emotions (i.e., bitterness, hatred, unforgiveness, hopelessness, depression) that he can manipulate through those circumstances. *Ha-Satan's* ultimate aim is to convince us to give up on YHVH, sink into a deep pit of despair, and give up on life. This has been a major generational battle on many sides of my family and, sadly, some have taken or attempted to take their own lives in the pits of despair. This is why the apostles repeatedly told us to rejoice at all times and in adversity (Phil. 4:4, Rom. 5:3, Rom. 12:12, 1 Pet. 4:12-13, James 1:2-4). Rejoicing in affliction and adversity is one of the most effective ways in which we are called to "resist the devil," so that "he will flee" (James 4:7).

No Weapon Shall Prosper

David managed to elude Saul's attempt against his life and, consequently, *ha-Satan's* attempt to wreck him emotionally. As a result, Saul became horribly terrified of David because he recognized that the Spirit of YHVH was with David as his helper. Likewise, when we elude *ha-Satan's* attempts against our life, he flees recognizing that the Spirit of YHVH is with us as our "Helper" (John 14:26 AMP). Saul was petrified of David, recognizing that he could do nothing to destroy him, so he decided to appoint David as captain over his troops and sent him to the battlefield, hopeful that he would be destroyed in warfare. However, "David behaved himself wisely in all his ways; and the LORD was with him" (1 Sam. 18:11-14). Likewise, *ha-Satan* tries to destroy us through spiritual warfare. But as it was with David, so it is for every believer with whom is the Spirit of YHVH—"no weapon formed against" us "shall prosper" (Isa. 54:17).

Because David was so untouchable under YHVH's favor and protection, Saul absolutely dreaded David (1 Sam 18:15). David was a man after YHVH's own heart, one in the image of YHVH's own Son *Yeshua*, the Good Shepherd who laid His life down for the sheep. Because David's identity was completely rooted in who he was in YHVH, David had no need to fear his enemy. If we are also fashioned after YHVH's heart and rooted in our identity in Him, we have no need to fear our enemy, *ha-Satan*. In fact, the enemy dreads this type of believer. Granted, it never motivates him to give up on his attempts to destroy us.

I have a powerful personal testimony to this end that occurred during the writing of this book. Shortly after I started writing, I had a prophetic dream about a demonic council convened against me. They had pronounced a judgment of death against me like a mafia hit. I grabbed my family, and we ran as far as we could until we reached a rest area in the wilderness. We all ducked into a janitor's closet and prayed. We heard what sounded like janitor's keys clanging as someone approached. I awoke from the dream in a pool of sweat with my heart pounding and immediately proclaimed, "Thank you YHVH that no weapon formed against me shall prosper and that You have set Your angels to guard over me." I understood the Father was telling me the key to overcoming this demonic attack was through our family uniting in prayer.

At the same time that I had this dream, I experienced a sudden onset of physical illness. Though I had never suffered from an ear infection in my lifetime and had a strong immune system, I suddenly had the worst ear infection my medical provider had ever seen in her career. It took four weeks of antibiotics to clear up the fluid in my ear. It returned twice over the year I spent writing this book, each time requiring long-course antibiotics to completely clear up the infection. As the first volume approached the end of the editing process, my appendix ruptured and sealed itself back over. This rupture happened before any of the usual symptoms of appendicitis had even manifested in my body. I was hospitalized for over a week after my appendectomy due to intra-abdominal abscesses.

I knew that the enemy was trying to fulfill the death decree against me, but I had no fear. Every step of the way, I continually praised and thanked YHVH that He was covering me, protecting me, and would not allow any weapon formed against me to prosper. In fact, the morning before the pathology reports on my abscesses were complete, I encouraged a concerned family member with the promise of Isaiah 54:17. I read the rest of the verse and realized that as a servant worshipper of YHVH, He had assigned me the heritage of condemning every voice that rose against me in judgment. So, I possessed my heritage and condemned the judgment of death as null and void in the mighty name of *Yeshua*.

Later that same morning, one of my friends from my local home fellowship group arrived at my hospital room wearing a T-shirt that had Isaiah 54:17 printed on it. Coincidence or God-o-wince? The *Ruach ha-Kodesh* prompted her to lay hands on me and sing "There is Power in the Name of Jesus." I immediately understood why YHVH instructed her to sing that particular song.

My fevers had returned, and my white blood cell counts had started increasing again overnight. Having a former career in health care, I knew in my heart that I had an antibiotic-resistant super germ and that the genetic mutation that caused it was the chain that *Yeshua's* mighty name would break. As soon as my friend left, I turned on Hillsong Radio live stream and "There is Power in the Name of Jesus" immediately started to play, as though YHVH was confirming Himself with a second witness. My fever started to decline, and I started to feel better even before the pathology report came in later that night.

The next morning, I learned from the infectious disease specialist that my repeated long-course antibiotics for the ear infections had led to my normal gastrointestinal E. coli mutating into an antibiotic-resistant super germ called ESBL E. coli. It was the perfect storm that was meant to sink my ship. I immediately began a new antibiotic treatment that had effectively killed my super germ in the lab. Though YHVH can and does use doctors and medicine to heal us, I truly give all glory, honor, and praise to

His hand of healing on me. I have fully recovered to finish the work set before me.

In every way, the Heavenly Father protected my family from the enemy's plot to steal, kill, and destroy. In addition to protecting my life and health, He protected our finances. My husband has been a civilian technician in the Air National Guard. We normally have significant out of pocket expenses with our federal employee medical plan. However, because my husband was scheduled for a mobilization, we had Tricare coverage and had zero out-of-pocket expense. All glory, honor, and praise to YHVH for His perfect timing and provision! Truly, no weapon formed against us prospered. Halleluyah!

A Humble Servant

Even though David had sensational success and favor with both YHVH and man, he maintained an attitude of remarkable humility. Saul continually attempted to give David one of his daughters in marriage, but David did not even count himself worthy to be the king's son-in-law. He was anointed to be the next king, had experienced unprecedented victory in battle, and had won the hearts of Israel. Nevertheless, David said of himself, "I am a poor man, and lightly esteemed" (1 Sam. 18:17-23).

This humility in David was precisely why YHVH chose him to be the next king of Israel. His ego was not inflated by his anointing, his glorious success in battle, or the favor of the public. David's humility was genuine and it mirrored *Yeshua's* humility. Although *Yeshua* is King of kings and Lord of lords, Scripture says that He "made Himself of no reputation" (Phil. 2:6-8). Every disciple of Messiah *Yeshua* is called to model genuine humility such as this (1 Pet. 5:5).

The way in which David handled Saul's offers reveals another beautiful quality of his heart. It is clear that David trusted YHVH to bring him to the throne of Israel in His own way and timing. David could have easily presumed that becoming the king's son through marriage was an opportunity to move closer to his promised position as future king. However, David did not presumptuously leap at this golden opportunity, as many others would have. How often do we make presumptions about our circumstances? Do we leap into an opportunity believing it is YHVH's will for our lives, only to find out later that He had another perfect plan?

Schemers vs. Interceders

Despite David's denial of worth, Saul was insistent about David marrying one of his daughters. However, it became apparent that this was only another of Saul's schemes to destroy David's life. Saul acknowledged David's claim that he was a poor man and told him that he would accept a dowry price of one hundred Philistine foreskins. David thought this seemed a fair price to pay to become the king's son-in-law. So, without any hesitation or fear, David waged war against the Philistines and brought back double the requested bride price! Much to Saul's chagrin, David was unscathed through his scheme (1 Sam. 18:24-27).

The more Saul realized that his schemes were futile because YHVH was with David, the more his consternation grew. Likewise, the more *ha-Satan* realizes that his schemes against us are futile because YHVH is with us, the more his consternation grows. But just as Saul's realizations did not prevent him from continuing to scheme and plot against David's life, we can be certain *ha-Satan* will not stop trying to destroy us either. Saul was even willing to enlist his own children to help kill David. However, Jonathan loved David and honored his covenant friendship with him more than he feared his own father. Jonathan helped and covered David so that he could evade Saul's attempts on his life (1 Sam. 19:1-3).

Likewise, we should strive to love our brothers and sisters in Messiah as Jonathan loved David. No matter what or who *ha-Satan* enlists in his attempts to destroy our brethren—often through offense and man's judgment—we need to overcome the temptation of taking on another person's offense and judgment. We are called to honor the covenant relationships we enter into, whether they are with a spouse, spiritual brethren, or our church leadership. By walking in love and honoring our covenant relationships, we help and cover our brothers and sisters from *ha-Satan's* attacks, just as Jonathan helped and covered David.

Jonathan could have been more concerned about his own life and position as future king. He could have feared his father or feared what man could do to him more than he feared YHVH. However, Jonathan had a heart to lay down his life for his friend. He knew that his father's actions were not righteous and that Saul would just as soon turn against his own son for helping David. We need to be like Jonathan and be willing to lay our own lives down for that of our brothers and sisters in Messiah. We must be willing to fear YHVH enough to honor our covenant relationships more than we fear whatever man or the enemy could do to us.

I have found myself in such a position three times over the last decade. For example, before my family moved to the Midwest, I personally witnessed the unrighteous abuse of power by church leadership against a vulnerable sister in Messiah. It was clearly communicated that anyone who sought to stand in the gap for her would likewise be ousted from the congregation. Although I had favor in the sight of the leadership, I knew I would lose that favor if I chose to advocate for my sister in her distress.

My husband and I prayed and were clearly led by the *Ruach ha-Kodesh* to choose love over the fear of man. We advocated for brotherly love, peace, and reconciliation. The leadership would not reconsider their judgment against her or allow anyone to remain under their authority that chose to remain in unity with her, even though she had committed no sin worthy of excommunication according to the Scriptures. In submission to the *Ruach ha-Kodesh,* my family and I peacefully and voluntarily left the congregation so that we could continue to minister to the needs of our poor and vulnerable sister in Messiah. Sadly, we later saw the leadership lose their positions and the entire congregation was dismantled.

Though the experience was tragic all the way around and involved tremendous personal loss to us, my family and I will never regret the decisions we made. YHVH is ever faithful in restoring our loss. The spiritual lessons we learned and the covenant friendships forged in the fire were well worth the cost. Many of those spiritual lessons have lent to a greater understanding of David's circumstances. I don't think I would have been prepared to write *The Key of David* series if I had not walked through each of the three similar trials. I can certainly identify with Jonathan's heart for David.

Jonathan weighed the cost of loyalty and became David's mediator and intercessor against his enemy. Through his mediation and intercession, he caused David's enemy to be at peace with him and stop pursuing his life (at least temporarily). Likewise, we can become mediators and intercessors against the enemy of our brothers and sisters in Messiah, and cause the enemy to stop pursuing their lives. Because of Jonathan's intercession, David and Jonathan were able to remain in close fellowship with one another for a time and season (1 Sam. 19:4-7). When we become each other's advocates and intercessor's, we too can remain in close fellowship as brothers and sisters in Messiah, fulfilling the second greatest commandment of loving our neighbor as we love ourselves (Matt. 22:39).

Despite Jonathan's efforts, David's continued victory in warfare provoked Saul's jealousy, and he no longer feared that YHVH was with David. Saul made a second attempt to spear David through, but David evaded him once again. David ran home to his wife Michal, but she convinced him that his only hope to live was to flee from Saul. "Michal let David down through a window," "took an image [*teraphim*], and laid it in the bed," and claimed David was very ill in order to fool Saul's soldiers, who had come to capture and kill David at Saul's command (1 Sam. 19:8-14, *brackets mine*).

What Michal did may be another indication for why YHVH had rejected Saul as king of Israel. The Brown-Driver-Briggs Hebrew and English Lexicon, many Bible commentaries, and the Jewish Encyclopedia note that *teraphim* could be small or life-sized forms of a man, and their use was prevalent in ancient Israel.[4] Gill's Exposition of the Bible notes that the *teraphim* must have been "privately kept by Michal; for, had David known of them, he would not have suffered them to have been in his house." Gill goes on to say that "to consult such images was very far from David."[5]

Saul not only disobeyed YHVH's specific war instructions and regulations concerning the priestly sacrificial office, but he may have also violated Israel's covenant with YHVH by committing adultery with *teraphim* in his palace. If so, this may have led Saul's children into idolatry. The question remains, where did Michal get the *teraphim*? The point being made is that YHVH will not stay in covenant relationship with those who continually practice adultery (idolatry) any more than a man or woman will stay in covenant relationship with a spouse who is continually adulterous and unrepentant. Idolatry could be just another reasonable explanation for Saul's loss of the throne and the *Ruach ha-Kodesh*.

Saul's Mission Impossible

After David escaped out the window, he fled to Ramah, found Samuel, and reported all that had happened to him. Samuel immediately took David to Naioth (1 Sam. 19:18), which was the abode of the prophets in Israel. Naioth's name meaning, which we will explore shortly, is spiritually significant of where David was being protected from the schemes of his enemy.

Psalms 5, 11, 23, and 25 were possibly written from this very time in David's life.[6] As we look at YHVH's care over David in Naioth, we will certainly see how he could say, "Thou preparest a table before me in the presence of mine enemies" (Ps. 23:5), "let not mine enemies triumph over me...let them be ashamed which transgress without cause" (Ps. 25:2-3, *condensed*), and "let them [David's enemies] fall by their own counsels; cast them out in the multitude of their transgressions" (Ps. 5:10, *brackets mine*). Psalm 59 is definitely attributed to this time as he fled from Saul's watchman. Here, David had called upon YHVH to awaken, to look, and to help him against his enemies (Ps. 59:4-5). He proclaimed in faith that "God shall let him see his desire upon his enemies" that they would be scattered and brought down low (Ps. 59:10-11). David praised YHVH for being his strength, "defence and refuge in the day of trouble" (Ps. 59:16-17). This prayer of faith activated the miracle we are about to see.

Before we learn what YHVH did for David in Naioth, let us first look at the Hebrew word Naioth, which comes from *naveh,* which means: "comely, abode of shepherd, sheepcote, dwelling place, abide, pleasant place, abode of God" (H5116).[7] This reminds me of Psalm 91, "He who dwells in the secret place of the Most High shall abide under the shadow of the Almighty" (Ps. 91:1 NKJV). Though all scholars are not in agreement as to when Psalm 91 was written or whether Psalm 91 was penned by David or Moses,[8] the Septuagint assigned it to David. Therefore, he may have written it while thinking back on all of the experiences of YHVH's protection that he had, starting with this one in Naioth.

1 Samuel 19 records one of my favorite accounts of YHVH's divine protection in Scripture. News that David was hiding out with Samuel and the prophets at Naioth made its way through the grapevine to Saul, so he sent mercenaries there "to take David." However, the Spirit of YHVH overtook Saul's mercenaries upon arrival in Naioth "and they also prophesied" with the prophets. When Saul received word that his first mission to assassinate David had been foiled, he sent out a second team of mercenaries to seize David. They too were overcome by the *Ruach ha-Kodesh* "and they prophesied likewise." Saul was reticent to concede defeat and sent yet a third team of mercenaries who were also overcome "and they prophesied also" (1 Sam. 19:19-21). Saul was showing signs of insanity as he continued to "do the same thing over and over again expecting a different result." 9

Needless to say, Saul was supremely flabbergasted with the abject failure of his mercenaries. I can almost hear him shouting, "If you want something done right, you just have to do it yourself!" And, so he decided to take matters into his own hands. Saul personally traveled to Naioth planning to seize David himself, but upon his arrival the *Ruach ha-Kodesh* seized and overcame him and he "prophesied," "stripped off his clothes," paraded around Naioth buck naked, and "lay down naked all that day and all that night" (1 Sam. 19:22-24). That must have been quite a scene!

David's recorded prayers (Psalms 5, 25, and 59) had been answered! Because he continued to ruthlessly seek after David's life, Saul ended up stripped and naked before David, the prophets of YHVH, and the people around Naioth. Who says that YHVH lacks a sense of humor! One would think Saul would have gotten the message, after being thwarted at every attempt to take David's life, but he did not seem to be that intelligent.

Likewise, *ha-Satan* pursues every believer's life with the same level of insanity as Saul. Despite the fact that he is thwarted at every attempt to destroy our lives, *ha-Satan* continues to pursue us. The Scriptures indicate he will one day be overcome, prophesy who is truly Lord and King over all the earth, and be ashamed before the whole world as his destruction is fulfilled (Phil. 2:10-11, Rev. 19:19-21). Technically, *ha-Satan* was defeated at the cross of Messiah, but this has not stopped his pursuit of faith-filled anointed ones of YHVH. In the same way, this humiliating defeat for Saul would not keep him from pursuing David for many years to come.

Every disciple of *Yeshua* should consider that as long as we are being continually pursued by the enemy, we can take heart in our position as a faith-filled anointed of YHVH. However, if the enemy is not pursuing us to destruction, we may need to take a self-audit and ask ourselves the hard question of why the enemy does not consider us a threat to his kingdom. A smooth and easy life is not necessarily the indication of YHVH's blessing, favor, and protection. As we see in this chapter and will see throughout the rest of this study, David's life proves that YHVH's blessing, favor, and protection was on him through being constantly hunted by his enemies, who never overtook him. This is likewise the true indication of a faith-filled anointed believer whose life has YHVH's blessing, favor, and protection.

Yeshua seemed to support this concept when He said, "strait is the gate, and narrow is the way, which leads to life, and few there be that find it" (Matt. 7:14). The Greek word translated as strait is *stenos* and according to HELPS Word-studies, it is defined as "the closely-defined *path God ordains* to travel on to gain His *approval*" (G4728).[10] Furthermore, the word translated as narrow is *thlibo* and it has the following meanings: "I make narrow (strictly: by pressure); I press upon, (b) I persecute, press hard." According to HELPS Word Studies, *thlibo* is defined as: "rub together, constrict (compress), i.e. *pressed* together; (figuratively) *oppressively* afflict (distress), i.e. like when circumstances "rub us the wrong way" that make us feel confined (hemmed in); restricted to a "narrow" place" (G2346).[11] *Yeshua's* message to His disciples was that as long as they walked in the closely-defined path that YHVH ordained, they would suffer persecution, oppression, and pressure (Matt. 10:16-42). The Apostle Paul gave a second witness to the promise of persecution for "all that will live godly in Christ Jesus" (2 Tim. 3:12).

A Covenant of Protection

1 Samuel 20 reveals that while Saul was overtaken by the *Ruach ha-Kodesh*, David escaped and ran to find his covenant friend Jonathan. He asked Jonathan if there could ever be any peace between him and Saul (1 Sam. 20:1). Despite all the wrong Saul had done to him, David would not even consider writing Saul off as a lost cause, but earnestly desired to continue a peaceful relationship with Saul. How unique David's character was to his own time and culture, as well as our own modern time and culture!

Jonathan responded to David's desperate cry for peace with the house of Saul by cutting yet another covenant with him (1 Sam. 20:2-16). Jonathan and David agreed to a covenant promise with one another to protect each other's descendants forever, something that was out of the norm in the ancient Middle Eastern culture of kings and kingdoms. They had genuine brotherly love for one another (Rom. 12:10, 1 Pet. 3:8, 1 Thess. 4:9, Heb. 13:1-3). Jonathan, "loved [David] as he loved his own soul" (1 Sam. 20:17, *brackets mine*), fulfilling the second greatest commandment to love his neighbor as himself (Mark 12:30-31).

The multi-faceted, reciprocal covenant relationship between David and Jonathan was such a beautiful prophetic foreshadow of our relationship to the Son of the King of the Universe. It is a promise of mutual protection. David's promise of protection over Jonathan's future descendants points to something that applies to every disciple who has entered into a personal covenant relationship with *Yeshua.*

Every brother and sister in Messiah is a child of the King. Because of our undying love for Him, we should have an undying love for all of His children, a protective love. Yes, our brothers and sisters in Messiah are ultimately under YHVH's protection and have angels watching over them to protect them in all their ways (Ps. 91:11). However, YHVH also designed us to be watchmen over each other (Ezek. 33:7). Just as David would ultimately treat Jonathan's son as though he were his own son (2 Sam. 9), we should likewise treat all of YHVH's children as though they were our own.

The New Moon Test

After cutting covenant, Jonathan told David to go to the stone of *Ezel* (a memorial stone, stone of departure)[12] on the third day after the new moon festival and wait for word as to whether Saul would make peace with David or not (1 Sam. 20:18-19). It is indicated in the context of 1 Samuel 20:20-27, that they were holding a multi-day feast[13] in their observance of the feast of the New Moon (Num. 28:11-15). Saul excuses David's absence on the first night of the feast under the assumption he was ceremonially unclean, but he does not see fit to assume the same when David is absent the second night. Saul's actions give a clear indication that the second night was still part of the feast of the New Moon, for which a person would need to be ceremonially clean (1 Sam. 20:26-27).

In David's time, they did not yet know how to calculate the astronomical conjunction of the new moon. In the Middle East, the moon can be concealed (darkened) from one and a half days up to three and a half days, and it is commonly concealed (dark) for two and a half-days in modern Israel.[14] Under the circumstances, it is reasonable to assume that they held a multi-day feast of the New Moon. The feast would begin during the concealment of the moon and last through the confirmation of the new month by the sighting of the first sliver. How else could David and Jonathan have known for certain that the New Moon would be on the following day if they were to wait until the first sliver had been sighted?

If one does an internet search on these terms, there is no end to the arguments over whether the New Moon is to be celebrated when the moon is concealed (dark) or when the first sliver of the moon is witnessed. Each party to the argument presents convincing scriptural evidence for their interpretation and dogmatically proclaims to have the only correct interpretation. However, in David's time, they appeared to have universally and peacefully celebrated it for more than one day without disputation.

In our modern era, there are disciples of *Yeshua* who break fellowship with one another over harsh debates and arguments of whether to celebrate the feast of the New Moon at the conjunction or the first sliver sighting. Shouldn't we all be celebrating it in unity and peace? Is YHVH really going to be angry with us if we celebrate it more than one day as they did in David's time? Or is YHVH more likely to be angry with us over how we mistreat our brothers and sisters (His children) with disrespect, dishonor, and disdain over the issue?

Such questions can be extended to other issues of doctrine and interpretation within the body of Messiah. A variety of divisive arguments have arisen over the correct day and way to observe YHVH's feasts. There are also divisive arguments over the pronunciation of YHVH's name or His Son's name, the ways in which His instructions should be observed, and even the shape and expanse of the heavens and earth. Does YHVH really want members of the household of faith arguing and fighting, sometimes to the point of the death of their relationship? The Scriptures speak at length about maintaining brotherly love and unity[15] with one another (Rom. 14:10,19, Rom. 15:2,5-6, 1 Thess. 3:12-13, 1 Cor. 1:10, 3:1-3, Col. 2:2-3). Wouldn't YHVH be far more pleased to see us hold the unity of our relationships with one another in the highest regard by celebrating together in peace? Over the course of the last decade, I have been strongly convicted by His *Ruach ha-Kodesh* that YHVH is much more concerned with how we obey the second greatest commandment of loving our neighbor.

In fact, the Apostle Peter confirmed that a believer's highest end goal is love. In 2 Peter 1:5-11, Peter outlined the seven-tiered spiritual exercise program that, when practiced diligently, would lead to abundant spiritual fruitfulness and ensure our calling and election to enter the eternal Kingdom of Messiah *Yeshua*. As we exercise our faith, we develop virtue, then knowledge. Knowledge is only the second tier of our spiritual exercise program. It is not the end goal.

We are not meant to camp out on the second tier of knowledge and never reach the pinnacle of love. If we have all knowledge but do not have love, we are nothing (1 Cor. 13:2). When knowledge is exercised with incorrect technique, it leads to arguments, divisions, and schisms over doctrine and interpretations within the body of Messiah. However, when knowledge of our Creator and His heart is exercised correctly, we develop the fruit of the Spirit (Gal. 5:22-23).

Tiers three and four of our spiritual exercise program are the fruits of self-control and patience. The more we know Him, the more we will be like Him. As we exercise the fruits of self-control and patience, we develop godliness (godly character). The more our character becomes aligned with YHVH's, the more we develop the brotherly love that Jonathan had for David, wherein we will be willing to lay our lives down for one another no matter the personal cost.

The more we practice brotherly love, the more our spiritual trainer (the *Ruach ha-Kodesh*) will work in us to develop the highest form of love that includes love for our enemies. This highest form of love is the seventh tier of our spiritual exercise program and our ultimate goal to attain (2 Pet. 1:5-11). Throughout our study of David's life, we will witness how YHVH continually trained him toward such love. Let us also press on to reach the pinnacle of love together, my brothers and sisters!

A Father Betrays His Son

Before leaving David to attend the New Moon celebration, Jonathan shared a secret code by which he would covertly communicate to David whether Saul was at peace with him or not. Saul noticed David's absence the first night of the feast, but he did not think much of it. On the second day of the feast, Saul observed David's lack of attendance and asked Jonathan about David's whereabouts. Jonathan told his father that David had requested to celebrate the feast with his family, a request that Jonathan granted.

Saul was absolutely livid with Jonathan for excusing David. He accused Jonathan of being perverse and rebellious (1 Sam. 20:20-30). Yet perversity and rebellion was behavior that Saul was demonstrating himself. Isn't it ironic how often we can sometimes accuse others of the very things we are guilty of? The problem with Saul was that he could not really see with that colossal beam in his eye. It is often the same with us (Matt. 7:3), but thanks be to YHVH for His mercy and forgiveness the moment we take responsibility and repent.

When Jonathan jumped in to defend David's life, Saul saw that his son's heart was for David. In jealousy and rage, Saul hurled his spear at his own son—the very same son he was just concerned about protecting (1 Sam. 20:32-33). Isn't it sad how quickly a person can turn on their loved ones when they take offense to their actions? How often are we guilty of doing this to some degree?

Evil Separates Friends

Like David, Jonathan evaded his father's spear and fled from his presence. He ran out with his young assistant to where David was hiding near the stone of Ezel and shot three arrows into the field. David and Jonathan had previously arranged this act with the arrows as their special code. Jonathan told the lad, "Make speed, haste, stay not!" David understood the message loud and clear, and his heart was shattered. Jonathan sent the lad back home while he stayed behind to say goodbye to his covenant friend (1 Sam. 20:34-40).

As Jonathan approached him, David abased himself before Jonathan by bowing to his honor three times, and they kissed on the cheek (a common ancient Middle Eastern practice amongst covenant friends). They wept together for the loss of their close fellowship (1 Sam. 20:41-42). As the king of Israel, Saul should have been a catalyst for unity by leading David, Jonathan, and all the people of Israel in YHVH's covenant laws. Instead, his emotional offense was separating David and Jonathan.

Sadly, I have witnessed this type of thing happen far too often in the body of Messiah. Churches split over emotional offenses, as well as differences in doctrines and interpretations. That is precisely *ha-Satan's* goal: to divide and conquer the unity of the body of Messiah through offense. Divisions and schisms within the body hurt and separate far too many brothers and sisters. In the process of a church split, brethren may lose their close fellowship with one another. Also, division within a church body can sometimes interfere with each person's relationship with the Heavenly Father. Tragically, I know two people who were so emotionally devastated by a church split that they have left the faith altogether. They were disillusioned with the Heavenly Father because the church leadership grossly misrepresented His nature and character through their divisiveness.

A Higher Calling

At this point in David's journey, he had lost everything but his anointing and promise due to the work of the adversary. He was living the high life as captain of the king's army, personal minstrel to the king, husband of the king's daughter, and best friend of the king's son. Now, David was forced to leave all that and lose the precious fellowship of everyone he knew and loved.

YHVH was releasing David from his former life and calling him into the unknown territory of the Judean wilderness. At this time, David probably did not understand that, if he was truly to walk in the fullness of his anointing, he could no longer remain yoked together with Saul. Saul was full of a wicked spirit and his house may have been full of idolatry. If David were allowed to comfortably remain with him, Saul's lifestyle would only defile David and his future dynasty.

Through all of it, David was probably crying out, "Why God? Why are you allowing this to happen to me? It doesn't compute with your promises and with the anointing you gave me." Like many of us who face similar trials, David probably did not realize that these circumstances were the result of YHVH's hand of protection over him and his future. YHVH would sanctify David and keep him undefiled so that he could successfully fulfill the purpose for which he had been anointed.

David chose to praise YHVH in these crushing circumstances. Some biblical scholars attribute Psalm 26 to this time in David's life.[16] David said, "I will wash my hands in innocence; so I will go about your altar, O LORD, that I may proclaim with the voice of thanksgiving, and tell of all your wondrous works. LORD, I have loved the habitation of your house, and the place where your glory dwells" (Ps. 26:6-8 NKJV).

We do not always understand why YHVH allows certain circumstances to happen in our lives. And we may ask the same questions that I speculate David asked, "Why me? Why is this being allowed to happen in my life?" Sometimes, YHVH needs to separate us from our home, our family, and even our friends. This separation may happen through painful circumstances, such as what David experienced.

However, if we truly love YHVH, and we are called according to His purposes, we can trust that He is working every circumstance together for our good—even our most painful life circumstances (Rom. 8:28). He may be using the wilderness journey to save us and our future calling from being contaminated and defiled. We can trust YHVH's purposes and praise Him even in the midst of the most painful situations, just as David trusted Him. As we will see in a future chapter, YHVH had an awesome plan to build David an incredible palace of his own in Jerusalem. Therefore, David was never meant to stay comfortable in Saul's palace.

No doubt it hurt David immensely to be separated from his covenant friend Jonathan. However, their brotherly love for one another and the promises they had made to each other would be a blessing for David to hold onto in the days ahead. No matter what his future held, David knew he would always have a friend in Jonathan, and that was worth gold.

YHVH is calling each of us to be that kind of friend to all of our brothers and sisters in Messiah. Now more than ever, we need each other as persecution and attacks from our enemy intensify in these last days. Personally, I hope to be that kind of friend. Will you?

"A man that hath friends must shew himself friendly: and there is a friend that sticketh closer than a brother." (Prov. 18:24)

"This is my commandment, That ye love one another, as I have loved you. Greater love hath no man than this, that a man lay down his life for his friends. Ye are my friends, if ye do whatsoever I command you." (John 15:12-14)

JOURNEY JOURNAL

1. Do you personally identify with any of Jonathan's characteristics or experiences? If so, which one(s)?

2. Do you personally identify with any of David's characteristics or experiences? If so, which one(s)?

3. Do you personally identify with any of Saul's characteristics or experiences? If so, which one(s)?

4. How has this chapter's study affected your perspective on persecution and pressure versus a life of smooth sailing?

5. How has this chapter's study affected your perspective of how we should relate to one another through our differences of opinion and biblical interpretation in the body of Messiah?

6. Did you experience any personal conviction as you read this chapter and answered the questions presented? What were you convicted about? (Conviction is meant to lead us to prayers of repentance, wherein we receive YHVH's grace, mercy, and forgiveness.)

7. How has this chapter's study encouraged you to greater love for YHVH and your neighbor?

4
INTO THE GREAT UNKNOWN

Life doesn't always go the way that we expect. We have goals, hopes, dreams, and even promises of how our future will look. However, life has a way of suddenly taking us down unexpected roads. Those roads seem to lead away from our goals, hopes, and dreams. In fact, some catastrophic events may seem to lead us far outside of the imagined landscape of our lives. We may find ourselves staring into a vast and seemingly unending desert landscape. In such moments, we may be tempted to believe that YHVH has abandoned His promises to us.

Our study resumes in 1 Samuel 21. A broken-hearted David has been left standing before his own desert landscape, the Judean wilderness. In light of YHVH's promises to him and his dire circumstances, David wondered what his future held. Where was he supposed to go? What was he supposed to do now? How could this dry, barren wasteland possibly be part of YHVH's plan to lead him to the throne?

The Sacrifice of Praise

What is our first thought for seeking refuge in times of adversity? In David's case, his first thought was to seek refuge in the dwelling place of YHVH's presence. In 1 Samuel 19, David fled from Saul to seek refuge with Samuel and the prophets. However, he knew he couldn't go to Ramah again as it would likely be the first place that Saul went looking for him. Instead, David chose to go to the tabernacle in Nob (1 Sam. 21:1 KJV). By this time, Saul had moved the tabernacle of Moses from Shiloh to a place near his home town of Gibeah called Nob.[1] This occurred sometime after the Philistines had defeated Israel's armies and captured the Ark of the Covenant.

Considering the word origin of Nob, the fact that Saul decided to move the tabernacle there has prophetic significance. On the surface, Nob can mean a place of "exaltation, elevation, and proclamation" (H5011).[2] It is the same as the word *nowb,* which means "fruit of the lips, or praise" (H5108).[3] I am reminded of the words of the author of Hebrews: "Let us offer the sacrifice of praise to God continually, that is, the fruit of our lips giving thanks to his name" (Heb. 13:15).

Interestingly, Nob's word origin, *naar,* means to "abandon, reject, abhor, or make void" (H5010).[4] The tabernacle was supposed to be a place of exaltation, elevation, and proclamation of YHVH's name. It was supposed to bring Him glory through the fruit of praise on the lips (thanksgiving). However, because of the rebellion of the priests (Eli and his sons) and King Saul, Nob became a place that had been abandoned, rejected, and made void of YHVH's presence.

Likewise, the heart of every disciple of Messiah is a living tabernacle (1 Cor. 3:16). Like David, our hearts can be a place of exaltation, elevation, and proclamation of YHVH's name and glory through the fruit of praise on our lips. Or, through our own rebellion as kings and priests (Rev. 1:6, 5:10), our hearts can become a place that has been abandoned, rejected, and made void of YHVH's presence. However, His presence returns when there is repentance and restoration of our thanksgiving. Halleluyah!

Covert Mission of the King

In his distress, David approached the tabernacle and found the high priest, Ahimelek. After telling him a little story about being on a covert mission for the king, David asked Ahimelek for bread (1 Sam. 21:1-2). It is quite easy and tempting to judge David for failing to trust in YHVH's provision and protection, to call him a liar and a man ruled by fear. It is possible that David was wondering who he could trust and who would be on his side when King Saul had a bounty on his life. I have been in similar situations and pondered these questions myself.

Understandably, David might have been afraid to tell Ahimelek the truth because of the priests' loyalty to Saul. There were two religious camps in Israel at the time of Saul. One camp was Samuel and the prophets of YHVH who were in Ramah and Naioth. Samuel was officiating sacrifices to YHVH, which appeared to be wholly acceptable to Him (1 Sam. 7:9, 16:1-3). Samuel was the biological son of Elkanah, a Levitical priest of the family of the Kohathites (1 Chron. 6:33). The Kohathites were the porters, gatekeepers, and singers in the tabernacle. Samuel was also like an adopted son to Eli, the former high priest. Eli essentially raised him, but Samuel did not become corrupted like Eli's sons. Samuel and the prophets with him were not loyal to Saul, but only to YHVH and his anointed king.

The second religious camp in Israel was the priestly class in Nob. Many of the priests in Nob, including Ahimelek, were descendants of Eli. They were loyal to Saul, whom YHVH had rejected as king. As descendants of Eli, their hearts may have been quite corrupt, giving David all the more reason to fear them.

I would be willing to give David the benefit of the doubt in this situation. It is quite possible that he inquired of YHVH and received instructions to act covertly. If the King of kings gave David a mission and instructed him to go to the tabernacle under His covering, David would have been telling the truth. However, David was clearly lying about having Israel's armies with him because, in truth, he was alone.

As we saw in the first chapter, YHVH instructed Samuel to conduct a covert operation to protect David's life; YHVH did not want Saul to know that a new king was being anointed. In the second volume of this book series, we will discuss how YHVH may have authorized another covert mission for one of David's loyal servants during Absalom's rebellion. With all this in mind, it appears reasonable that YHVH may have given David a covert mission to Nob.

Even if David lied out of fear and desperation for his life, do we have a right to judge him for it? *Yeshua* didn't seem to judge him for it. In Matthew 12:4, *Yeshua* actually used the example of David receiving and eating the consecrated showbread as a proof text to defend His disciples for picking grain to eat on the Sabbath. In fact, in Matthew 12:3-8, *Yeshua* gave multiple examples that supported the kingdom principle that the preservation of life supersedes law; it is permissible to break YHVH's law *only if it is necessary to save a life.*

In the next chapter, we will discuss the larger implications of David's visit to Nob. Ultimately, YHVH would use this event to fulfill the judgment He spoke against Eli and his descendants. All the more reason we must be careful not to judge the situation before its time (1 Cor. 4:5).

The high priest, Ahimelek, informed David that the only bread on the premises was the consecrated showbread (also known as the bread of the Presence). By the law of YHVH, only the Aaronic priests and Levites were permitted to eat the showbread (Lev. 24:5-9). After David assured Ahimelek that he and his companions had kept themselves from sexual relations with women and were therefore consecrated, Ahimelek gave David the showbread (1 Sam. 21:3-6).

It is highly likely that David was given the showbread from the previous week. This bread was set aside as the daily portion of bread for the priests and Levites; it was not the showbread that was currently consecrated to YHVH on the table of showbread. This means that the priests and the Levites were willing to sacrifice their daily provision of bread (their only daily living) to feed David and Israel's army. The priests were willing to preserve the lives of Israel's soldiers over their own lives. What an example they set for us! Are we willing to sacrifice our daily bread for a brother or sister in need?

After receiving the bread, David told Ahimelek that his mission was so urgent and he had left in such haste that he had no weapons with him. David asked if there were any weapons on hand. Ahimelek offered him the only sword on the premises—the sword of Goliath. This was probably the largest sword available in the world. Truly, David was the rightful owner of this sword because he had conquered its former owner. He gladly received it (1 Sam. 21:8-9).

The account of David's tabernacle visit was a beautiful prophetic picture for him and for every disciple of Messiah *Yeshua*. David had been rejected and exiled under threat of death by the king of Israel. David was being driven out of the culture and the world he had known and called into the unknown of the wilderness. He came before the high priest and was given consecrated bread and a very impressive sword.

I wonder if David understood the prophetic significance of what was happening in his life at this very moment. Keep in mind that the earthly high priest is a foreshadow of the heavenly eternal high priest, *Yeshua* (Heb. 4:14, 5:5-10). *Yeshua* is the consecrated "bread of life" (John 6:35). He is the biggest sword in the entire known universe, "the sword of the Spirit, which is the word of God" (Eph. 6:17). *Yeshua* is the Word which "was made flesh, and dwelt among us" (John 1:14).

Like David, every disciple of *Yeshua* that is truly a person after YHVH's own heart has been anointed and called to be a king and priest. We have faced our personal Goliaths and experienced the defeat of our enemy through the cross. We have also experienced hate and exile from the culture who recognizes that YHVH is with us. As we continually seek refuge in the dwelling place of YHVH, we will personally encounter our high priest, *Yeshua*, and receive the same gifts that were given to David. *Yeshua* will provide us with bread (every word that proceeds from the mouth of the Father) and the sword of the Spirit; we will be prepared for whatever lies ahead on the way He is calling us. When we have such an encounter with Him, it is only natural that our lives become a place of exaltation, elevation, and proclamation of His name and glory by the fruit of praise on our lips.

While YHVH was provisioning David, Saul's chief shepherd, Doeg, was in the tabernacle. Scripture states that Doeg was "detained before the LORD and saw everything" (1 Sam. 21:7). The question is what does it mean that he was detained before YHVH? Was Doeg detained from saying anything to the high priest that would expose David's deception about his mission? Or did YHVH prevent Doeg from leaving the tabernacle before David arrived because He wanted word to get back to Saul? It may be a little of both, but it was certainly the latter, as we will discuss in the next chapter.

Driven into Enemy Territory

After seeing Doeg, David departed from Nob. It is not clear from the text what ultimately drove David to flee into the enemy territory of Gath, in the land of the Philistines. However, it is possible that the sight of Doeg—whose name root means "anxiety, fear, dread" (H1672)[5]—sparked fear of Saul in David and compelled him to flee. In *The Treasury of David*, Charles Spurgeon suggests that Psalm 27 was inspired at this very occasion.[6] In the face of anxiety, fear, and dread, look at how David encouraged himself: "The LORD is my light and my salvation; whom shall I fear? The LORD is the strength of my life; of whom shall I be afraid? Wait on the LORD: be of good courage, and he shall strengthen thine heart: wait, I say, on the LORD" (Ps. 27:1, 14).

David's psalm gives us the key to overcoming the dark spiritual force behind anxiety, fear, and dread: know that YHVH is your salvation from every enemy and wait for it with confident expectation. Through our certainty in YHVH's faithfulness, our hearts are strengthened and filled with courage. Anxiety, fear, and dread shall not overtake us when we stand firm in such faith and confident expectation.

David appeared to be standing very firm in confident expectation of YHVH's salvation from his enemies, as he entered Gath. Perhaps, he may have been a tad too confident. It was pretty gutsy for David to enter Philistine territory carrying Goliath's sword (1 Sam. 21:10). Was it solely his confidence in YHVH that compelled him to take this bold step, or is it possible that David thought the Philistines would fear him because of his massive victories against them? If such was the case, that might have been a sliver of pride peeking out of his heart. Have you ever felt so confident in YHVH's salvation that you hastily took a bold step into enemy territory like this? I have, and it turned out a lot like David's experience did.

Needless to say, the Philistines didn't fear David. In fact, they alerted the local ruler, King Achish, that the mighty warrior and future king of Israel was right there under his nose. Psalm 56 captured David's thoughts about his circumstances. David said to YHVH, "What time I am afraid, I will trust in thee. In God, I have put my trust; I will not fear what flesh can do to me. When I cry unto thee, then shall mine enemies turn back: this I know; for God is for me" (Ps. 56:3-4, 9).

Even in his faith, David was mortified of King Achish, and he pretended to be insane (1 Sam. 21:11-13). I think he must have been a little insane to have fled for refuge from Saul into the land of his arch-enemies. The Philistines hated David with a passion for ravaging them in warfare. Civilization in enemy territory must have appeared to be a better option to him than the unknown of the Judean wilderness!

Fit to be King?

I wonder how some in the modern church would have judged David if they had been alive in his time. On Christian blogs, social media, and through YouTube videos, I have seen many judgments against anointed leaders. In the absence of our Bibles, how would we feel about a man who lied to the high priest and took forbidden bread from YHVH's tabernacle? How would we feel if that same man publicly displayed signs of mental illness? Would we believe that he was qualified to be YHVH's anointed and chosen leader? Or would we have judged him to be unfit for leadership?

Painfully, I can imagine all the internet and social media slander that David would have received: "David broke YHVH's law, deceived the priest, and took what was unlawful! He is a drooling madman who has totally lost his mind! He is definitely no anointed leader of YHVH's people!" I can even imagine the viral YouTube videos showing footage of David's dastardly deeds and warning everyone in the world to beware of him. David would be called a criminal, liar, madman, and one who was unfit for leadership. All of these judgments would come complete with a slew scriptural support for the case against him.

Perhaps you laugh at my imaginations, but sadly, this is the behavior of many who call themselves disciples of *Yeshua* (even pastors). I have seen many web pages dedicated to the defamation of specific pastors, teachers, and ministries. Sadly, the authors of these web pages believe they are doing YHVH's work and being a blessing to the greater body of Messiah. I have spent a lot of time travailing in prayer over such things. Was the prophet Micah alluding to this time also when he prophesied, "They all lie in wait for blood; every man hunts his brother with a net" (Mic. 7:2 NKJV)?

This issue has personally touched my life because my congregation and pastor have been victim to public slander by other "Christians." My pastor's family is one of the most beautiful families I have ever had the blessing to know intimately. His teenage daughters are the most humble, honorable, and respectful young ladies, who manifest many gifts of the *Ruach ha-Kodesh*. The entire family has ministered to my family greatly, and they have saved many marriages that were in deep trouble. Yet there are other pastors and ministry leaders who dedicate their web pages to defaming my pastor and others in ministry.

It breaks my heart to hear brothers and sisters slander one another in this way. It breaks our Heavenly Father's heart as well. Such behavior should not be seen or heard among His children! *Yeshua* said everyone would know the identity of His disciples because they would see our love for one another (John 13:35). According to the Apostle Paul, those who love readily believe the best in others, not the worst (1 Cor. 13:7 AMP). In other words, love upholds a presumption of innocence in the absence of firsthand, reliable, verifiable, substantive proof of guilt. According to Proverbs 10:12 and 1 Peter 4:8, "love covers a multitude of sins" rather than exposing them publicly.

Despite David's shortcomings, was he any less YHVH's chosen and anointed king of Israel? Certainly not! Do we have the right to judge who YHVH has chosen and anointed to be leaders over His flock? We should be very careful not to judge and slander other brothers and sisters in our misguided zeal (James 4:11, Luke 6:36-38). Though I have never dedicated web pages to such, I have also been guilty of past judgment and slander in misguided zeal; the *Ruach ha-Kodesh* corrected and convicted me, and I had to repent. If we have likewise been guilty of such behavior, let us all repent and work on loving one another better.

All Things Together for Good

Thankfully, David's ruse of insanity worked to fake out the enemy and save his life. Surely, King Achish would have killed David on the spot had he not believed David was genuinely insane and no longer a threat to his kingdom. Achish commanded his servants to get the madman out of his presence (1 Sam. 21:14-15). Despite what others might judge as a total failure of judgment or weakness in David's faith, YHVH's hand of protection was clearly on him.

Through the words of Psalms 34, which David penned at this time, we can see that David's faith was significantly strengthened through these circumstances. He said, "I sought the LORD, and he heard me, and delivered me from all my fears. This poor man cried, and the LORD heard him, and saved him out of all his troubles. The angel of the LORD encampeth round about them that fear him, and delivereth them. The righteous cry, and the LORD heareth, and delivereth them out of all their troubles" (Ps. 34:4, 6-7, 17 KJV).

YHVH can take even our most egregious mistakes and turn them into blessings. Therefore, we really should withhold judgment in everything, because we do not always know what is happening behind the scenes (1 Cor. 4:5). YHVH is sovereign and He is working "all things together for good" (Rom. 8:28). He can use any person, in any situation to forward His purposes. He can even use our weakness and failure to show His strength and goodness. Instead of judging, it is best if we simply trust that YHVH knows what He is doing with His people.

Throughout this extended study, we are going to see that each point in David's life (including this ruse of insanity) was training him to be a godly king. YHVH could not truly set David on the throne of Israel until he went through every point of training. Everything that the enemy was allowed to do to David, everything David was allowed to do, and everything that YHVH would allow in David's future was working together with the good purpose of shaping him into the best king and shepherd of Israel that he could be. History speaks of the fruit of YHVH's work in his life, for David was the best king that Israel has ever known.

Through this crazy mess of wandering into enemy territory, it would seem that YHVH taught David a valuable lesson in humility. It was a bit bold for David to walk into Gath with Goliath's sword. By carrying it, he probably thought that no one would dare take him on. But he quickly learned that, if he wanted to make it out of Philistine territory alive, he had better abase himself. There is nothing more humbling than acting like a toddler, scribbling "on the doors of the gates," and drooling all over oneself (1 Sam. 21:13)!

Remember, that it was pride that destroyed Saul. David could not have even a sliver of pride if he was going to be the king that YHVH had anointed him to be. So it is with us who have been called to be kings (Rev. 1:6, 5:10). We cannot have one shred of pride in us if we are going to be the kings that YHVH has anointed us to be.

If we find ourselves staring at a vast, unknown landscape, we must trust that we are going to encounter YHVH there. The Most High will have some things He wants to provide us with as we seek refuge in His dwelling place (Ps. 91). He might also need to purge us of some things, such as pride. The difficulties will all work together for good—even if we give in to fear and make a mistake or two along the way. In the process, we must never beat ourselves up. We need only trust in YHVH's faithfulness, just as He was faithful to David.

"And we know that all things work together for good to them that love God, to them who are the called according to his purpose. For whom he did foreknow, he also did predestinate to be conformed to the image of his Son, that he might be the firstborn among many brethren. Moreover whom he did predestinate, them he also called: and whom he called, them he also justified: and whom he justified, them he also glorified." (Rom. 8:28-30)

"For I know the thoughts that I think toward you, saith the LORD, thoughts of peace, and not of evil, to give you an expected end. Then shall ye call upon me, and ye shall go and pray unto me, and I will hearken unto you. And ye shall seek me, and find me, when ye shall search for me with all your heart." (Jer. 29:11-13)

JOURNEY JOURNAL

1. Do you personally identify with any of David's characteristics or experiences? If so, which one(s)?

2. Which kind of living tabernacle will you choose to be? What are some things you can do to make yourself a living tabernacle that is a place of exaltation, elevation, and proclamation of YHVH's name and glory through the fruit of praise on your lips?

3. Have you ever made decisions out of anxiety, fear, dread, or even pride, leading you down paths you should not have traveled? How has YHVH protected you through those times and grown your faith and maturity through them?

4. How has this chapter's study affected your perspective on the calling of a disciple of *Yeshua* as it relates to judging and exposing other believer's shortcomings?

5. Did you experience any other personal conviction as you read this chapter and answered the questions presented? What were you convicted about? (Conviction is meant to lead us to prayers of repentance, wherein we receive YHVH's grace, mercy, and forgiveness.)

6. How has this chapter's study encouraged you to greater love for YHVH and your neighbor?

5
DEN OF THIEVES

The most humiliating circumstances can often lend to some of the most valuable lessons and growth of our lives. Undesirable experiences can challenge our sense of pride, and supremely test our faith in YHVH's promises. Such experiences can become a bountiful harvest of good fruit or bad fruit depending on how we handle them. The fruit we produce also depends on how others relate to us as we go through trials and how we respond to those individuals in return. If we maintain our trust in YHVH's sovereign plan and His character, then our experiences will always bring about a bountiful harvest of good fruit in us. If we do not maintain trust, the results can be disastrous—for us and for those around us.

Remember the Victories

In 1 Samuel 22, we will witness how David, and those around him, navigated through a set of humiliating circumstances. After

David successfully escaped from King Achish, he retreated into the wilderness of Judah. He took refuge in the cave of Adullam, which overlooked the valley of Elah (1 Sam. 22:1 KJV).[1] The recent turn of events was humbling for David. It was only natural for him to return to a place that would remind him of an exceptional victory of faith. It was in the valley of Elah that David defeated Goliath (1 Sam. 17). Though the text does not make it overtly clear, I believe YHVH's hand orchestrated David's steps to return to this place because he needed to be reminded of his identity. Likewise, when circumstances in our lives seek to bring us down low, YHVH will always seek to remind us who we are in Him.

David's life had taken a drastic turn. He went from chasing down his enemies in victory to running away from them in what seemed like defeat. Perhaps David was hoping to meet YHVH amidst the terebinth trees of Elah once again. Certainly, YHVH had a purpose for leading David to this place at this very time. As David had just been exiled, betrayed, and outcast by Saul, he needed to be reminded that *that giant* had been defeated in his life. As we discussed in Chapter 2, Goliath's name means exiled, betrayed, and outcast. YHVH did not want David to succumb to the emotional defeat of anxiety and insecurity because of the downturn in his circumstances. Likewise, we sometimes need to walk around the same old mountain to be reminded of how YHVH helped us overcome our last battle there.

Refuge in the Father's Judgment

Every move in David's journey was ordained by YHVH for a good purpose. We are going to see that more clearly as we dig into the name meaning of David's refuge. The word translated as cave is *mearah* which means "cave, den, *a place of refuge*" (H4631).[2] Its root *uwr* means "to be exposed or bare, naked" (H5783).[3] Don't you think that David must have been feeling a little exposed or emotionally bare at this point? He had certainly been stripped bare of everything he knew in life up to this point.

Adullam (H5725) comes from the passive participle *adlay* meaning "father of Shaphat" and also means "retreat or refuge" (H5724).[4] *Shaphat* means "to judge or govern" and has the connotation of "entering into YHVH's judgment" or of "looking for YHVH to argue our case" (H8199).[5] David might have been wondering if his present circumstances indicated that he was receiving YHVH's judgment for something he might have done. He was also clearly seeking YHVH's judgment and advocacy in all that had transpired against him of late.

From the Psalms that are attributed to David during this time in his journey, we know that judgment was certainly on his mind (Ps. 7, 57, 63, 142).[6] David recorded, "I poured out my complaint before him; I shewed before him my trouble. Attend unto my cry; for I am brought very low: deliver me from my persecutors; for they are stronger than I" (Ps. 142:2, 6). Psalm 7 recorded some of David's cries to YHVH: "O LORD my God, in thee do I put my trust: save me from all them that persecute me, and deliver me. Arise, O LORD, in thine anger, lift up thyself because of the rage of mine enemies: and awake for me to the judgment that thou hast commanded. O let the wickedness of the wicked come to an end. He ordains his arrows against the persecutors" (Ps. 7:1, 6, 9, 13).

Yet even in the midst of David's cries for help against his adversary, he found an occasion to praise YHVH. Psalm 63 is one of my all-time favorite psalms of David to sing. Many wonderful modern worship songs have been born out of David's recorded praises to YHVH in the midst of his adversity. "O God, thou art my God; early will I seek thee: my soul thirsteth for thee; to see thy power and thy glory, so as I have seen thee in the sanctuary. Because thy loving kindness is better than life, my lips shall praise thee. Thus I will bless thee while I live: I will lift up my hands in thy name. My mouth shall praise thee with joyful lips. Because thou hast been my help, therefore in the shadow of thy wings will I rejoice" (Ps. 63:1-5, 7, *condensed*).

As David sat overlooking the valley of Elah, he reminisced about the sanctuary at Nob and the wonderful provisions YHVH had bestowed upon him there. David's tabernacle (his heart) was filled with the fruit of joyful praise on his lips. In the midst of his circumstances, he found hope in remembering the great victory over Goliath and the Philistines through YHVH's glorious power. And David looked with expectation to see YHVH's power and glory again in this place. Though he was facing trouble of many kinds, he rejoiced (James 1:2). David's example is one that we can follow in the midst of our tribulations.

David understood that being under the Father's wings meant being under the covering of the Father's judgment *(shaphat)*. And to be under the covering of YHVH's judgment is to be in a place of retreat and refuge *(mearah)*. It is easy to think that seeking YHVH's judgment is about seeking His discipline for those who have committed injustice against us. However, I am going to suggest that David would learn what seeking YHVH's advocacy truly means. Later, David's actions prove that he learned the same lesson every disciple of *Yeshua* must learn.

Yeshua said, "But the Advocate, the Holy Spirit, whom the Father will send in my name, will teach you all things and will remind you of everything I have said to you" (John 14:26 NIV). The word translated as Advocate is *parakletos* and is further defined in the HELPS Word-studies as "a legal advocate who makes the right judgment call because they are close enough to the situation" (G3875).[7] Seeking YHVH as our advocate does not always necessarily mean that we are seeking for Him to argue our case and bring the one who injured us to justice. *Yeshua* said that in His role as Advocate, the *Ruach ha-Kodesh* would teach us all things and remind us of everything *Yeshua* said to us. The *Ruach ha-Kodesh* reminds us to love our enemies (Matt. 5:44) and to have mercy and refrain from judgment (Luke 6:36-38 KJV). He also teaches us to forgive in the same way we have been forgiven, as many times as necessary (Matt. 6:14-15, 18:21-22).

I wonder if David had some kind of supernatural pre-incarnate encounter with *Yeshua* (perhaps even in this cave) and learned these things from Him. Though the prophet Micah lived long after David's time, he did prophecy that an heir (the promised heir of the Davidic covenant), the glory of Israel would come to Adullam (Mic. 1:15). Is it possible that *Yeshua* already had come in David's time? A just and devout man named Simeon prophesied over baby *Yeshua* that he was "the glory of thy people Israel" (Luke 2:32). In the last days of David's life, he said, "the Rock of Israel spake to me, He that ruleth over men must be just, ruling in the fear of God —he shall be as the light of the morning, when the sun riseth" (2 Sam. 23:3-4).

The Rock of Israel is Messiah *Yeshua* (1 Cor. 10:1-4). Throughout the rest of our study, we will see how David lived out this message of love, mercy, and forgiveness toward Saul (and many others). He lived out this message even as Saul continued to ruthlessly pursue him. David must have learned this supernaturally because it is not our natural human response to persecution.

I have personally experienced supernatural learning of this nature through my own wilderness experience of tremendous injustices committed against myself and beloved brothers and sisters in Messiah. In my spiritual immaturity, I once looked upon YHVH as my advocate to bring down severe justice for the wrongs committed. However, as I continued to pray and submit myself to the *Ruach ha-Kodesh's* work in me, I was matured to a place of being able to love and pray for YHVH's kindness to lead the offenders to repentance. The more I submitted to His work in me, the more He empowered me to be the one who reflected His kindness to those who were unkind to me. He is continually refining me in this area, just as we will see Him refine David in the chapters ahead.

The Power of Unity

While David was hiding out in the cave of Adullam, his brothers heard about his circumstances. David's brothers and *"all his father's house"* went down to meet him in the cave (1 Sam. 22:1). Thankfully, David's family had become a true family to him —family that sticks together no matter what. They could have been afraid for their own lives. After all, Saul was willing to kill his own son Jonathan because he helped David. Yet the fear of what Saul or the government of Israel would do to them did not deter David's family; they were eager to stand with their brother and minister to him in his time of need.

Such needs to be the case for us, if we call ourselves disciples of *Yeshua*. We are children of the Most High *Elohim*, and a family member to every other disciple of *Yeshua*. All members of the Father's house are called to "have fervent and unfailing love for one another" (1 Pet. 4:8 AMP). Notice what Scripture says of David's family— *"all his father's house"* came to meet him. I believe this statement has prophetic significance for us as a body of Messiah that is divided into almost 40,000 denominations. A time is coming when fear of our rulers and governments is something we will have to overcome. We need to stand by each other and minister to each other in times of need, taking no thought for our own lives. *Yeshua* is abiding in each one of His disciples (John 4:4). If we are willing to lay down our lives for each other, we are laying them down for Him (Matt. 16:25).

There is also prophetic significance in what happened immediately after David's family came together in unity to attend to him. 1 Samuel 22:2 states that "every one that was in distress, and every one that was in debt, and every one that was discontented, gathered themselves unto him; and he became a captain over them." Bear in mind that David was both a biological forefather and an archetype of the Messiah. Can you see the results of brotherly love and unity among all the Father's house? All the distressed, indebted, and discontented rallied around David, and he became their leader. This is what *Yeshua's* final prayer before His crucifixion was all about. Let us look at what He said:

> *"Neither for these alone do I pray [it is not for their sake only that I make this request], but also for all those who will ever come to believe in (trust in, cling to, rely on) Me through their word and teaching, That they all may be one, [just] as You, Father, are in Me and I in You, that they also may be one in Us,* **so that the world may believe and be convinced that You have sent Me.** *I have given to them the glory and honor which You have given Me, that they may be one [even] as We are one: I in them and You in Me, in order that they may become one and perfectly united,* **that the world may know and [definitely] recognize that You sent Me** *and that You have loved them [even] as You have loved Me." (John 17:20-23 AMPC)*

What did *Yeshua* say was the purpose of all believers being one and perfected in unity? Please allow me to repeat that *the result of all believers being one and perfectly united is that the world comes to the knowledge and convincing belief of Yeshua as the Messiah!* The early Acts church, that we all say we want to reflect, had that kind of unity (Acts 1:14, Acts 2:44, Rom. 15:6). The gospel was spreading like wild-fire, until factions, divisions, and schisms started rising up among them; over time, the "church" became a place of institutionalized denominations with many different doctrines and interpretations.

YHVH is able to use all things that are meant for evil for good. Many have still come to the saving knowledge of *Yeshua* since the first century. However, I just want to make all believers aware that our being one and perfected in unity is a *huge* threat to *ha-Satan*. Our unity is probably his most substantial target for destruction because he does not want the whole world to come to the saving knowledge of *Yeshua*. Why? Because he hates YHVH for kicking him out of heaven and condemning him to the lake of fire for all eternity (Rev. 20:10).

Therefore, *ha-Satan* does not want what YHVH wants, and YHVH wants all people to come to repentance and everlasting life (John 3:16, Ezek. 18:23). This is precisely why *ha-Satan* went hard after the unity of the body of Messiah in the first century and has continued ever since. He uses everything he possibly can, including using us as weapons against each other—*if we allow him to*. He does this primarily through manipulating our emotional system through offense and judgment. The moment he can get a believer to take up offense and judgment against another believer, he can conquer and divide relationships in the body of Messiah.

In Acts 15:36-41, we can see a perfect example of how *ha-Satan* used emotional offense to divide close brothers and co-laborers of the gospel. Paul and Barnabas were preparing to set out for another gospel mission together. Barnabas wanted to take his cousin John Mark with them. However, John Mark deserted them on a previous mission, and Paul was still offended over it; he did not trust John Mark enough to take him with them again. Scripture does not tell us what Barnabas and Paul argued over at this point. However, it is plausible that Barnabas wanted Paul to forgive John Mark and give him a second chance, but Paul refused to do so.

Barnabas was, after all, the one who convinced the apostles of Jerusalem to forgive Paul for his horrendous transgressions against the disciples of *Yeshua* before his conversion. Barnabas convinced them to give Paul a chance to prove himself to be a true convert (Acts 9:26-27). Barnabas likely reminded Paul of this very fact as he pled for Paul to forgive John Mark. Paul was still young in his newfound faith in *Yeshua* and still heavily influenced by his former training as a Pharisee. Pharisees were heavily unbalanced on judgment for transgressions. Therefore, Paul was unwilling to relent in his position and grant mercy at that time.

Paul's unwillingness to humble himself and grant mercy and forgiveness as freely as it had been granted to him resulted in separation. The brothers divided their ministry and moved in different directions. However, Paul's later writings indicate that the *Ruach ha-Kodesh* worked in him over time. He was convicted to forgive and reconcile his broken relationship with John Mark and possibly even Barnabas. We see evidence of a reconciled relationship years later in Paul's letters.

It is evident that Mark was close to Paul while he was imprisoned. Paul referred to Mark as his "fellow labourer" (Philem. 1:23-24), "profitable to me for the ministry" (2 Tim. 4:11), and Paul instructed the Colossians to "receive him" (Col. 4:10). Paul also made a friendly mention of Barnabas in 1 Corinthians 9:6, possibly indicating reconciliation of their relationship.[8] Many of his later writings indicated that the *Ruach ha-Kodesh* had matured Paul into a more merciful and freely forgiving believer whose aim was to emulate *Yeshua*.[9] Emulating *Yeshua's* freely forgiving nature is our best defense against the enemy's schemes to divide and conquer the unity of the body.

David's Mighty Misfits

For the sake of this study in 1 Samuel 22, I would like to get back to digging a little deeper into the Hebrew of verse 2: "Every one that was in *distress*, and every one that was in *debt*, and every one that was *discontented*, gathered themselves unto [David]; and he became a captain over them." Those who are in distress are defined as: "in straits, stress, in distress, anguish and its root speaks of being in a narrow place or confinement (figuratively/abstractly)" (H4689 *matsoq*).[10] This is reminiscent of Joseph when he was thrown into prison in Egypt. In Psalm 142:7, David even likened his place in the cave of Adullam to a prison.

Those who are in debt are defined as: "to beguile, deceive, delude, to become a creditor, lend on usury (interest), or to be indebted to a creditor" (H5378).[11] In Israel, these individuals were considered to be lawbreakers if they were exacting usury out of their fellow Israelites. This word has the connotation that they are deceitful in their lending practices. Those who are discontented are defined as: "bitter, bitterness (of soul), discontented, fierce (-ness of temper, like a bear robbed of whelps), seriously distressed, chafed" (H4751).[12] What a ragtag group of followers! Perhaps now my chapter title of "Den of Thieves" makes sense.

Surely YHVH could not use a group of distressed, deceitful, indebted, bitter, and fierce-tempered misfits in His kingdom, could He? Yet how often do we judge this type of person and assume they cannot be useful in YHVH's kingdom work until they get their lives perfectly in order? Yes, YHVH has some serious work to do in them before they can be all that they are called to be. But we will see how He used David's crew of misfits to make gains in His kingdom, even through their purging and refining process. Even at this point in the saga, YHVH used them to minister to David and to each other.

David could have been prideful as YHVH's next chosen king of Israel. He could have assumed that being an esteemed leader meant being surrounded with the best and the brightest people that money could buy—the most "together" people. However, YHVH brought David a group of embittered, hot-tempered, and stressed out misfits to lead and train in warfare. In fact, these misfits resembled the group that rallied around *Yeshua* during His earthly ministry. It is certainly not the type of group most kings, leaders, or pastors would choose for sure. However, it was what YHVH chose for the dream team that He was assembling together to be His royal army of Israel. A real dream team they became as we will see in future chapters and as one can read about in 2 Samuel 23:6-39 and 1 Chronicles 11:10-47.

We should never let anyone look down on us for our circumstances in life because YHVH might be calling us to His army. Likewise, we should never look down on others because YHVH might be calling them to His service as well. How do we know they are not His choice to serve with us? If He brought them, He wants to use them.

We must be careful not to judge or hinder whoever YHVH might want to use in His service. We can see from this chapter's study that people do not have to have their lives all together before they can be used in His kingdom work. No matter how polished or messed up someone may look on the outside, we really cannot know their heart until they are tested and proved in front of us. Only YHVH truly knows the heart. We should give everyone the benefit of the doubt and trust YHVH's judgment.

David and his new army ultimately left Adullam and traveled to the next point of their journey, which was Mizpah of Moab. Mizpah means "watchtower, lookout, observatory, outlook point for military purposes" (H4707-H4708).[13] David was concerned about Saul's unrelenting pursuit as well as his aging parents' ability to survive the harsh desert environment. Therefore, he asked the local Moabite king to look out for his parents and offer them a place of refuge in his kingdom. The Moabite king agreed. Meanwhile, David stayed in "the hold [castle, *net of God's judgment,* defense, fortress]" (H4686)[14] until YHVH called him, through the prophet Gad, to leave (1 Sam. 22:3-5). David trusted in YHVH's judgment to keep his parents safe.

His Word Engraved Upon the Heart

After praying for protection (as recorded in Psalms 64 and 141) David obediently left his parents in Moab, and went to "the forest of Hareth" (1 Sam. 22:5). The prophetic significance of Hareth is very interesting. The root of Hareth is *charath* and it means "to grave, engrave, engraved" (H2802-H2801).[15] *Charath* is used in Exodus 32:16 to speak of YHVH engraving His law upon the stone tablets with His finger. I believe that YHVH took David and his army to Hareth to engrave His law upon the tablet of their hearts. You might be thinking, "What? That is the new covenant!" Let us explore this thought a little further before coming to any conclusions. The understanding that we have of the new covenant comes from Jeremiah's prophecy:

"Behold, the days come, saith the LORD, that I will make a new covenant with the house of Israel, and with the house of Judah: Not according to the covenant that I made with their fathers in the day that I took them by the hand to bring them out of the land of Egypt; which my covenant they brake, although I was an husband unto them, saith the LORD: But this shall be the covenant that I will make with the house of Israel; After those days, saith the LORD, I will put my law in their inward parts, and write it in their hearts; and will be their God, and they shall be my people. And they shall teach no more every man his neighbour, and every man his brother, saying, Know the LORD : for they shall all know me, from the least of them unto the greatest of them, saith the LORD: for I will forgive their iniquity, and I will remember their sin no more. Thus saith the LORD, which giveth the sun for a light

*by day, and the ordinances of the moon and of the stars for a
light by night, which divideth the sea when the waves thereof
roar; The* LORD *of hosts is his name: If those ordinances
depart from before me, saith the* LORD, *then the seed of Israel
also shall cease from being a nation before me for ever. Thus
saith the* LORD; *If heaven above can be measured, and the
foundations of the earth searched out beneath, I will also
cast off all the seed of Israel for all that they have done, saith
the* LORD." *(Jer. 31:31-37)*

Writing His Word upon the hearts of Israel is certainly not a
"new" thing that YHVH wanted to do. When the next generation of
Israelites were preparing to enter the Promised Land, Moses
reiterated the laws of Sinai to them. He said, "These words, which
I command thee this day, *shall be in thine heart*" (Deut. 6:6,
emphasis mine). He also said, "You shall therefore impress these
words of mine *upon your heart* and on your soul" (Deut. 11:18
BSB, *emphasis mine*). Proverbs 7:3 also seems to indicate that
having YHVH's laws written on the tablet of our hearts was His
original intention from the beginning and not a new thing. In fact,
the root of the word translated as "new" in Jeremiah 31:31 is
chadash and it means "renew or repair" (H2318).[16]

It is important to recall that the old covenant, made between
Israel and YHVH at Mt. Sinai, was a marriage covenant. The
people broke that covenant through idolatry, an act that YHVH
viewed as adultery. Due to the repeated and unrepentant idolatry
(adultery), YHVH divorced Israel (Jer. 3:8). Through the prophet
Zechariah, YHVH also declared that He had broken the "covenant
He had made with all the people" (Zech. 11:10-11 KJV). That is
what divorce is, the agreement by both parties to break off or end
their marriage covenant. However, YHVH also promised Israel

that He would take her back and renew an unshakable covenant with her (Isa. 54:6-10).

Many believers are familiar with the Torah's prohibition of remarrying an adulterous wife after she has married and divorced another man (Deut. 24:1-4). YHVH came in the form of *Yeshua*, died, and resurrected, making a way for His Bride, Israel, to become born again of the Spirit (a new man). This made a way for YHVH's legal remarriage to Israel, as the old had "passed away" and "all things had become new" for both parties (2 Cor. 5:17). It was as if Israel was entering into the marriage covenant that YHVH had originally intended—and with a totally clean slate. This is really no different than a couple who divorced because of adultery only to later renew their covenant vows with a new marriage ceremony. They will still have the same marriage covenant expectations of each other, but there is now a renewed commitment to keep the vows which had been previously broken.

For the most part, Israel at large did not have YHVH's law written upon their hearts. However, there was always a small remnant throughout the generations that did. All the "greats" of the Bible like Joshua, Deborah, Samuel, David, Elijah, Jeremiah, Daniel, and many others obviously had YHVH's laws written upon their hearts. It is what made them who they were.

But YHVH's ultimate desire is to have His laws written upon the hearts of all of Israel (native-born and grafted in), and that is the point He was making in Jeremiah 31. Like many of us, David and his men were raised in a time when their generation and the generations before were not taught or led in the knowledge of YHVH's Word. Therefore, this place of engraving was a necessary part of their faith journey. To know the Word of YHVH—not just in their heads but in their hearts—would prepare them to be the best king and royal army of Israel. This is also a necessary part of our faith journey that will make us the best kings and priests in YHVH's Kingdom (Rev. 1:6, 5:10).

The Dreaded Massacre of Nob

While David and his men were hiding out in Hareth, Saul learned of his whereabouts. Saul was stark raving mad at everyone for letting David get away again. Saul reminded all the people around him that he had the power as king to bless them and lift them into positions in the kingdom. He had a pity party; he falsely accused David of lying in ambush against him and accused everyone else of deserting him. His emotional immaturity was quite evident at this point.

In an effort to manipulate people, Saul offered a field, vineyards, and captain position in his army to anyone who would help him find and destroy David (1 Sam. 22:6-8). Remember how Saul's fleshly behavior is a prophetic picture of our adversary, *ha-Satan*? Yes, our adversary also tempts people with promises of position and possession if they will only help him destroy YHVH's anointed.

Do you remember Saul's chief shepherd, Doeg? In the last chapter, we saw that YHVH detained him in the tabernacle in Nob while David received provisions. Well, Doeg wanted one of those fields, vineyards, and promotions for himself, and was eager to grab his golden opportunity. He finally opened his mouth and reported to Saul all he witnessed in Nob concerning David (1 Sam. 22:9-10).

Of interesting note is the root meaning of Doeg's name and the fact that he was chief of Saul's shepherds. *Da'ag* means "to be anxious or concerned, to fear, dread, or to be worried" (H1672).[17] Remember that Saul's behavior is a prophetic pointer to *ha-Satan*. Therefore, Saul's chief shepherd is also a prophetic pointer to a chief false shepherd in *ha-Satan's* kingdom—anxiety, fear, dread, and worry. These things are spiritual and not from YHVH (2 Timothy 1:7). However, Doeg (anxiety, fear, etc.) was detained at the tabernacle in order to bring about YHVH's judgment against Eli's descendants.

Upon hearing this news from Doeg, Saul summoned Ahimelek, the high priest. Ahimelek could not understand why Saul was angry with David. When Saul falsely accused the high priest of conspiring with David against him, Ahimelek reminded Saul how it had been his long-held practice to inquire on behalf of David. Ahimelek tried to convince Saul that David was still his trusted servant and, therefore, no threat to him. But Saul's heart was hardened. He was unwilling to listen to priestly reason and was ready to kill anyone who had covered for David in any way. Saul wanted everyone in Israel to fear him only. Therefore, he decided it was necessary to make an extreme example, to kill even the priests and Levites who dared threaten his position by helping David (1 Sam. 22:11-17).

Needless to say, none of Saul's servants wanted anything to do with killing the priests and Levites—except Doeg. Doeg already proved himself to be a man of selfish ambition (James 3:16). He saw this situation as an opportunity to make a name for himself and rise to substantial power in Saul's kingdom. Therefore, Doeg gleefully went and brutally slaughtered eighty-five men of YHVH.

However, Doeg did not stop at the priests and Levites; he annihilated every man, woman, child, and animal in Nob. Doeg wanted to make a strong point that anyone who crossed Saul and helped David would suffer in the same way (1 Sam. 22:17-19). His actions were hallmark indications of a spirit of anxiety, fear, and dread in operation.

Why did YHVH allow this atrocious slaughter when He could have stopped it at any time? Because He used this entire scenario to fulfill the word of prophecy that he gave to Eli in 1 Samuel

2:30-34. Ahimelek and many of those in Nob were third and fourth generation descendants of Eli. The priests and Levites in Eli's day had become corrupt. Scripture says that Eli's sons "were *sons of Belial* [18]; they knew not the LORD" (1 Sam. 2:12).

The priests were taking the fat of sacrifices, which was punishable by death (according to Lev. 7:25). They were also taking a larger portion of the peace offerings than what YHVH had allotted to be the priestly portion. The peace-offering (Lev. 3) was meant to be for a fellowship meal between the offerer, the priests, and YHVH. Each person had a designated portion they were to enjoy. But the priests were taking part of the offerer's portion for themselves.

The priests were also not leaving any portion of the offerings for the poor, orphans, and widows. Eli's two sons, Hophni and Phinehas, were exceedingly wicked beyond the other priests and Levites. They were taking these unauthorized portions by force. They were also engaging in sexual fornication with the women who served around the tabernacle (1 Sam. 2:22).

Eli tried to correct his sons, but they got angry and threatened to kill him. So, Eli shrank back in dread and enabled them to continue sinning against YHVH and the people of Israel (1 Sam. 2:23-25). According to the law and as the high priest, he should have killed Hophni and Phinehas. Instead, he offered mercy to wicked and unremorseful men in order to save his own skin, not because he had the heart of the Heavenly Father. Eli was guilty of letting the fear of man rule in him instead of the fear of YHVH.

For this, YHVH became vehemently enraged against Eli and his sons. He sent a prophet to Eli to inform him, "Them that honour me I will honour, and they that despise me will be lightly esteemed...thou shalt see an enemy in my habitation...there shall not be an old man in thine house for ever...all the increase of thine house shall die in the flower of their age" (1 Sam. 2:30-34, *condensed*). Additionally, YHVH spoke to Eli through a young Samuel. Samuel prophesied that, because Eli did not rebuke his sons after hearing the words of the first prophet, his curse was sealed; there would be no pardon available to him through any sacrifice (1 Sam. 3).

So, as you can see, YHVH allowed this situation with Doeg to develop. It ultimately fulfilled YHVH's righteous and sovereign judgment against a wicked priestly system that was oppressing, violating, and neglecting the very people they were supposed to be shepherding. YHVH rightly expects His shepherds to care for His flock, especially the weaker of His flock— the poor, orphans, and widows. Throughout Scripture, He has extensively communicated His expectations of His shepherds. They will be accountable to His fury if they fail to protect the sheep they have been entrusted with.

Through the prophets Jeremiah and Ezekiel, YHVH warned Israel's shepherds, "Woe be unto the pastors that destroy and scatter the sheep of my pasture! Ye have scattered my flock, and driven them away, and have not visited them: behold, I will visit upon you the evil of your doings" (Jer. 23:1-2). YHVH continued to warn the shepherds saying, "Woe be to the shepherds of Israel that do feed themselves! Should not the shepherds feed the flocks? The diseased have ye not strengthened, neither have ye healed that which was sick, neither have ye bound up that which was broken, neither have ye brought again that which was driven away, neither have ye sought that which was lost; but with force and with cruelty have ye ruled them. Behold, I am against the shepherds; and I will require my flock at their hand, and cause them to cease from feeding the flock; neither shall the shepherds feed themselves any more; for I will deliver my flock from their mouth, that they may not be meat for them" (Ezek. 34:2, 4, 10).

The Apostle James clearly understood the stark warnings and heavy accountability which applied to those who would be shepherds or teachers of YHVH's flock when he declared, "My brethren, let not many of you become teachers, knowing that we shall receive a stricter judgment" (James 3:1 NKJV). Peter the Apostle also vehemently exhorted the elders to shepherd YHVH's flock with great care, to avoid being motivated by monetary gain, and to avoid lording over the flock in abuse of their authority (1 Pet. 5:1-4). Paul the Apostle also taught Timothy the expectations of overseers of the flock: they must be of blamelessly honorable behavior, not abusive, greedy, or prideful (1 Tim. 3:1-7). These three witnesses from the New Testament confirmed what the two witnesses of the Prophets already established about YHVH's expectations for those who would oversee His sheep.

The account of Nob's slaughter serves as a grave reminder to shepherds everywhere of what it means to fall into the hands of the Owner of the sheep. The fate of the priests also reveals to us an important spiritual truth. The dread of his sons ruled in Eli's heart and kept him from obeying YHVH's instructions. And dread was the very thing that destroyed his descendants and all those who lived around them. Likewise, we must take care not to allow fear, anxiety, worry, or dread to dissuade us from obeying YHVH's instructions. If we do, we may open a spiritual door that leads future generations to be destroyed by these spiritual principalities and powers. Doesn't this principle provide us with a much different perspective on the slaughter at Nob?

A Remnant Redeemed

Despite all the tragedy at Nob, there was redemption. YHVH allowed one descendant of Eli to escape His judgment. Abiathar was a fourth-generation descendant of Eli, doomed by the prophecy to die. However, he managed to escape Doeg's slaughter at Nob, and retained the priestly ephod in his care (1 Sam. 22:20, 23:6). Do you suppose Abiathar slipped YHVH's notice, or do you think YHVH had a purpose in allowing him to be the sole survivor of this slaughter?

As He often does, it is plausible that the Father was preserving a remnant, this time in order to prosper David. Abiathar's name means "the great one is Father" (H54).[19] Is it possible that Abiathar lived up to his name, believing that there was no greater one than the Heavenly Father? Is it possible that he was the only descendant of Eli who had a sincerely repentant heart for all that his forefathers had done? Despite the word YHVH had given that every descendant would die, perhaps He saw something in Abiathar's heart that was worth preserving. YHVH alone is Judge and can show mercy to whomever He wants.

Second, Abiathar's salvation alone points to the one thing that can help us overcome the destructive force of *ha-Satan's* chief shepherd (fear, anxiety, dread, and worry). This surviving shepherd (priest) reminds us that the Great One, YHVH, is Father. Our Father works "all things together for good" (Rom. 8:28). He loves us so much He was willing to send His "only begotten Son" to take the death penalty that we deserved for our sins (John 3:16). If we fully believe in the character of our Father, then there is *nothing* at all that should bring us fear, anxiety, dread, or worry.

Death is about the scariest thing for most everyone to face. Yet we do not need to fear death because we have a great Father who made a way for us to overcome death through the blood of the Lamb. Physical death is not the end, but the beginning of a glorious spiritual resurrection to eternal life in a perfect Kingdom with no suffering, pain, disease, or sin. Therefore, how can we allow ourselves to entertain fear, anxiety, dread, or worry for even a moment? Which shepherd are we choosing to follow?

Narrowly escaping the slaughter at Nob, Abiathar ran for his life and found David in the wilderness of Hareth. He told David all that had happened. Understandably, David was crushed! We hear his laments in Psalms 35 and 52. David wrongfully assumed responsibility for the bloodshed because he had gone to the tabernacle for refuge (1 Sam. 22:20-23). He did not realize that YHVH was using the situation to carry out his judgment against Eli's house.

Perhaps David never heard the report about Eli from Samuel during their brief interactions with one another. In the last chapter, I posed a theory that YHVH truly sent David on a mission to the tabernacle, implying that David was not lying to the high priest. From this perspective, it now seems to be a reasonable possibility.

At this time, David offered Abiathar refuge. Future chapters will reveal that Abiathar remained faithful and served David as a priest all the days of his life. YHVH had now provided David with a prophet (Gad), a priest, and an army. Preparations for David's future kingdom were well advanced.

YHVH was building David up to enter his kingship, providing faithful men to serve him. YHVH was doing this because of David's faithfulness. Many others faced with a similar downturn in their circumstances might waver in doubt and begin to question YHVH's sovereignty and goodness. Some would even walk away from Him. However, David remained faithful to YHVH at every turn, even when he felt like a prisoner.

Like David, the disciples of *Yeshua* are being prepared and tested for fitness as future kings. We should be those who continue to trust in YHVH's goodness, giving Him praise in the most distressing times of our lives. As we remain faithful to Him through every challenge, we will be prepared to enter into our promise with everything we need to be kings in YHVH's Kingdom, just as David was. In the following chapters, David's preparations for his kingdom rule will be brought to completion through a relentless onslaught of tribulations. We stand to learn invaluable lessons from his example to help us navigate our own training through trials in the days ahead.

> *"I cried unto thee, O LORD: I said, Thou art my refuge and my portion in the land of the living. Attend unto my cry; for I am brought very low: deliver me from my persecutors; for they are stronger than I. Bring my soul out of prison, that I may praise thy name: the righteous shall compass me about; for thou shalt deal bountifully with me." (Ps. 142:5-7)*

> *"Be merciful unto me, O God, be merciful unto me: for my soul trusteth in thee: yea, in the shadow of thy wings will I make my refuge, until these calamities be overpast. I will cry unto God most high; unto God that performeth all things for me. He shall send from heaven, and save me from the reproach of him that would swallow me up. Selah. God shall send forth his mercy and his truth." (Ps. 57:1-3)*

JOURNEY JOURNAL

1. Do you personally identify with any of David's characteristics or experiences? If so, which one(s)?

2. How has this chapter's study affected your perspective of seeking YHVH's judgment when you have been wronged?

3. How has this chapter's study affected your perspective on the importance of unity within the body of Messiah?

4. How has this chapter's study affected your perspective on the usefulness of broken people in YHVH's Kingdom?

5. How has this chapter's study affected your perception of the New Covenant?

6. What have you learned about the source of fear, anxiety, dread, and worry, and how they operate in our lives to bring us to destruction?

7. Did you experience any other personal conviction as you read this chapter and answered the questions presented? What were you convicted about? (Conviction is meant to lead us to prayers of repentance, wherein we receive YHVH's grace, mercy, and forgiveness.)

8. How has this chapter's study encouraged you to greater love for YHVH and your neighbor?

6

THE RELENTLESS PURSUIT

Every one of us has an enemy; some of us have many. They pursue us like a predator stalks its prey. We can easily grow weary and bitter in our effort to escape our enemy's plots. We might wonder where YHVH is in the midst of the onslaught. Why is He allowing it? Is He really for us?

In this chapter, we are going to discuss how YHVH used Saul's relentless pursuit to train David and his followers. He shaped them into mighty men of faith, who learned how to trust in YHVH's covering and rescue. We will also see that YHVH used this crucible to conform David into *Yeshua's* image of humble love and forgiveness.

Overcoming Insecurity and Wavering Faith

David learned that the Philistines were attacking and plundering "the threshing floors" of *Keilah*, a town in the Judean wilderness. *Keilah* was located close to where he and his men were hiding from Saul. David did not want to presume anything, so he asked YHVH if he should go to battle against the Philistines and deliver the people of *Keilah* (1 Sam. 23:1-2 KJV). This is a wonderful example of David's leadership skills that we can all learn from. Just because we see someone afflicted by an enemy, we should not presume that it is our role to deliver them. It is best to seek YHVH first and ask Him if we are supposed to get involved.

YHVH answered David's inquiry, told him that he should go up against the Philistines at *Keilah*, and that He would give him victory there. The root meaning of the name *Keilah* is prophetically significant. *Qala'* means to "carve out, sling out, sit insecurely, and waver" (H7049).[1] When David shared YHVH's instructions with his men, they were fearful, insecure, and wavering in their faith as to whether they could overcome the enemy. They preferred to continue hiding out in the cave. At this, David did not merely try to convince the men, but he took it to YHVH in prayer again, and YHVH reassured him of victory (1 Sam. 23:2-4).

After David shared YHVH's promise of victory, his troops chose faith and went up with him against the Philistines at *Keilah* (1 Sam. 23:5). Through faith in YHVH's promises, they overcame their weakness of fear, insecurity, and wavering and rescued the inhabitants of *Keilah*. As believers and followers of the Son of David (*Yeshua*), we have this same overcoming power. We will conquer our weaknesses when we choose to walk in faith and believe the promises that YHVH has confirmed to us.

Saul heard that David delivered *Keilah* from the Philistines, and he made an assumption based on the circumstances. His human reasoning told him that YHVH had given David into his hand by allowing David's whereabouts to be known. Saul thought he had David cornered and that he would be easy pickings. So,

Saul summoned his troops to "besiege David and his troops" (1 Sam. 23:7-8). Saul's behavior is the mark of ungodly leadership. He moved based on sight or how the circumstances appeared to be (2 Cor. 5:7). He leaned on his own understanding (Prov. 3:5-6) and made assumptions rather than seeking YHVH for His insight into the situation.

David learned that Saul was aware of his location and sending his army out after him. However, David did not make any assumptions or allow himself to be ruled by circumstance, his own understanding, or by fear. Instead, he inquired of YHVH via the priestly ephod. David asked YHVH all the questions flooding his mind. Would the people David just delivered from the Philistines, "deliver him up into his [Saul] hand," or would they be faithful to cover for David the way he just covered for them (1 Sam. 23:9-12, *brackets mine*)?

Psalms 17, 31, 35, and 140 most likely record David's full supplications before YHVH at this time.[2] His supplications are such a model for us to follow, so let's look at what he uttered when he learned that his enemy was coming to kill him. He said, "I have called upon You, for You will hear me, O God; Incline Your ear to me, *and* hear my speech. Show Your marvelous lovingkindness by Your right hand, O You who save those who trust *in You* from those who rise up *against them.* Keep me as the apple of Your eye; Hide me under the shadow of Your wings, From the wicked who oppress me, *From* my deadly enemies who surround me. Arise, O LORD, Confront him, cast him down; Deliver my life from the wicked with Your sword" (Ps. 17:6-9, 13 NKJV).

David continued to supplicate, "In thee, O LORD, do I put my trust; deliver me speedily: be thou my strong rock. For thou art my rock and my fortress. Pull me out of the net that they have laid privily for me: for thou art my strength" (Ps. 31:1-4 KJV, *condensed*). "Plead my cause, O LORD, with them that strive with me: fight against them that fight against me. Take hold of shield and buckler, and stand up for mine help. Draw out also the spear, and stop the way against them that persecute me: say unto my soul, I am thy salvation. Stir up thyself, and awake to my judgment, even unto my cause, my God and my Lord" (Ps. 35:1-3, 23).

YHVH's Shroud of Covering

David may not have known it, but he also prophesied as he poured out his supplications. He declared, "O GOD, the Lord, the strength of my salvation, thou hast covered my head in the day of battle" (Ps. 140:7). We are going to see shortly that YHVH would certainly "cover" David's head and conceal him from his adversary. This is actually a prayer strategy that a dear sister in Messiah taught me: we can pray forward in thanksgiving for the breakthrough that we need as if it is already done. Yes, YHVH covered David's head in the day of his battle with Goliath. Now, David desperately needed YHVH to do the same in the day of battle against Saul. So, we see David praying something forward that will ultimately be answered in an awesome way.

Faithfully, YHVH answered David's inquiries. YHVH informed him that it was unsafe to remain in *Keilah* because the people would surely turn him over to Saul. What gratitude they had for their deliverer! Many of us may be able to relate to how David must have felt in this moment. Many of us have had people in our lives that did not reciprocate the good we did for them, especially when we were in need.

After learning he would be betrayed by the very people he had saved, David and his men immediately left *Keilah*. Saul learned that they skipped town and called off his army from pursuing them. David and his men found refuge in the strongholds of "the wilderness of *Ziph* in a wood." The Bible says, "Saul sought [David] every day, but God delivered him not into his hand" (1

Sam. 12-15). Clearly, Saul's assumption that YHVH had handed David over to him was totally wrong!

The Hebrew word translated as "in a wood" is *choresh,* which means "a wooded height or shroud" (H2793).[3] A shroud "covers or envelopes to conceal or obscure something from view."[4] YHVH was covering David and enveloping him to conceal him from Saul's view, just as David had proclaimed in Psalm 140:7. The truth about who YHVH is and what He does for His chosen was being further sealed upon David's heart through this situation.

Nothing that happened to David was by accident or coincidence! Every place David visited in his wilderness wandering was divinely ordered to strengthen his faith. In the same way, every stop in our own wilderness is orchestrated to build our faith. Embrace every trial with this perspective in mind and learn all that you can at every stop in your life's journey.

While David and his men camped out in *Choresh,* Jonathan set out to find and comfort his friend. Jonathan's own father could not find David because YHVH had shrouded him, but YHVH allowed his covenant friend to find him (1 Sam. 23:16)! YHVH can hide us from our enemies while allowing our covenant friends to find us.

Jonathan reassured David and told him that Saul knew he would never find David and that David would one day be king of Israel. Then Jonathan cut a third covenant with David, and the friends agreed that Jonathan would be second to David when he came into his kingdom (1 Sam. 23:17-18). Once again, Jonathan displayed great love for his covenant friend. He was willing to lay down his own life for David—his birthright to be the next king of Israel. It is possible that David penned Psalm 17 around the time of this final encounter with Jonathan.[5]

Shortly after Jonathan left David, YHVH's shroud seemingly lifted as the local Ziphites learned of David's whereabouts and ratted him out to Saul. They revealed that David was hiding "in the wood, in the hill of *Hachilah*" (1 Sam. 23:19), which means "dark" (H2444).[6] David had been shrouded in darkness. This was the place that YHVH chose to preserve David and his warriors from the enemy who was seeking after their lives.

Though Psalm 139 may be ascribed to a later time in David's life, he may have been pondering the events of *Hachilah* as he penned the words, "If I say, 'Surely the darkness shall cover me; even the night shall be light about me. Yea, the darkness hideth not from thee; but the night shineth as the day: the darkness and the light are both alike to thee" (Ps. 139:11-12). As believers, we can often find ourselves in dark places. We may even feel like YHVH led us there. Lacking understanding, we may question why we are there. During these times, it is possible that YHVH is shrouding us from the enemy. However, we can rest in the knowledge that He has us covered and enveloped no matter where we are; the light of His presence will be with us in the darkness.

Scouted Out by the Enemy

Recognizing that David was divinely shrouded, Saul asked the Ziphites to "scout out" and record David's comings and goings. Saul needed to know David's patterns so he could easily find and trap him. Saul acknowledged that David "deals very subtilly [cunning, prudent]" (1 Sam. 23:21-23, *brackets mine*). David acted with care and thought for the future. He was wise, sensible, and well-advised in all of his ways.

Saul was just like the enemy of our souls. *Ha-Satan* also scouts us out in order to identify our patterns or areas of weakness, and then trap and destroy us. This is why it is so essential for us to remain in the Spirit, always inquiring of YHVH and being equipped with His wisdom, just as David was. As long as David was submitted to the *Ruach ha-Kodesh*, he was able to escape the plots of his enemy every time!

Because of his rebellion and idolatry, Saul no longer had the Spirit of YHVH in him or with him. As a result, he had to enlist men to help him strategize against his enemy. The fact that he had to seek earthly wisdom in place of godly wisdom is significant to the life of every believer. We need to audit our lives to see how much we must rely on others to navigate through life and overcome our enemy. If we must rely heavily on our own understanding and the counsel of others to guide our decisions, then we may want to ask ourselves some questions. If we are not as in tune with the *Ruach ha-Kodesh* as David was, it could be that something in our heart may be blocking us from hearing YHVH (Isa. 59:1-4).

The Ziphites began scouting out *Hachilah* for Saul, completely unaware they were "in the dark" about David's whereabouts. The *Ruach ha-Kodesh* led David to the wilderness of *Maon*, located six miles southwest of his refuge in the desert wilderness of the Judean hills (1 Sam. 23:24). [7] We know that David prayed when Saul learned of his whereabouts from the Ziphites because Psalms 13 and 54 record it. It is very likely that YHVH responded to these supplications and prompted David to move to the wilderness of *Maon*. For the Ziphites, searching for David was like looking for a needle in a haystack! *Maon* means "habitation, residence, and dwelling place" (H4583-H4584).[8] I personally believe David was the author of Psalm 91.[9] Through this trial, he learned that as long as his dwelling place was in the shadow of the Most High, he would be protected from his enemy.

The Rock of Security and Refuge

David chose to hide "down into a rock" when he heard that Saul was having the area combed for him (1 Sam. 23:25). The Hebrew word for rock is *sela*, which means "rock, cliff, or crag." According to the Brown-Driver-Briggs Hebrew and English

Lexicon, *sela* is "figurative of security." A crag in a cliff is a place of refuge for wild animals where they can escape a predator or storms. Strong's Exhaustive Concordances defines *sela* as "a ragged rock, stone, stronghold, and fortress (figuratively)" (H5553). [10] As we have already seen, a stone is indicative of *Yeshua*. Truly, He is our escape from the predator, *ha-Satan* (1 Pet. 5:8), and all the storms our adversary tries to bring against us.

David certainly learned that YHVH was his security, his rock, his stronghold, and his fortress. We saw David declare this in many psalms (Psalms 18, 27, 43, 91, 141, etc.). YHVH helped David and his men overcome insecurity and wavering faith at *Keilah*. At *Choresh-Hachilah*, YHVH demonstrated his ability to shroud them in darkness and hide them from their enemies. Now, He had brought them to a place of security, His hiding place from the storm of Saul's army. YHVH ordained the steps of David and his army so that they would learn who He is and learn how to overcome their weaknesses. YHVH is likewise doing the same for us as we follow the leading of the *Ruach ha-Kodesh*.

While David and his men took refuge in the rock, Saul was on the other side of the same mountain and closing in fast. As soon as David and his men became aware of Saul's location, they scrambled "to get away for fear of Saul." Just in the nick-of-time, as Saul was about to discover David's hiding place, "a messenger" brought Saul news that the Philistines had invaded the land of Israel (1 Sam. 23:26-27). Talk about a divine diversion! YHVH used the archenemies of Israel to save David and his mighty men from their most immediate enemy, Saul. Saul had no choice but to leave his pursuit of David and take care of the real threat to Israel. Look at YHVH's salvation!

Separating the Sheep from the Goats

To commemorate what YHVH had done for him, David named

this rocky hiding place *Sela Hammachleqoth,* which means "rock of the divisions" (H5555) (1 Sam. 23:28).[11] YHVH made a division between His chosen (the sheep) and His rejected (the goats). If you recall from our previous chapter, David took refuge in the Father's righteous judgment. This division at *Sela Hammachleqoth* was part of how YHVH carried out His righteous judgment.

Interestingly enough, after Saul departed to fight the Philistines, David moved to the "strongholds at *Engedi*" (1 Sam. 23:29). *Engedi* is a word that is constructed of two Hebrew words, *ayin* (fountain) and *gedi* (young goat).[12] *Ayin* is also the name of a Hebrew letter, one that represents spiritual eyesight.[13] Perhaps this was where David learned to have spiritual eyes to see the spiritual goats.

Even though David may have had spiritual eyes to recognize Saul as a spiritual goat, *Yeshua* (the Good Shepherd) is the only one with the scepter of authority to execute this judgment. The true purpose of *Yeshua's* separation and division is to protect His anointed ones and keep their enemies (a rebellious and idolatrous people) from overtaking and destroying them. Separating the sheep from the goats is something that *Yeshua* does (Matt. 25:31-46). Taking this judgment upon ourselves is not something we have been called to do.

David's narrative begs me to ask myself and every other disciple of *Yeshua* some serious questions. Which side of the rock of the divisions are we on? Are we on the side of YHVH's chosen and anointed ones who are full of the *Ruach ha-Kodesh?* Or are we on the side of the enemy who is devoid of the *Ruach ha-Kodesh* and pursues YHVH's anointed for destruction? These are questions we need to ask if we find ourselves in offense against YHVH's anointed and are being led away from them in separation and division.

We should be careful to check our own heart motives and the motives of those who might be leading us away from YHVH's anointed through offense. We may believe in our hearts that we are zealously pursuing YHVH's anointed for all the right reasons, just as Saul probably believed in his pursuit of David. Regardless of what Saul believed in his heart, YHVH was not behind what he was doing. YHVH had to bring out the Philistine army against Saul to divert him away from his pursuit of David. We can avoid finding ourselves in unnecessary battles if we will just take a step back from the offense, do our own heart audit, and prayerfully seek YHVH's direction to ensure that our hearts remain aligned with His.

Godly Division vs. Ungodly Division

Now that we have taken some time to ponder those questions, I want to look a little deeper at the word *machaloqeth* used in naming of this rock of the divisions. *Machaloqeth* means "division, course, or portion" (H4256).[14] It is used in the Scriptures to describe how the priests and Levites were separated impartially by lot (by chance) into divisions or groups (1 Chron. 26-27). This division was necessary to give them an equal share in ministry and to prevent burn out. When done properly and for the right reasons, this was a good use and purpose of division or separation in the Levitical priesthood. The ministers of YHVH were all on the same team. They were serving the same *Elohim* in His prescribed manner and according to His specific instructions, but they were simply taking shifts.

Machaloqeth has its root in the word *chalaq* (H2505),[15] which was also used to describe the separation of soldiers into divisions (Gen. 14:15). Each division was assigned with specific assignments toward fighting the same enemy. They were all part of the same team, serving the same king or Commander-in-Chief. These divisions were certainly not meant to judge, criticize, correct, slander, humiliate, or create infighting. The division was not intended to pit soldiers against one another as enemies, encourage them to win people to their side, and destroy each other.

A nation's military is divided into many different branches, which are each further divided into numerous wings, squadrons, units, battalions, etc. What would happen if there was infighting in our military the way that there is infighting across denominations in the body of Messiah? Consider the following scenario, if you will: imagine if our military branches suddenly decided to stop following the orders of their Commander-in-Chief. Over time, the soldiers begin to lose sight of the fact that they are working together on the same team to fight against a common enemy. In place of solidarity, the soldiers become offended over their differences and judge the way their fellow soldiers operate. If the soldiers in our military began to look at each other as the enemy, things could get really ugly, really fast! Can you imagine all the warfare training and munitions they would use against each other instead of the real enemy? That is a terrifying thought!

Unfortunately, this is exactly what has happened far too often in the body of Messiah since the mid-first century. When the *Ruach ha-Kodesh* came upon the believers in the book of Acts, they were in true unity (in "one accord") and they had "everything in common" (Acts 1:14 NKJV, Acts 2:44 NIV respectively). In this perfect unity, when the believers of the Acts "church" were moved by the *Ruach ha-Kodesh* in everything, they were a force to be reckoned with! The hearts of many were converted to the truth. Miraculous healings were the norm every day. Believers were affecting supernatural events through corporate fasting and prayer and the "church" was growing exponentially. If the church would have continued in this perfect unity, the power of the *Ruach ha-Kodesh* and the gospel message would have continued to spread like wild-fire. Through unity, all the world may have been saved by now (John 17:20-23), and *ha-Satan* would have lost *all* of his ground!

Certainly, *ha-Satan* could not give up his territory, so he had to act and act fast! The history of the early church proves that he quickly came into the body of Messiah from many directions. *Ha-Satan* began to manipulate people's thoughts and emotional systems through offense. He got people to act according to their emotions and their personal or collective opinions instead of allowing the *Ruach ha-Kodesh* to move them. *Ha-Satan* effectively created unholy divisions and separations in the body of Messiah (the priests and army of the King of kings). Division occurred, in part, through arguments and disagreements over interpretations and doctrines.

Many in the modern church wonder why we are not experiencing the same level of power and manifestations of the *Ruach ha-Kodesh* as the Acts church did. We seek the healing miracles, resurrection of the dead, and other miraculous manifestations of YHVH's power in us just as the apostles displayed. However, because the body of Messiah is divided in the wrong way and for the wrong purposes, it is hindering the work of the *Ruach ha-Kodesh*. Some members of the body are more focused on treating those who are different from them as though they are an enemy. They judge and condemn one another as heretics and cult followers, instead of remembering that we are all different members of the same body. They forget that each member has a specific purpose and function to work together in keeping the body alive (1 Cor. 12:12-27).

We need to let the hand be the hand and the kidney be the kidney. Each member should focus only on their own role and function, which is to live out YHVH's love and the gospel message. And we will flourish best when we allow other members to focus on doing the same. The body cannot live and function properly when it gets its wires crossed and sees its fellow parts as the enemy. In the human body, this type of dysfunction is called autoimmunity. The immune system, which is supposed to root out external threats that invade the body, gets hijacked into viewing the body's organs as the real threat. When the immune system attacks the body's organs, it creates inflammation and pain.

From everything that I have witnessed in over two decades among numerous denominational backgrounds, it seems that much of the modern church has spiritual autoimmunity. Our spiritual immune system has been hijacked into thinking that our fellow body members are the real enemy instead of the real external threat, *ha-Satan*. As a result, we have a modern church that is often full of inflammation (pride) and pain. People often leave the church more hurt and broken than when they came in.

I cannot tell you how many people I have encountered over the years, who have completely walked away from the faith because of this spiritual autoimmunity. They experienced so much pride, judgment, hypocrisy, and hurt at the hands of the church (including the church leadership). It is gut-wrenching to hear and to experience! May we each be moved to humble ourselves and repent if we have played a part in this problem (2 Chron. 7:14).

Several years ago, I had a vision of the bride of Messiah that absolutely crushed my heart. It convicted me as I could feel that it also devastated *Yeshua's* heart. I saw the bride, but instead of looking radiant, pure, and spotless as the Bridegroom desires, she looked like a discombobulated wreck. Her garments were tattered and stained with blood, and she had self-inflicted wounds all over herself. In her hands were two-edged swords (the Word of God), which she had used to cut into all her members.

I clearly understood what YHVH was showing me through this vision. Those who confess His name are spending too much time harshly judging, criticizing, and slandering one another over our differences. We are using His Word to inflict injury on one another, instead of loving one another as a body fit together, all with unique callings, functions, and purposes (1 Cor. 12:12-27).

Instead of allowing our hands to wrestle against each other, we must remember: "We wrestle not against flesh and blood [our fellow human], but against principalities, against powers, against the rulers of the darkness of this world, against spiritual wickedness in high places" (Eph. 6:12 KJV, *brackets mine*). Therefore, "the weapons of our warfare are not carnal [the things of the flesh: arguments, etc.], but mighty through God to the pulling down of strongholds; casting down imaginations, and every high thing that exalts itself against the knowledge of God, and bringing into captivity every thought to the obedience of Christ" (2 Cor. 10:4-5 KJV, *brackets mine*). The cure for our spiritual autoimmunity and the discombobulated state of the bride is taking on the yoke of humility and gentleness toward one another (Matt. 11:29). We must strive to love each other with compassion, just as the Father loves each one of us. Most of all, we must refrain from judging or condemning one another (Luke 6:36-37) as cult followers or lost heretics.[16]

Let us remember that the four Gospels clearly reveal that the Pharisees and Sadducees of the first century were deeply and bitterly divided and prideful. They believed they had all truth and doctrine figured out. They thought that anyone who differed from them was a lost heretic and unworthy of fellowship, or guilty of blasphemy and worthy of death. They even condemned *Yeshua* as a demon-possessed heretic and blasphemer worthy of death. But *Yeshua* proved how little they truly understood when it came to the Word of YHVH. Is it possible that, in our modern times, *Yeshua* might have to prove how little we truly understand?

Yeshua spent much of his three years in earthly ministry clearing up misinterpretations of doctrine among less than a handful of religious sects (denominations). It is reasonable to think that He will likewise spend His millennial reign clearing up misinterpretations of doctrine amongst nearly forty-thousand religious sects (denominations). His mission will be to train us for the Heavenly Kingdom we are to inherit and rule with Him after this earthly kingdom passes away (Rev. 21). To prepare ourselves for this day, it would be best if we humbled ourselves. There are such uncharted depths and mysteries in the Word of YHVH and in the nature of YHVH that we have yet to grasp. It is very possible that we have some things wrong with our doctrines and interpretations. Instead, let us focus more of our spiritual energies on living out the grace and love of YHVH toward one another.

Saul's Bathroom Break

Now that we have taken the time to ponder this weighty subject of unity, let us return to the vicious game of hide-and-seek between Saul and David. In 1 Samuel 24, Saul finished fighting with the Philistines and returned to his pursuit of David. He learned that David was hiding out in the wilderness of *Engedi*. So, Saul decided to personally go along with "three thousand chosen" warriors to search for David among "the rocks of the wild goats" (1 Sam. 24:1-2).

Saul probably thought the odds were in his favor because his army outnumbered David and his men five to one. While David certainly acknowledged the odds against him, he knew who ultimately protected him. He cried out and praised the One who had always helped him and who he knew would remain faithful to help him.

David's praises are recorded in Psalms 16, 57, and 108.[17] He declared, "In thee do I put my trust. Because He is at my right hand, I shall not be moved. My heart is glad: my flesh shall also rest in hope" (Ps. 16:1, 8-9, *condensed*). "In the shadow of thy wings will I make my refuge, until these calamities be overpast. He shall send from heaven and save me from the reproach of him that would swallow me up. My heart is fixed, O God, my heart is fixed: I will sing and give praise" (Ps. 57:1, 3, 7, *condensed*). "Through God we shall do valiantly: for he it is that shall tread down our enemies" (Ps. 108:13).

While David praised YHVH and thanked Him in advance for His salvation, Saul closed in on David amidst the cliffs of *Engedi*. Saul suddenly realized he needed to relieve himself, so he slipped into a cave for privacy (1 Sam. 24:3). Little did he know that he had chosen the very cave that David and hundreds of fierce warriors were hiding in. David's men immediately jumped to conclusions. They believed that YHVH was giving Saul over to David to defeat once-and-for-all so that David could finally come into his anointing as king (1 Sam. 24:3-4). They trusted in their perception of the circumstance and leaned on their own understanding.

It does not appear that David inquired of YHVH before agreeing with the counsel of his men. David stealthily approached Saul, raised his weapon, and slashed off the corner of his garment (1 Sam. 24:4). It is extremely important to note the significance of David cutting the corner of Saul's garment. The Bible says, "David's conscience bothered him because he had cut off the hem of Saul's robe" (1 Sam. 24:5, AMP).

The Hebrew word translated as hem is *kanaph*, which means "wings, extremity, or corner." It is the same word used in Numbers 15:37-41 and Deuteronomy 22:12 in reference to the four corners of the men's garments in Israel. They were to have the tzitzit (tassels) hanging from the four corners as a reminder to obey YHVH's laws (H3671).[18] Surely, as David held the *kanaph* in his hand, he was reminded of YHVH's commandments. His conscience was pricked by the two-edged sword of YHVH's Word, and he was deeply convicted by the *Ruach ha-Kodesh* not to touch YHVH's anointed. He later codified his inner convictions in Psalm 105:15. David immediately repented and convinced his men to back off from their position to take this golden opportunity to kill Saul. Thankfully, they submitted to their leader (1 Sam. 24:5-6).

David's Kindness Leads Saul to Repentance

It would have been disastrous to David's reign if he had made a different choice in this moment. If David and his men chose to kill Saul and take the kingdom by force, those who were loyal to Saul would have taken offense. As a result, many in Israel might have denied him as king, and David would have begun his reign in a lot more turmoil than necessary. It was crucial that David leave Saul's removal from the throne completely to the hand of YHVH.

Saul remained completely unaware of all that transpired while he was relieving himself and left the cave. David ran out after him, humbled himself before Saul in repentance for cutting off his garment, and appealed to him for peace in their relationship. David told him that, even though Saul was out to take his life, he would not repay evil for evil by doing the same (1 Sam. 24:7-11).

It is amazing that David was the one humbling himself in repentance after all that Saul had done to him. Shouldn't it have been the other way around? David said, "The LORD judge between me and thee, and the LORD avenge me of thee: but mine hand shall not be upon thee" (1 Sam. 24:12). David set an example for the true mark of a leader after YHVH's own heart.

David's example should certainly be our life philosophy: let YHVH judge and avenge and let not our hands have anything to do with it. This is the Proverbs 10:12 principle: "Hatred stirs up strife, But love covers and overwhelms all transgressions [forgiving and overlooking another's faults]" (AMP). [19] Through his wilderness wandering, David learned that judgment belongs to YHVH alone. He did not have to plead his own case or defend himself in any way. Many arguments and relationship breakdowns arise when we plead our own case and judge between ourselves and the person who offended us or betrayed our trust.

We must resist the temptation to become our offender's prosecuting attorney (accuser of the brethren), judge, jury, and executioner. Instead, we must take a deep breath, a big step back, and look at their heavenly defense attorney (1 John 2:1). He is the same heavenly defense attorney we have been given. We will not have to look at our brother's or sister's defense attorney for too long to see the nail scars in His hands and feet. Those scars will remind us that *Yeshua* has forgiven us a huge debt we could never repay! When we sincerely look at Him and His scars, we can't help but step down from the judgment seat and forgive our offender, just as YHVH has forgiven us. If we struggle with forgiveness, we must recall what *Yeshua* said: "But if you do not forgive others [nurturing your hurt and anger with the result that it interferes with your relationship with God], then your Father will not forgive your trespasses" (Matthew 6:15 AMP).

David must have had a supernatural revelation about forgiveness to have abased himself like this. David sought restitution of a peaceful relationship from someone who was actively out to destroy him and displayed no signs of remorse. To forgive in this manner is so far removed from our natural human response. Yet look at the fruit that David's humble actions produced! Saul accepted his submission and declared that David was more righteous than himself. With thanksgiving, Saul acknowledged that David did not take advantage of the situation and kill him, and commended his actions as being supremely unique (1 Sam. 24:16-19KJV).

Saul also blessed David and confirmed David's calling as the next future king of Israel. Saul then humbled himself before David and pled for his life and the lives of his descendants. David vowed that he would not cut off Saul's descendants from the kingdom of Israel, and they parted ways in peace (1 Sam. 24:20-22).

What an incredible result David's humility produced in Saul! It is the same result that will be produced every time we take the position of humility and submission as David did. David could have made the choice to act presumptuously and accept the unanimous counsel of his men. Yet by killing Saul and taking his promised position by his own hands, David would have brought the curse of YHVH's law and judgment upon himself and greater warfare against his reign. However, because David remained in tune with YHVH's Spirit and His law (truth), he ended up with blessings and peace from his enemy.

If we likewise follow David's example (which is ultimately *Yeshua's* example), our enemies will also be made to be at peace with us. Our humility and forgiveness can even produce the fruit of repentance in them, which is what we ultimately want. How often does that come about when we defend ourselves, argue our case, or enlist others to argue our case? Pretty much *never!*

Let us strive to take the humble position with our offenders and go our way in peace. More than dancing as David danced, or singing as David sang, we need to make peace with our adversary like David did. This is what the *Ruach ha-Kodesh* has commanded us to do through Paul's inspired words when he wrote, "If possible, as far as it depends on *you,* live at peace with everyone" (Rom. 12:18 AMP, *emphasis mine*). It is all about each one of us and what we can do, not about the other person and what they could have or should have done.

"The L ORD judge between me and thee, and the L ORD avenge me of thee: but mine hand shall not be upon thee." (1 Sam. 24:12)

"My little children (believers, dear ones), I am writing you these things so that you will not sin and violate God's law. And if anyone sins, we have an Advocate [who will intercede for us] with the Father: Jesus Christ the righteous [the upright, the just One, who conforms to the Father's will in every way—purpose, thought, and action]." (1 John 2:1 AMP)

JOURNEY JOURNAL

1. Do you personally identify with any of Saul's characteristics or experiences? If so, which one(s)?

2. Do you personally identify with any of David's characteristics or experiences? If so, which one(s)?

3. Did you personally identify with any of the characteristics or experiences of David's men? If so, which one(s)?

4. How has this chapter's study affected your view of the importance of unity in the body of Messiah?

5. Can you see how YHVH has ordained every single step in your life to teach, train, and prepare you to prosper in His kingdom? What are some examples of YHVH's training and preparation in your life?

6. Did you experience any personal conviction as you read this chapter and answered the questions presented? What were you convicted about? (Conviction is meant to lead us to prayers of repentance, wherein we receive YHVH's grace, mercy, and forgiveness.)

7. How has this chapter's study encouraged you to greater love for YHVH and your neighbor?

7

A BRIDE ADORNED

Life is a colossal series of tests. The moment we complete one test, another is certain to follow. Tests are immeasurably beneficial for us, though most of us never really look forward to or enjoy taking them. However, every test has a single purpose at heart: to measure how well we have assimilated what we have learned and to reinforce each spiritual lesson in us. If we fail to excel on any given test, we inevitably return to study more intensely in preparation for the final exam—*if* we desire to make the grade. Such it is in the spiritual school of life. Throughout 1 Samuel 25-26, we will witness how David was tested to measure his grasp of the lessons he learned throughout his kingdom preparation in the wilderness.

To Show Forth His Glory

Since we last saw David, Samuel the prophet had passed on

from this life. After completing his time of mourning over Samuel's death, David was led into "the wilderness of Paran" (1 Sam. 25:1 KJV). Paran is quite an interesting place when we take into account David's actions in the last chapter. To briefly recap, David humbled himself before his enemy (Saul) and repented for what he had done wrong against him (cutting the corner of his garment). David sought peace and reconciliation in their relationship without Saul first showing any sign of repentance or making restitution for his actions. David displayed forgiveness, grace, and mercy while Saul was yet sinning against him, a beautiful prophetic reflection of what *Yeshua* did for humankind.

From a prophetic perspective, David's current stop in his wilderness wandering is amazing! The root meaning of Paran is to "beautify, glorify, adorn, or show forth His glory" (H6286).[1] As has been the case at every stop in David's journey thus far, the name of this location hints to the spiritual refining process that YHVH was about to perform in David and his men. Through this refining process, they would be better prepared to rule and reign over Israel. Israel (whether natural-born or grafted-in) is YHVH's bride, and He is to be glorified through her (Isa. 44:23). Though it was David's first time in Paran, it was not the first time YHVH sought to beautify, glorify, adorn, or show forth His glory in His chosen in the wilderness of Paran.

If you remember the story of Numbers 13, it was during Israel's sojourn in the wilderness of Paran that ten of the twelve chosen princes of Israel failed their faith test. The princes allowed fear, doubt, and unbelief in YHVH's faithfulness to rule in them, which led all of Israel to do the same. In failing their faith test, that generation lost their promised inheritance from YHVH. Only two of Israel's chosen princes, Caleb of Judah and Joshua of Ephraim, passed the test. Caleb and Joshua were ruled by YHVH's Spirit and truth and, therefore, were able to inherit their promise from

YHVH. They were the only two Israelites who allowed themselves to be adorned, beautified, and to show forth YHVH's glory. This leads me to believe that David's test results in the wilderness of Paran would ultimately determine his receipt of his promised inheritance as king of Israel.

David's latest actions toward Saul began his beautification and adornment as a bride who would show forth the glory of the Bridegroom (to be conformed into His image) (Isa. 61:10, 2 Cor. 3:18). Part of David's beautification process was to learn how not to allow his circumstances or emotions to lead him and resist the urge to operate in offense. Likewise, this is the same beautification and adornment process of every believer in Messiah *Yeshua*. We must learn how to take off the enemy's garments of offense and emotional reactions in the flesh and to clothe ourselves with Messiah *Yeshua* (Rom. 13:14). We are called to clothe ourselves with *Yeshua's* "compassion, kindness, humility, gentleness, and patience" (Col. 3:12-17 AMP).

David's New Test Subject

Though David displayed a supernatural understanding of YHVH's love toward his enemy, he still required further refining in the art of overcoming emotional reactions to offense. He had just barely passed his test with Saul. David nearly conceded to the uninspired counsel of his men to murder Saul.

There is an old adage which says that it is easier to forgive an enemy than a friend. In my personal experience, I have seen the opposite of this adage. It is often times easier to forgive someone who is part of our family, with whom we have once enjoyed the benefits of a healthy relationship. It can be much harder with someone we have no personal investment with, and therefore nothing to lose. Hence, David was due for a test to ascertain whether he could faithfully walk in supernatural love and forgiveness with everyone that YHVH placed in his path.

Near David's hideout in Paran was the estate of a wealthy man named Nabal. Nabal's name means: "foolish, senseless, disgraceful, ignoble, and vile" (H5036).[2] The Bible describes Nabal as a man who "was churlish and evil in his doings" (1 Sam. 25:3 KJV). The Hebrew word translated as churlish is *qasheh* and it means "hard, severe, difficult, fierce, cruel, harsh, obstinate, stubborn, intense, vehement, and stiff-necked" (H7186).[3] Most of us undoubtedly have someone who immediately pops into our mind when we read that description!

As if being churlish was not enough, the Hebrew word translated as evil above is the same word used to describe the evil spirit that tormented Saul (H7541).[4] Through the power of the *Ruach ha-Kodesh,* David had overcome his test against the evil spirit that operated in Saul. The time had arrived to test whether he would respond in the same Spirit towards another person operating under the influence of the same evil spirit. This is a perfect reflection of our own spiritual testing process. YHVH continues to test us until we maintain a consistent response in the Spirit instead of the flesh.

Have you ever wondered why we are repeatedly tested by the same type of people? It is all part of our beautification process as a bride of Messiah. Repeating our spiritual tests gives that sense of going around the same old mountain a whole new perspective, doesn't it? If we are not ascending as we round the mountain, perhaps we are failing to correctly apply the lessons we were taught the first time around. Therefore, we must master our lessons well enough to advance to the next level of our journey toward the mountaintop.

Nabal, David's new "test subject," had a wife named Abigail. The Bible describes Abigail as "a woman of good understanding and a beautiful countenance" (1 Samuel 25:3). The Hebrew word translated as good understanding is *sekel* and it means "prudent, insightful, intelligent, discrete, wise" (H7922).[5] In light of Nabal's character, one can say that opposites really do attract! However, their marriage was most likely arranged by their fathers and not the result of their attraction for one another. It is quite unlikely that a wise and prudent lady would be attracted to such a man.

In the 21st Century, we may view such arranged marriages as archaic and horrible, but there is actually beautiful prophetic significance to them. Our Heavenly Father often arranges opposites in marriages so that each spouse will balance the other and make each other better. That character improvement will happen *if* we submit to YHVH's hand on our lives in this process. Marital clashes produce fiery sparks between spouses and are evidence of the "iron sharpens iron" process (Prov. 27:17 NIV). Even if it feels unpleasant at times, this sharpening process is for our good so that we can be made useful to YHVH. Certainly, a man like Nabal needed to be sharpened by a woman like Abigail. We will observe shortly that she was Nabal's saving grace from certain destruction at the hands of David. More importantly, Abigail was David's saving grace from certain destruction at the hand of his true adversary, *ha-Satan*.

The Audacity of Stinginess

While David and his mighty men stayed in Paran and warded off the Philistines, Nabal and his family benefited immeasurably from the resultant peace. David figured that was worth something, and this wealthy man had much to offer him and his men who were in need. He sent ten of his mighty men of valor to greet Nabal with blessings of peace and a prosperous life. They reminded Nabal of all the benefits they had provided to help keep his family, flocks, and property safe from the Philistines (1 Sam. 25:5-9). There is no record that David inquired of YHVH before going to Nabal to ensure his thoughts were in submission to His will.

David's appointed messengers respectfully requested that Nabal provide sustenance for them in-kind. However, Nabal rashly refused to fulfill their reasonable request, and brought an allegation against them, falsely accusing them of representing some runaway slave and not really David (1 Sam. 25:10-11). If Nabal was truly harsh, severe, and evil in all of his business, it is certainly possible that he had a slave or two run away from him. Although his reaction may not have been justified, this perspective makes his refusal to feed David and his men a little more understandable. However, based on the description of his personality, it is also entirely possible that his denial was a lame excuse. Perhaps, Nabal really was the most selfish and stingy jerk on the planet, unwilling to share his wealth with anyone.

Regardless of Nabal's heart motivations, when news returned to David that his reasonable request was denied, he was *livid!* I can only imagine the thoughts that must have raced through his mind in his anger, "You mean after all that I have done for him, this is how he repays me! *The nerve!*" David did not think twice, and it does not seem that he paused to inquire of YHVH first. He commanded his men to "buckle on their swords" and prepare to go kill Nabal. Off they marched in a swirling ball of fury toward Nabal's house (1 Sam. 25:12-13)!

Nabal's wife Abigail received word that David and hundreds of his mighty men were storming like a tornado to render devastation against her husband and his entire household. Her servants reported all that had transpired between David and Nabal. She made haste to prepare a veritable buffet in an attempt to pacify the fierce anger of David and his men (1 Sam. 25:14-18). She knew the way to a man's heart!

While Abigail prepared for his arrival, David hashed over his offense with Nabal the whole way. He informed his men that he would be cursed if he spared a single male alive in Nabal's household. David was furious and ready to annihilate everyone (1 Sam. 25:21-22). I can certainly relate to David's emotional response. Can you?

The Spiritual Weapon of Offense

However, little did David comprehend it at the time, but this was the very situation through which the Father was looking to beautify and adorn him with glory. Meanwhile, David's true adversary, *ha-Satan,* was hoping to disqualify him and make him a stench before YHVH and the people of Israel. *Ha-Satan* was tempting David to sin in his anger before the sun had even set on the day of his offense (Eph. 4:26). Oh, had David done well to take his wrathful thoughts captive through prayer before rashly and unwittingly committing folly in the eyes of YHVH and all the people of Israel (2 Cor. 10:5)!

We would prosper to take heed of the message the *Ruach ha-Kodesh* is conveying through David's example. The very moment our Heavenly Father is trying to perfect His glorious image in us, our adversary, often operating through another person, likewise tempts us through offensive circumstances. If we respond to offense in cruel wrath and vengeance, like David was about to do, it would be a complete misrepresentation of YHVH's merciful nature and disobedience to His Word (Ps. 37:8-10, Rom. 12:19). Such an action by a professed disciple of *Yeshua* is hypocritical and also tantamount to taking YHVH's name in vain, a violation of the third commandment.[6]

Ha-Satan's ultimate aim is to disqualify us from promotion in YHVH's kingdom through sin. Our adversary seeks to steal, kill, and destroy YHVH's image and glory in and through us, because of our hypocrisy. Such hypocrisy serves as a double-whammy because it often produces false judgments against the Heavenly Father in those who are witness to it. Sadly, hypocritical sin and misrepresentation of the Father's glorious image by those who call themselves His children is *ha-Satan's* most effective weapon of mass destruction (WMD). Christian hypocrisy causes more people to walk away from a relationship with their loving Creator than any other weapon in *ha-Satan's* arsenal. Our only guard against this WMD is to remain aware and alert to his schemes. On a daily, hourly, and momentary basis we must "take captive every thought," inquire of YHVH before *any* reaction and submit them "to the obedience of" Messiah *Yeshua*. *Yeshua* was our example in that He laid down any and all emotional reaction to offense, except His undying, unconditional, and sacrificial love for His offenders (2 Cor. 10:5 NIV, AMP).

A Wise Woman Comes to David's Rescue

In his fury, David was far removed from even considering what YHVH would have him do in this situation. Thankfully, through a willing vessel that was in tune with His *Ruach ha-Kodesh*, YHVH was busy preparing "a way to escape" that David could "stand up under" (1 Cor. 10:13 KJV, BSB). Abigail was willing to submit herself to YHVH's wisdom and instruction so that a counterattack could be leveled against the adversary's WMD. It is ironic that YHVH was using the beautiful wife of the very man the adversary was operating through (Nabal) to offer a way of escape to David.

Abigail hastened to meet David along the way and came riding on a donkey. The moment Abigail laid eyes on David she abased herself before him. She offered up her own life as a ransom for everyone that David was determined to kill, including her foolish husband (1 Sam. 25:20-24 KJV). Her actions were a pure reflection of YHVH's heart for her husband and their entire household, including all their servants. Abigail's actions also served as a prophetic pointer to the Messiah, *Yeshua*, who would one day come riding to Jerusalem on a young donkey (Zech. 9:9, Matt. 21:5, Luke 19:32-37). He too would be willing to offer up His life as a ransom for all who faced the penalty of death for their sins (Matt. 20:28, Mark 10:45, 1 Tim. 2:5-6).

Abigail's self-sacrifice was an unparalleled and astonishing act of wisdom, one that many women might think was totally crazy. Would we even dream of following her example or would we consider her to be "off her rocker?" After all, her husband, Nabal, had to have been the most atrocious husband on the planet!

Nabal's servants certainly did not have a high opinion of him. They said to Abigail, "he is such a son of Belial,[7] that a man can not speak to him" (1 Samuel 25:17). We all know the type. Such men can be terribly abusive (verbally, emotionally, and sometimes physically) to their family and to everyone else for that matter. Yet, Abigail was willing to lay down her life as a living sacrifice for Nabal and all who were under her care. She was a beautiful example of godly servanthood to follow!

Many women, if they found themselves in Abigail's position, would easily plead for the lives of their servants and children. But how many women would jump at the chance to hand their jerk of a husband over to David and thank him for ending their torment? Quite truthfully, how many women would have divorced such a man a long time ago? How could Abigail have possibly remained by the side of this pitiful man and be willing to lay down her life for him? I know we do not presently live under the same ancient Middle Eastern culture where a woman's very survival was largely dependent on her marriage. Yet there are still many rich truths to consider in Abigail's example.

First, Abigail means "my father is joy" (H26).[8] I believe she was a woman whose strength to endure life with such a man came from the joy she had in her Heavenly Father (Neh. 8:10). Second, Abigail was truly a unique woman of inner beauty of the heart, endowed with "a meek and quiet spirit" (1 Pet. 3:4-6), and wisdom and understanding from the *Ruach ha-Kodesh* (Isa. 11:2, 2 Cor. 3:18). These godly attributes caused her to display supernatural love. Abigail's heart was called to travel a hard road and lay herself down for all who were under her care, even her undeserving husband. This was clearly not a heart merely ruled by survival instinct or fear of losing her livelihood.

Abigail's example to women is stellar for another reason. She further set the example of godliness by humbly asking David for the opportunity to speak before her husband's death sentence was carried out upon her (1 Sam. 25:24). This was another mark of her uniqueness as a godly woman. Many of us do not ask permission to speak our words of wisdom (our opinion). More often than not, we just blurt out whatever is on our mind, and it can often make matters worse. Not so with Abigail. She understood respect and honor for those in a position of authority.

David graciously permitted Abigail to speak her piece. When she did, she displayed another godly example of wisdom and understanding for handling conflict. She did not judge or accuse David of overreacting. Nor did she try to defend herself, her household, or even her husband in any way. The first thing Abigail did was validate David's reason for being offended by acknowledging the folly and disgrace of her husband's behavior.

However, Abigail did not stop at merely acknowledging David's feelings. She said, "Please pay no attention, my lord, to that wicked man, Nabal" (1 Sam. 25:25 NIV). The wisdom within her was evoking the Proverbs 19:11 spiritual principle, which says that "it is to one's glory to overlook an offense" (NIV). Remember, this was wisdom inspired by the *Ruach ha-Kodesh* before Solomon ever codified it in writing, and we will see it evoked by others in David's life in Volume Two of our study series.

Abigail further advised David that YHVH had restrained him from taking vengeance into his own hands. If David had killed Nabal for a reason that is not authorized by YHVH's law, it would have brought a curse upon his kingdom reign (Rom. 12:19, Deut. 32:35). Furthermore, such an action would have caused the people of Israel to fear David; they would end up serving him out of fear instead of love and loyalty. In addition to warning David, Abigail also invoked blessings over David and his kingdom reign and pled for forgiveness of her household (1 Sam. 25:26-31 KJV). I can almost hear her words echoing through her example, "Forgive Nabal, for he knows not what he does."

The Beauty of a Teachable Heart

Thankfully, David was not so blinded by wrath that he could not hear YHVH's Spirit of wisdom and understanding speaking to him through Abigail. He immediately recognized YHVH's grace in sending this willing vessel, Abigail. He was grateful that YHVH would intercept him and keep him from doing something incredibly foolish and wrong (1 Sam. 25:32-34). David had a humble, pliable heart and a teachable spirit; he did not reject Abigail's words on the basis that she was a woman or the wife of such a worthless man. He also did not write her off and assume that she was serving her own best interests to save her family. David refused to judge her.

I believe the *Ruach ha-Kodesh* used Abigail's actions and gentle words of wisdom to prick David's conscience and remind him who he was deep down inside. She reminded David of his shepherd's heart and his willingness to lay his life down for his father's sheep. Abigail also caused David to remember the lesson he had just learned with Saul but had quickly forgotten the moment a stranger offended him.

Abigail's example and admonishment encouraged David to be the man that he was—a man after YHVH's own heart. He humbly received and agreed to her wisdom, calmed down, and commanded all of his men to stand down. He then blessed Abigail and sent her home with a vow of peace towards her and her entire household (1 Sam. 25:35). We would do well to learn from Abigail and David's example of submission if we desire peace at the end of a serious conflict of emotions.

The Folly of an Unteachable Heart

With her mission before YHVH accomplished, Abigail departed from David, leaving him and his men well provisioned with the food she had prepared for them. She returned home only to discover Nabal holding his own immense banquet. He was drunk and celebrating himself pridefully as though he were a king (1 Sam. 25:36). After all she had just laid on the line for him, Abigail had every right to be furious and bite his head off. Isn't that what many women would feel like doing if they were in her shoes?

However, instead of ripping Nabal to shreds for being such a loser, she had the wisdom to let him sleep it off. This gave her time to calm down before she opened her mouth. Women of faith would do well to follow her example here! When Nabal awakened in the morning, Abigail told him how she had saved him from certain death at the hands of David (1 Sam. 25:37).

When Nabal heard her words, he had the opposite reaction from David. He did not have a humble and teachable heart that was open to receiving wisdom from this beautiful woman, nor was he grateful for her sacrificial love. His prideful heart refused to repent, and it became physically hardened "as a stone." Ten days later, Nabal died at the hand of YHVH (1 Sam. 25:37-38).

As one of my pastors often says, "What happens in the physical is always a picture of what is already at work in the spiritual." Nabal's heart was spiritually hardened like a stone because of pride, and he was already spiritually dead because of it. His pride made him unwilling to budge at anyone's words, including the *Ruach ha-Kodesh* manifesting through his wife.

Nabal was the prophetic foreshadow of every prideful person. Even more, he foreshadows those who have been invited by the *Ruach ha-Kodesh* to serve King *Yeshua* out of gratitude for His sacrifice to protect them from eternal death. Those who reject that invitation and serve themselves as king instead will likewise find spiritual death as their end. We should be careful not to follow in Nabal's footsteps.

YHVH is Judge

David learned of Nabal's death and declared, "Blessed be to the LORD, that hath pleaded the cause of my reproach from the hand of Nabal, and hath kept his servant from evil: for the LORD hath returned the wickedness of Nabal upon his own head" (1 Sam. 25:39). David learned an indispensable truth that we all can glean from: we must let YHVH take our case for the insults and offenses committed against us.

We do not need to take up the case for ourselves or enlist others to do so. We must lay the offense down at the feet of *Yeshua* and leave it there for Him to deal with as He sees fit. YHVH will judge between us and our offender. However, this act of submission to YHVH is far easier said than done. Our tongues might bleed as we would likely have to bite them far more often than we are used to! However, until humble submission becomes our first and natural response to offense, we will continue being tested in this area.

The Beautiful Bride and Her Bridegroom

With Nabal dead, David sent for Abigail to become his own wife. Abigail's response to David was another incredible prophetic pointer to Messiah *Yeshua*. She was a considerably wealthy woman who was accustomed to having many servants at her service. And yet she responded to David, "let thine handmaid be a servant to wash the feet of the servants of my lord" (1 Sam. 25:39-41). What a beautiful foreshadowing of the night when the King of the Universe, one of unending wealth and hosts of angelic servants at His service, would humble Himself as a servant to wash the feet of His disciples (John 13:1-17)!

Abigail ultimately accepted David's offer to become his bride (1 Sam. 25:42). This whole narrative is a beautiful prophetic foreshadow when we consider that David is YHVH's king and the forefather and archetype of *Yeshua*, our Bridegroom. Abigail was a woman full of wisdom and understanding. She adorned herself and prepared much food to humbly bring before the future King David that she might be found pleasing in his sight. She was willing to lay down her own life as a living sacrifice before him. As a result, David gave Abigail a vow of peace to cover her household, and he ultimately took her as his own bride.

Isn't this a beautiful reflection of our relationship to our Bridegroom, *Yeshua*? He is coming to this earth in wrath and fury to judge the wicked. But He is also coming to find His bride, the wise virgin (Matt. 25:1-12) who has made herself ready and brings forth much fruit (Gal. 5:22-23). His bride is humble and submitted before Him and her lamp is full of oil (symbolic of the *Ruach ha-Kodesh*). *Yeshua* is looking for a bride who is beautifully adorned. His bride must strive to pass her tests to be a perfect reflection of Him and must be willing to lay her life down for the undeserving (Rom. 12:1-2). Most of all, she must live out the gospel instead of just speaking it, an example which will show forth His glory to the ends of the earth.

Are we that kind of bride? Have we mastered the test yet? If not, let us study our Bridegroom further so that we will be prepared to master the final exam at the last day.

The Final Exam

In his confrontation with Nabal, David did not quite pass his test with flying colors. In fact, had it not been for the intervention of the *Ruach ha-Kodesh* via Abigail, David would have blown it. YHVH was looking for a first response that would be born of the Spirit. So, David was in need of further refining and testing, and he was about to get it!

In 1 Samuel 26, David returned to *Hachilah*. He had taken one step forward and two steps backward. Sometimes in our own faith journey, we may find that we are repeatedly taking one step forward and two steps backward. If this is the case, we may need to ask ourselves if we are failing to comprehend and apply a lesson that YHVH is trying to teach us. Saul came out to *Hachilah* with "three thousand chosen" warriors to hunt David down (1 Sam. 26:2). Wait a minute! Didn't Saul make a covenant of peace with David the last time he brought three thousand warriors against David in *Maon*? Unfortunately, evil doesn't honor covenants. Besides, YHVH was truly in charge and needed to continue testing David until he produced the first fruit that He was looking for.

David spied Saul's encampment and waited until Saul and his army were asleep in their camp. Ahimelech, Abishai, and David stealthily descended to the camp and entered Saul's tent unnoticed. Once again, Abishai jumped to the conclusion that Saul had been delivered into David's hands. He ardently begged David to let him personally finish Saul off for him (1 Sam. 26:3-8).

Didn't zealous Abishai learn anything in *Maon*? David immediately commanded Abishai to calm down and reminded him that it was a sin to kill YHVH's anointed. He also passed on the lesson he had learned through Nabal by saying, "As the LORD liveth, the LORD shall smite him; or his day shall come to die; or he shall descend into battle and perish (1 Sam. 26:9-11).

Although David knew that YHVH had spiritually removed His anointing from Saul, he recognized that YHVH had not yet physically removed Saul from his position. David believed that, when YHVH was ready, He would make him the new king; YHVH would make it happen in His own way, in His own time, and by His own hands. David did not believe that his hands were to have anything to do with Saul's removal from the throne of Israel. He just needed to wait and be ready to step into his calling and anointing when that time came. He did not need to interfere in the process or have anyone act on his behalf, besides YHVH.

Therefore, David simply took Saul's "spear and the cruse of water from Saul's bolster." David and his two comrades escaped Saul's tent and the camp without being noticed, "because a deep sleep from the LORD was fallen upon them." David and his men went a good distance away from Saul's camp before shouting to awaken the warriors within it. He publicly denounced Abner, the captain of Saul's army. Abner had allowed the king's enemy to sneak within striking distance of Saul and confiscate his spear and water pot from his bedside (1 Samuel 26:12-16).

Saul awakened, immediately recognized David's voice, and called out to him. David asked Saul why he continued to pursue him when David had proven his loyalty in the cave in *Maon* (1 Sam. 26:17-18). Certainly, David could have called Saul on the carpet and reamed him out for his failure to uphold his recent covenant vow. However, once again David humbled himself before Saul, calling himself nothing more than "a flea" (1 Sam. 26:19-20).

This was an amazing and unnatural response to someone who had just broken his covenant of peace, returned to pursuing David's life, and showed no sign of repentance. But this was exactly the first response that YHVH was looking for in David and the very reason He had brought Saul out here to test David once more.

Just as David's kindness and humility toward Saul produced fruit the last time they met in *Maon*, Saul again responded by acknowledging his sin toward David. He promised David he would do him no further harm. Saul abased himself before David, called himself a "fool," and admitted that he was in error to continue pursuing David. He blessed David and they parted ways in peace (1 Sam. 26:21, 25). This time, Saul's repentance appeared to be genuine, as he did not continue to pursue David's life afterward.

David passed this test with flying colors! He proved himself to be the more mature, stronger man of faith by humbling himself before his enemy. David did not defend his rights, expect his feelings to be validated, nor demand restitution for the hurt that Saul had caused him. If he had, it would have only stirred up more conflict and kept him in the cycle of taking one step forward and two steps back. Instead, David died to himself, took "the yoke of meekness and humility" upon himself (Matt. 11:29 YLT), and sought peace and reconciliation of his relationship with Saul. This produced the fruit of humility and repentance in his opponent.

A Pure Reflection of the Bridegroom

David's actions were counter-culture. Even within the church, we live in a culture that says we must defend our rights and expect our feelings to be validated by others. We are also taught to demand restitution of all our losses before giving a moment's thought to reconciliation of relationship. Yet is this the example *Yeshua* displayed for us?

Did *Yeshua* defend His rights at all? No. Although He was innocent of every charge against Him, *Yeshua* willingly went to the cross, silent as a lamb to the slaughter (Isaiah 53:7). Did *Yeshua* ever demand anyone validate His feelings? No. As He endured the horrendous physical and emotional pain of the cross, He laid down His feelings and chose forgiveness as He cried out, "Father forgive them for they know not what they do" (Luke 23:34). Did *Yeshua* demand restitution of all before He gave a moment's notice to the thought of reconciliation of relationship? No. He gave His all to restore our relationship with Him while we were yet sinners and had made no efforts toward restoration. His example should give us cause to reconsider how we are counseling people, even in the church. Are we teaching the disciples of *Yeshua* to be a pure reflection of their Master?

Now, I feel a necessity to clarify to the reader that I am *not* advocating that we enable abusive people to run roughshod over us or others. YHVH's Word is clear that we need to repent and make restitution for our wrongdoings (Exod. 22, Lev. 5:16, Lev. 24, Num. 5). It is one of the many practical ways that we fulfill the second greatest commandment of loving our neighbor as we love ourselves. However, each person is ultimately accountable to YHVH for how they keep or fail to keep His commandments.

We most certainly should admonish and patiently exhort one another to fear YHVH and keep His commandments, and to do so out of a pure heart of love. However, we cannot mandate such behavior by our brothers and sisters. We must refrain from mandating obedience through emotional manipulation, which includes using our relationship with them as leverage. If we use emotional manipulation, we could potentially create an impure motive in that person's heart to keep YHVH's commandments, a motive other than love. This is a motive by which they will be judged. Sometimes, we do not know what we do.

No one appreciates insincere repentance and restitution that is driven purely out of a selfish desire to regain relationship. We should desire the same thing for our neighbor that YHVH ultimately desires from all humanity: voluntary and sincere repentance and restitution. YHVH wants us to be moved by love to make things right, to bless and please the ones we have offended. He allows His kindness to lead people to sincere repentance (Rom. 2:4), and so should we since we are made in His image and likeness.

At *Hachilah*, David mastered the lesson of how kindness leads to repentance. This is what YHVH aimed to teach him through all of this treachery, and the affliction from the evil spirit operating through Saul and Nabal. If we find ourselves facing similar treachery and affliction, it is possible that YHVH is trying to teach us this same lesson. Through David's counter-culture actions, he became a beautifully adorned reflection of His Heavenly King. *Yeshua* displayed His glory through his own example of humility, forgiveness, and selfless love.

Because David ultimately submitted to the *Ruach ha-Kodesh* and did not react in the flesh at all this last time, he was done being tested through Saul. Likewise, when we choose to react according to the leading of the *Ruach ha-Kodesh*, we will find that our time of testing ends. Adorned in *Yeshua's* image, we will find ourselves advancing to the next level toward our spiritual mountaintop. Let us encourage one another to remain submitted to the *Ruach ha-Kodesh* in all things at all times. The final exam is coming soon!

"But we all, with open face beholding as in a glass the glory of the Lord, are changed into the same image from glory to glory, even as by the Spirit of the Lord." (2 Cor. 3:18)

JOURNEY JOURNAL

1. Do you personally identify with any of Abigail's characteristics or experiences? If so, which one(s)? If not, why? How can you work toward modeling her example?

2. Do you personally identify with any of Nabal's characteristics or experiences? If so, which one(s)?

3. Do you personally identify with any of David's characteristics or experiences? If so, which one(s)? Could you respond to Saul in humility as David did? Why or why not?

4. How has this chapter's study affected your perspective of our adversary's use of offense to disqualify and destroy us? How are we to respond to offense to overcome his schemes?

5. How has this chapter's study affected your perspective about godly conflict resolution?

6. Did you experience any other personal conviction as you read this chapter and answered the questions presented? What were you convicted about? (Conviction is meant to lead us to prayers of repentance, wherein we receive YHVH's grace, mercy, and forgiveness.)

7. How has this chapter's study encouraged you to greater love for YHVH and your neighbor?

8
SIDETRACKED BY FEAR

Just when we think we have arrived at the perfect level of faith, a test will come along and reveal where we have areas of weakness that need to be strengthened. These are the spots and wrinkles in our spiritual bridal garment that need to be cleansed and ironed out, often through fiery trials. But we can rejoice because, in the end, those trials will develop patient endurance in us and bring us closer to perfection (James 1:2-4). In 1 Samuel 27, we are going to see that David's beautification and adornment process was not entirely complete. His garment still needed a bit of ironing.

Fear: Deceiver of the Heart

Despite the amazing covering and favor that YHVH provided against Saul, David said in his heart, "I shall now perish one day by the hand of Saul." He then decided to retreat in fear into enemy territory, back into the land of the Philistines (1 Samuel 27:1 KJV).

Notice how the Scriptures indicate that David said this in his heart, not that YHVH had told him. We need to be careful of the things that we say in our hearts or of following our hearts as "the heart is deceitful above all things, and desperately wicked" (Jer. 17:9).

This thought in David's heart was actually the complete opposite of what YHVH had told him and faithfully showed him throughout his time in the Judean wilderness. Any thought that does not originate from the *Ruach ha-Kodesh* is from an evil source and needs to be tested (1 John 4:1). These evil thoughts will always be the antithesis of YHVH's spoken promises to us or the antithesis of our personal experience with Him. David should have taken this thought captive and brought it into submission or alignment with YHVH's promises (2 Cor. 10:4-5), but he did not. YHVH promised David that he would be the next king of Israel; this was an automatic promise that YHVH would protect him until He physically placed David on the throne. YHVH's word *never* returns to Him void (Isa. 55:11)!

If David had had perfect trust in YHVH's promises without a shred of doubt, he would have never fretted for one moment over Saul. David would have been in perfect peace; "For God has not given us the spirit of fear, but of power, and of love, and of a sound mind" (2 Tim. 1:7). Of course, I personally can't judge David in this regard. I have been just as guilty of imperfect trust in YHVH's promises. I too have allowed doubt and fear to rule in my heart in the course of my faith journey. Thankfully, there is forgiveness and mercy for that folly as soon as we recognize it, take responsibility, and repent.

We can still learn much about ourselves by examining David's mistakes. Wisdom learns from the mistakes of others. It amazes me how the spirit of fear often drives us into situations more dangerous than the threats we fear. David was more afraid of Saul and his three thousand men (who had never overtaken him) than he was of the Philistine kings and their myriads of warriors. The Philistines hated David more vehemently than Saul did. Did David forget that humiliating episode where he barely escaped death at the hands of those in Gath?

Throughout his wilderness wandering, YHVH repeatedly preserved David from the hand of Saul, and twice YHVH established peace between them. So, why was David operating in fear? He never should have aligned himself with this thought that was meant to take him off course. It seems insane that he would choose to take refuge in the land of his archenemy rather than remain in the refuge of YHVH that had preserved him this whole time.

Unfortunately, this goes to show the power that fear can have over us if we give it any traction in our hearts and minds. Any time fear of anything, except the fear of the LORD, is at play in our decisions, we need to *stop* and carefully consider what we are about to do! If we move in fear, it can severely take us off course, delay our progress, or completely derail us from our destiny.

Moving in fear is precisely what the children of Israel did when the ten spies gave a bad report. They feared the giants in the land and did not believe YHVH's promises. The Israelites were about to receive their blessing of the Promised Land. However, their alignment with the spirit of fear cost them forty more years in the wilderness, and an entire generation never reached their calling to enter the Land. Only Joshua and Caleb refused to align themselves with fear and chose to align themselves with YHVH's promise. As a result, they were preserved alive and allowed to lead the next generation into their promised inheritance (Num. 13:25-14:45). Fear and anxiety were also the reason that YHVH sent home twenty-two thousand warriors (out of thirty-two thousand) from Gideon's army; YHVH was unable to use them in the initial and

most glorious battle against Israel's oppressor, the Midianites
(Judg. 7:3).

I wonder if, at this point in his journey, David was on the cusp
of receiving his kingdom promise. In a royal position, YHVH
would be able to use David to deliver Israel from her oppressors,
the Philistines. Is it possible YHVH saw this little shred of
wavering faith inside David's heart and knew that it had to be dealt
with? Did YHVH allow this test by the spirit of fear so that David
could overcome this weakness? An effective king and shepherd of
YHVH's flock cannot be swayed by fear; they must be prepared to
face even death at the hands of an adversary for the sake of the
flock! David was once this type of man, as he fought off a bear and
a lion for the sake of his father's sheep. However, fear can cause us
to forget who we are in YHVH.

Oppression Brings Forth the Light

In spite of our fear, YHVH is faithful and sovereign. He is
always covering us, and I believe nothing is allowed to touch us or
test us without His consent. We see evidence of this concept
through the story of Job. Furthermore, YHVH is always working
"all things together for good to them that love" Him and are
"called according to His purpose" (Rom. 8:28). We are going to
see that this was precisely what He was doing for David, even in
enemy territory.

Following after his heart, David took his mighty men "unto
Achish, the son of Maoch, king of Gath" (1 Sam. 27:2). Gath
means "winepress" (H1661),[1] and the root of Maoch means
"oppressed, pressed, struck, bruised, squeezed, and
pierced" (H4600).[2] Led by his own heart and by fear, it does not
appear that David inquired of YHVH before he decided to flee into
Philistine territory. However, I believe that YHVH still ordained
this destination (Prov. 16:9). Just as we have discussed in previous

chapters, no stop on David's journey was an accident or coincidence. Prophetically speaking, YHVH was taking David and his men to the winepress, under the son of oppression. He would press them in order to bring out the useful substance within them.

Symbolically, the Scriptures liken YHVH's chosen people to olive trees and grapevines (Ps. 52:8, 128:3, Jer. 11:16, Zech. 4, Rom. 11). In ancient Israel, both olives and grapes were predominantly pressed for their very useful substance within. The outer shell—the skin and the flesh—along with the seed was removed. The oil and juice produced through the pressing process were put into use. Some of the olive oil was used to light the menorah in the Sanctuary, which was referred to as the light to the nations.

Spiritually, this is the reason why we are pressed, bruised, struck, squeezed, and pierced through testing. YHVH desires to remove our outer shell, the thick skin that is our protective mechanism— our flesh (Rom. 8:6-10). He also seeks to remove the perishable seed of the forbidden fruit that lies deep within every human since the fall in the Garden of Eden (1 Pet. 1:23). Through the pressing process, His purpose is to produce the oil for our lamps to light up the world (Matt. 5:14, 25:1-13) and the fruit of the Spirit (Gal. 5:22-23). And this was how YHVH planned to use the sixteen months that David and his men would stay in Philistine territory.

The Hand That Turns the Heart of Kings

Just as He did the last time David wandered into Gath, YHVH once again turned the heart of King Achish to fulfill His plan for David. Achish once looked down upon David as an archenemy and a madman and had cast David away from his presence. Now, he looked upon David with favor. As we saw in Chapter Two, Achish suffered tremendous defeat at David's hand. Not only did David defeat Achish's champion, Goliath, but David also led Israel's army to pursue Achish's army all the way to Gath, overcoming them with an impressive slaughter. Only YHVH could move upon Achish's heart and cause him to look upon David with favor like this (Prov. 21:1).

In fact, David had so much favor with Achish that he was able to ask him for a place for him and his men to call home within the land of the Philistines. Achish granted his request and gave him *Ziklag*. While they were living in *Ziklag*, David and his men conducted covert missions against the enemies of Israel. During this time, Achish believed they were fighting against Israel, even though David did not intentionally lead him to believe such. David merely disclosed the location of his raids in the Negev, an area where the Amalekites, Girzites, and Geshurites lived and routinely pilfered the Israelites. David never said that he was conducting raids against his own people in these areas (1 Sam. 27:5-11).

Even though David had moved to Philistine territory in fear, YHVH used him in this place to rid the surrounding lands of Israel's enemies. As a result, David would enjoy more peace when he finally made it to his promised throne. This is more proof that YHVH can take what is meant for evil and turn it around for our good, just as He did for Joseph (Gen. 50:20). YHVH can even redeem our mistakes when we operate in fear.

King Achish believed that David and his men were championing his cause (1 Sam. 27:12). He thought that David had become an enemy of Israel. As the Philistines gathered their armies together to wage war against Israel, Achish trusted David and his men enough to invite them into battle with him. David did not say yes or no to Achish, but simply responded, "Surely, you know what your servant can do" (1 Sam. 28:1-2 NKJV).

Surely Achish knew that David was a mighty man of war. Achish had been on the wrong side of David and saw the collateral damage that David and the men under his leadership could inflict. Now that he trusted David was for him and not against him, this was precisely the reason that Achish wanted the all-star David on his team. Achish informed David he would make him one of his chief guardians. It seems that David and his men joined the Philistine armies encamped against Israel in *Shunem* (1 Sam. 28:2-4). *Shunem's* root meaning is "quietly" (H7766),[3] but somehow, I doubt the Philistines were quiet while they prepared to destroy Israel!

When Emotions Lead Us Astray

In contrast, Saul and Israel's army encamped at *Gilboa* (1 Sam. 28:4). *Gilboa's* root meaning is "fountain of ebullition" (H1533).[4] Ebullition means "a sudden outburst of emotion or violence."[5] On many occasions, Saul surely displayed himself as one who sprung up with sudden outbursts of emotion and violence. Isn't it amazing how YHVH orchestrates Israel's physical battles in locations that reveal the hidden spiritual battle? Through His attention to detail in the Hebrew language, we learn a valuable lesson. Those who were the victors in this epic battle were the ones who encamped in the place of rest or quiet (*Shuni*). Meanwhile, the army that was devastatingly defeated encamped at the fountain of sudden outbursts of emotions (*Gilboa*). Where are we encamped in the day of battle, my brothers and sisters?

Needless to say, at the sight of the massive Philistine army gathered against them, Saul's heart became overwhelmed with sheer terror. He was shaking in his boots! (1 Sam. 28:5). Understandably so because he no longer had the Spirit of YHVH with him or the mighty warrior David to lead his army. Also, Samuel the prophet, who had also led Israel to glorious victory over the Philistines (1 Sam. 7), was dead. Saul had nothing going in his favor at this point. It would seem that many of his soldiers saw the writing on the wall; 1 Chronicles 12 indicates that around this time, there were men of Israel's army that defected from Saul and joined David in *Ziklag*.

In the face of such dismal circumstances, Saul fasted and "enquired of the LORD," but received no response (1 Sam. 28:4-6). This was the sad state of a rebellious heart that refused to keep the commandments of YHVH (Isa. 59:1-13). Unfortunately, in his petitions, Saul was "asking amiss" (James 4:1-6 NKJV). He was only seeking YHVH out of his desperation and fear, to save his life and his position, not because he had a heart to seek YHVH. How often do we find ourselves in the same boat as Saul where we receive no response to our petitions? If we do find ourselves petitioning YHVH with the wrong motive, it is always an opportunity to search our hearts for sin. We can come to YHVH in a sincere prayer of repentance and receive the forgiveness He is ever ready to grant.

Fear's Folly Hastens Destruction

Saul was desperate for guidance, and he feared that this battle would be his end. He did not know where to turn for answers, so he decided to go to a medium. Keep in mind, Saul had just ordered all the mediums and the spiritists to be "put out of the land" of Israel (1 Sam. 28:3 NKJV). The Hebrew word translated as "put" in this verse is *sur,* and it can actually mean "behead" according to Strong's Exhaustive Concordance (H5493).[6] From the medium's response to Saul, we may be able to deduce that he had beheaded the other mediums and spiritists. Perhaps Saul was trying to fulfill the laws of Exodus 22:18 and Leviticus 20:27, which required the death of anyone who was practicing witchcraft or necromancy. Was Saul trying to earn YHVH's favor back through following the law? Of course, such an attempt could not save Saul because the law cannot save. Additionally, his efforts were futile because true obedience, out of love for YHVH and His ways, was not in his heart.

When YHVH did not answer Saul's petitions, Saul was quick to violate the very law he was just trying to uphold. His violation of the law was punishable by death and was the very thing that set Saul's final judgment in motion. YHVH could have carried out His judgment against Saul at any time and fulfilled the death sentence that He rendered through Samuel the prophet. However, YHVH's appointed time for Saul's death had not yet come.

Any of the spears that Saul threw at David or Jonathan could have killed them. If that had happened, Saul would have been worthy of the death penalty according to YHVH's law. Additionally, Saul could have been judged as worthy of death for ordering the slaughter of the priests in Nob (even though YHVH permitted this event in order to carry out His judgment against Eli). Of course, YHVH was preserving David and would not allow Saul to kill him. Additionally, Jonathan was destined to die alongside Saul, so allowing his death to happen at an earlier time was clearly not in YHVH's plan. If Saul would have met his judgment at an earlier time, David and his men would not have experienced their faith-building lessons in the Judean wilderness. These lessons were essential to grow their faith and character and to foster spiritual maturity.

Sometimes in life, it seems as though YHVH is not moving, judging, or correcting someone who has wronged us. In reality, YHVH is working everything together for good in His way and according to His perfect timing. When we do not see our enemy being held accountable for their actions, we need to trust and wait on YHVH to do it. If David had circumvented YHVH's judgment process with Saul, he would have missed a lot of blessings and experiences with YHVH during his wilderness wandering. David and his men would not have intimately known the depth of YHVH's salvation and covering.

David could have spent all of his time looking for and asking YHVH for His judgment upon Saul. David's men were constantly thinking about it, and many of David's prayers reflect that he thought about it to some degree. However, David was a man after YHVH's own heart. He repeatedly showed kindness, honor, and mercy to Saul, which was the opposite of what everyone else thought Saul deserved. But this was what YHVH required of David, "to do justly [exercise YHVH's judgment], to love mercy [goodness, kindness], and to walk humbly with [his] God" (Mic. 6:8 BSB, *brackets mine*). David trusted in YHVH's timing. He was about to come into his promise because he "waited patiently for the LORD" (Ps. 40:2 KJV) and allowed the universal Judge to bring Saul to His perfectly timed end.

In Saul's desperation for answers, his men told him of "a woman that hath a familiar spirit at Endor." So, Saul disguised himself and went to her under the cover of night to seek her services. The medium did not recognize Saul, but she was clearly afraid that she would be turned in and put to death if she performed the service he was requesting. He swore by the name of YHVH that no harm would come to her. Saul then requested that she conjure up the spirit of Samuel the prophet so that he could learn his fate (1 Sam. 28:7-11).

Of course, Saul already knew his ultimate fate. YHVH had already told him through Samuel the prophet many years prior. Saul was just afraid of his fate and wanted to know how and when it would happen. No doubt his motive was to somehow change, avoid, or fight against YHVH's judgment. Saul was not the least bit submitted to YHVH's sovereign hand over his life. Otherwise, he would have had no occasion to fear like this. He would have just thought, "OK, I have been prideful and rebellious toward

YHVH, and He has justly rejected me. Whatever seems good to YHVH to do to me, so be it."

Such an admission of guilt was actually the response that Eli the priest gave when a young Samuel delivered the word of judgment from YHVH. Eli submitted himself to the sovereign hand of YHVH's judgment and accepted his fate (1 Sam. 3:18). Saul, on the other hand, did not once submit himself or accept his fate. In studying the book of 1 Samuel, we have watched Saul fight to hold onto his kingdom position and destroy any and all who dared threaten it. Saul's behavior is the hallmark of a rebellious heart.

Of course, asking for Samuel the prophet was a dead giveaway to the medium that the man before her was Saul and this really freaked her out. Saul reassured her once again that no harm would come to her for her service to him (1 Sam. 28:12-13). Not only did Saul break YHVH's law by consulting this medium, but he took YHVH's name in vain and promised her protection from the law. Saul added sin upon sin when he failed to carry out the requirement of the law and put the medium to death for her witchcraft. Saul was piling the curse of death upon himself.

It is amazing what people are willing to do when they are afraid to lose something. In the face of death, they can refuse to submit their lives into the sovereign hand of YHVH. They can actually accelerate the very thing that they fear the most and bring it into immediate reality. Our destruction is the spirit of fear's ultimate goal.

Because of his disobedience to YHVH's instructions, Saul had been given over to a spirit of fear and his punishment had come due. He had fallen vastly short of perfect love for YHVH. Saul also failed miserably in the area of loving his neighbor as himself; his sudden outbursts of emotions led to violence and murder of his fellow humans. In all this, Saul had failed to reflect the image and likeness of YHVH in the earth.

We can glean much wisdom from taking heed to Saul's folly and listening to the wise counsel of John the Apostle when he said, "If we love one another, God dwelleth in us and his love is perfected in us. Herein is our love made perfect: because as he is, so are we in this world. There is no fear in love; but perfect love casteth out fear: because fear hath torment. He that feareth is not made perfect in love" (1 John 4:12, 16-17, *condensed*). John made it crystal clear that deliverance from the spirit of fear comes through being perfected in our love for YHVH and our neighbor, through walking in YHVH's image and likeness. Messiah *Yeshua* perfectly modeled this principle for us.

In response to Saul's request, the medium agreed to conjure up Samuel's spirit. When she described the spirit's appearance to Saul, Saul immediately recognized that it was Samuel's spirit and bowed himself to the ground. Samuel was totally perturbed with Saul for disturbing his rest. Saul explained why he was so distressed and pleaded for Samuel to tell him his fate. Samuel pointed out Saul's audacity; what made Saul think that Samuel would be able to give him an answer when the *Ruach ha-Kodesh* refused to respond to his prayer and fasting? Samuel reiterated Saul's judgment which he had spoken years before and informed Saul that YHVH had not changed His mind (1 Sam. 28:13-19).

Saul had broken the law repeatedly—and for nothing! He got no new information from Samuel. Nothing had changed for him, except now he was more worthy of his punishment than ever before. What Samuel did tell him is that he and his sons would die in the battle against the Philistines the following day. Now, Saul knew for sure how the battle would turn out (1 Sam. 28:19).

Saul was so terrified at this news that he became weak. He had been fasting all day and night hoping to get some answer from

YHVH. The woman and his servants tried to convince Saul to eat something before going back to the war camp, and he finally broke down and agreed to eat (1 Sam. 28:20-25)

The next day the Philistines gathered their armies together at *Aphek* while "the Israelites pitched by a fountain which is in *Jezreel*" (1 Sam. 29:1). The Hebrew word for fountain is *ayin* and it also means "eye, sight, outward appearance, confidence, knowledge, think best, whatever you like" (H5869).[7] *Jezreel* means "God sows" (H3157).[8] It certainly was not by accident that Saul and his army camped in this place where he would meet his end. The very sin that caused Saul's spiritual death (the removal of YHVH's Spirit) was doing what he thought best (or whatever he liked) instead of what YHVH instructed. *Jezreel* was symbolic of this sin, and it would be the very place where he met his physical death and where Israel would be utterly defeated by their enemy. YHVH sowed His judgment of Saul and it was about to be reaped.

David Preserved from Judgment

Before the Philistines started their attack on the Israelites, the Philistine princes suddenly recognized that David and his mighty men were bringing up Achish's rear guard. They vehemently protested David's presence among their armies to Achish, convinced that he would turn against them and fight on behalf of Israel. Achish staunchly defended David's honor, testifying of his conduct for the last sixteen months that he had lived in *Ziklag*. Achish said, "I have found no fault in him since he fell unto me unto this day." The princes were not the least bit moved by Achish's declaration of David's trustworthiness, and they angrily insisted the king send David and his men away (1 Sam. 29:3-5).

Achish conceded to the princes' demands and summoned David. He told David, "As the LORD liveth, thou hast been upright, and thy going out and thy coming in with me in the host is good in my sight: for I have not found evil in thee since the day of thy coming unto me unto this day." He told David that the Philistine princes did not share his esteem for David, and desired for David to be sent home (1 Sam. 29:6-7).

Can you imagine someone who was once your archenemy ever saying such wonderful things about you? Have you lived out your faith in the presence of your enemies in such a way that they would call you blameless in their sight (Acts 24:16, Phil. 2:14-16)? Clearly, this is what David had done.

In Babylon, the prophet Daniel also lived out his faith in such a way that his enemies and oppressors could find no fault in him. Both Daniel and David showed honor, respect, and love to their leaders, even though they were heathen pagan leaders (Rom. 13). As a result, YHVH gave them favor and honored position in an earthly kingdom, which also points to the favor and honored position they would receive in the spiritual kingdom.

Ultimately, David and Daniel's good conduct caused these earthly leaders to recognize that YHVH is the living *Elohim*. If you read 1 Samuel 29:6 in the original Hebrew, you'll see that Achish actually confessed that YHVH lives. How are our hearts, attitudes, words, and actions toward our leaders and our oppressors (even the most heathen, pagan ones) measuring up to the standards of excellence that David and Daniel set? As I look at myself and much of the church, I have to admit that we are falling way short. Are we willing to make the necessary changes in our hearts to bring ourselves up to their standards? If we do, we may also see contemporary pagan leaders acknowledge YHVH as the true and living *Elohim* in the same way that David and Daniel did.

Upon hearing of the Philistine princes' demands, David seemed to be sincerely disappointed that he was not allowed to go into battle against Israel. He asked Achish why he should not fight alongside him. Achish replied, "I know that thou art good in my sight, as an angel of God." The Hebrew word for angel is *malak*, which also means "ambassador, messenger, envoy, prophet, priest, teacher, king" (H4397).[9] As people who desire to pursue YHVH's heart, we should live in a way that our leaders see us as pleasing in their sight and as angels or ambassadors of YHVH.

Achish further explained that, despite his own high regard for David, the Philistine commanders insisted, "He shall not go up with us to battle." He told David to head home with his men first thing in the morning. David could have taken up offense against the Philistine commanders, but he chose to honor their request by leaving (1 Sam. 29:8-11). Of course, this was all YHVH's hand working in the heart of David's enemies. YHVH was determined to protect David's future and preserve the spiritual cleanness of his calling and anointing to the throne of Israel. David and his men could not take part in Saul's demise. The blood of the former king could not be on his hands or the hands of his men. Likewise, if we are called and anointed for an esteemed position of leadership within YHVH's kingdom, we cannot take part in overthrowing another leader in order to take up our position. We must let it all be at the hands of YHVH, otherwise, we will have iniquity found in us by both YHVH and men.

If David and his men had participated in this final battle, those loyal to Saul and Jonathan would surely have viewed their involvement as high treason. David's authority would never have been recognized and there would have been division in his kingdom from the very beginning. Such a situation would prove to be a hindrance to David and quite possibly would have kept him from having total victory over his enemies (such as the Assyrians and Ammonites as we will see in future chapters). We may never know how David's saga might have been changed for the worse if he or his men had been involved in this campaign to destroy Saul.

This was a campaign YHVH ordained to fulfill His judgment against Saul. It was to be carried out only by the hands of the enemy so that the blood guilt would remain on the enemy alone. We see this concept throughout Scripture. In Isaiah 10:5-19, YHVH used the enemies of Israel to execute His judgment on His people. He used Assyria as Israel's rod of discipline but was also using the situation to bring judgment against Assyria; the Assyrians would be held accountable for the blood of Israel. In this, we see that YHVH uses His own judgment on His people as a means to bring an even heavier judgment upon His enemy.

If we get involved and put our hands in this process, we put ourselves in the path of YHVH's judgment. Do we really want to do that? In light of YHVH's system of justice, let's take another look at the beginning of 1 Samuel 27:1. It's possible that the spirit of fear had a much larger goal in mind when prompting David to move into the land of the Philistines. Perhaps the ultimate goal was to get David to participate in the battle of *Jezreel*, putting him in the path of YHVH's judgment and destroying his calling. This should move us to pray for the same protection that David had. YHVH is able to turn the hearts of our enemies to work for our good. He can prevent us from taking part in anything that would incur His judgment upon us and therefore, stop us from experiencing the fullness of our calling.

The Heart Purified Through Trial

Even though YHVH faithfully protected David, David's true enemy, *ha-Satan,* was relentless against him. *Ha-Satan* was determined to destroy David during his stay in Philistine territory. David and his men spent three days away from *Ziklag* following Achish to *Aphek*. In that time, a band of Amalekite raiders came through *Ziklag*, took everyone and everything captive, and burned the camp to the ground. David and his men were so distraught at the sight of *Ziklag*, and the loss of their wives and children, that they "wept aloud until they had no strength left to weep." David's men blamed him for their loss because he had led them away for seemingly no reason. They became so "bitter in spirit" that they wanted to stone David to death (1 Sam. 30:1-6 NIV).

Can you imagine yourself in their shoes? These men had left their lives and spent the last few years following David. They had fought alongside him against his enemies and watched over his life because they believed David was the chosen and anointed leader of Israel. However, the moment he made a decision that appeared to have cost them everything, their love for him turned into hatred. They suddenly became his staunchest enemy, ready to end his life. That is what bitterness will do.

When we allow ourselves to become offended at a brother or sister and disobey YHVH's word by taking up a bitter root (Heb. 12:15), our love for them can quickly turn into hatred. Hatred of a brother or sister is equated to spiritual blindness and leads to death. It is an emotion that does not belong in the heart of any follower of *Yeshua* (1 John 2:9-11, 3:15, 4:20). Yes, at times a brother or sister may do something unthinkable, cost us everything, and seemingly becoming our adversary. Yet *Yeshua* commands us to love them, do good to them, pray for them, and bless them (Luke 6:27-28).

As David's men were picking up stones to throw at him, he "encouraged himself" in YHVH. He immediately called for Abiathar, the priest, to bring him the ephod so that he could inquire of YHVH (1 Sam. 30:6-7 KJV). Psalm 4 may have been written near this time and may give us a glimpse of his prayer.[10] Even in the midst of his closest friends and allies who were now intent on destroying him, David was assured of YHVH's protection. He declared, "The LORD will hear when I call unto him. Thou hast put gladness in my heart, more than in the season that their corn [grain] and wine increased. I will both lay me down in peace, and sleep; for thou, LORD, only makest me to dwell in safety" (Ps. 4:3, 7-8, *condensed*).

David's reference to the season of grain and wine alludes to both the spring feast of *Shavuot* (Pentecost) and the fall feast of *Sukkot* (Tabernacles). Both of these feasts represent celebrations of tremendous gladness, joy, and thanksgiving for the abundance of the harvest. In this dire situation, David encouraged himself by proclaiming he had more gladness in his heart than during these joyous feasts. Because he was assured of YHVH's salvation, he had peace so sweet that he could sleep like a baby. Would we be able to encourage ourselves like this in the midst of similar circumstances?

Despite his great display of faith, it is unfortunate that it took this dire situation to bring David back to inquiring of YHVH. In Scripture, there is no evidence that David inquired of YHVH since he was in *Engedi* (1 Sam. 24). If he had inquired of YHVH before going up to battle with Achish, he and his men might have been in *Ziklag* to protect their family and belongings against the Amalekite raiders. Furthermore, if David had inquired of YHVH before fleeing to Philistine territory out of fear, they likely would have never been in this predicament at all.

Nevertheless, David was facing a crisis, and he came to YHVH with a model prayer, asking what he should do. He did not come before YHVH with his own agenda, asking Him to help his cause. Nor did David cry out to YHVH to deliver him from the wrath of his men. David asked for direction in how to rectify this situation and whether he should try to get back what had been stolen from them. YHVH responded, "thou shalt surely overtake them, and without fail recover all" (1 Sam. 30:8-9).

Pursuit of the Real Enemy

David told his men of YHVH's promise to help them overtake the Amalekites and rescue their families. The men overcame their bitterness and joined David in the pursuit of their real enemy who had stolen everything from them. As long as we hold on to bitterness, we will fail to recognize that the real enemy is the thief who came to "steal, kill, and destroy" (John 10:10), not our loved one.

At first, all six hundred men joined David in this mission. But as they came to the *Wadi Besor*, two hundred of the men were so emotionally, physically, and spiritually exhausted that they just could not continue on (1 Sam. 30:9-10). Keep in mind, these men had just traveled approximately fifty miles on foot from *Aphek* to *Ziklag*. They experienced the devastating loss of everything in their lives and had spent their strength weeping in grief. Now, the men had traveled about another twenty-five miles on foot. They were in dire need of some uplifting news to revive their spirits, which made *Besor* the perfect resting place for them. The root word of *Besor* means "receive good tidings" (H1319).[11]

David and the other four hundred men left their weary companions behind at the brook and pressed forward in the pursuit of the enemy. Along the way, they came across an Egyptian slave who had been deserted by the Amalekites three days prior because he was ill and could not keep up with them. David and his men fed him and gave him water to drink to revive him. David asked him if he would be willing to help them find the Amalekites, and the slave was willing so long as they promised not to hand him over to his master. They agreed to his terms and he led them straight to camp where the Amalekites were busy reveling in all their spoils (1 Sam. 30:11-16).

Spirit Empowered Victory over the Enemy

David and his men wasted no time and attacked the Amalekites while they were celebrating. They battled the Amalekites "from the twilight even unto the evening of the next day" (1 Sam. 30:17).

Can you even imagine this? David and his men had just traveled a total of approximately one hundred miles on foot between *Aphek* and the Amalekite camp. You would think they would have camped for the night, gotten some much-needed shut-eye, and attacked in the morning when they were well rested. But, no! David would not spend one more night without his wives! He would attack the enemy when they least expected it and while they reveled in their success.

The fact that David and his men fought all night and totally whooped on the Amalekites was simply nothing short of a miracle! YHVH promised to be with him and give him victory, and He had clearly done this, "not by might nor by power," but by His strength. YHVH endowed David and his men with His *Ruach ha-Kodesh* as they fought (Zech. 4:6). There was no way they could physically do this in their own strength as physically and emotionally exhausted as they had to have been. When they were in *Ziklag*, they had wept in grief until they were out of strength.

None of the Amalekites escaped this battle, "save four hundred young men, which rode upon camels, and fled" (1 Sam. 30:17). David and his men recovered everyone and everything that had been taken from *Ziklag*. Not one person or thing was missing from all that David recovered. He also recovered all the spoils that had been taken during the Amalekite raids upon the land of Israel (1 Sam. 30:18-20).

Righteousness Seeks Unity in Blessing

David and his men began the long journey back to *Ziklag* with much spoil. As they reached the two hundred men who stayed behind at the *Wadi Besor*, David reached out and greeted his brothers by saluting them with *shalom*. Some of the men that had gone into battle with David were not so happy to see those who had stayed behind. They were offended that their comrades did not help rescue and retrieve all that was stolen. They did not want to share any part of these spoils they were bringing back and told David that their comrades should have no part; they should only be allowed to take their wives and children and leave (1 Sam. 30:21-22).

Those who had fought with David were suggesting a permanent separation from their comrades, who had stayed behind. The Bible actually calls these fighting men "wicked" and "men of Belial"[12] for having this attitude toward their comrades—their brothers (1 Sam. 30:22). The word for wicked in this verse is the same as the evil spirit in Saul (H7451).[13] Undoubtedly, YHVH did not care to see this spirit in his chosen army.

David also would hear nothing of the sort and informed these wicked men that *all* the spoils would be shared equally among all the men. He understood that their victory and the fact that they had anything to bring back was all YHVH's doing. These men saw the victory as being their own accomplishment and were taking pride in it. They did not want to share with their weaker brothers who simply did not have the emotional strength and spiritual maturity to carry on. According to the Scripture, YHVH saw this prideful and selfish mindset in them as evil and worthless.

David felt strongly that all of his men should have their fair share of the spoils, so much so that he later codified this into Israel's laws; all of Israel would receive their portion of war spoils whether they fought or not (1 Sam. 30:23-25). Not only did David command that his men receive their fair share, but he also sent the leaders of Judah (Saul's loyal subjects) the spoils that the Amalekites had taken from them (1 Sam. 30:26-31). David was a man after YHVH's own heart, following His law to return what was lost to its rightful owner. Once again, YHVH used what was meant for evil for good!

Fear Turned into Greater Faith

David may have been sidetracked by fear and experienced some really hard times and battles because of it, but he was not derailed by it. Ultimately, YHVH protected and restored him. YHVH also used David to bless his brothers in a way that might not have happened if he had not been in Philistine territory. Additionally, David and his men experienced an unprecedented miracle of YHVH's might and power; YHVH fought for them when they had no strength left in them.

There would now be fewer Amalekite raiders for the Israelites to deal with in the future under David's leadership. All things were working together for good. David and his men definitely learned some of the most valuable faith lessons of their lives while living in enemy territory. They were one step closer to their ultimate destiny.

If you have ever operated in fear and found yourself sidetracked, as I have, I pray that this chapter's study has encouraged you. YHVH can still use us to accomplish His will every bit as much as He used David. YHVH protects, restores, and matures those who belong to Him and are called according to His purpose. He works everything together for our good and brings us back on track toward our ultimate destiny to deliver His chosen from oppression. We will likely forever be delivered from a spirit of fear, as I believe David and his men were.

"For God hath not given us the spirit of fear; but of power, and of love, and of a sound mind." (2 Tim. 1:7)

"There is no fear in love; but perfect love casteth out fear: because fear hath torment. He that feareth is not made perfect in love." (1 John 4:18)

JOURNEY JOURNAL

1. Do you personally identify with any of David's characteristics or experiences in this chapter's study? If so, how?

2. Do you personally identify with any of Saul's characteristics or experiences in this chapter's study? If so, how?

3. How can you live your life before your authorities or enemies in such a way that causes them to acknowledge that YHVH lives or see you as a blameless ambassador of YHVH?

4. Where do you usually find yourself encamped in the day of battle? In the rest and quiet of YHVH's peaceful presence or bubbling up with sudden outbursts of emotion or violence? What is your plan to ensure you remain victorious in every battle?

5. Describe your walk with YHVH and your prayer life. Do you regularly make time for prayer and fasting, or is prayer and fasting something you reserve only for desperate times?

6. Have you ever allowed your love for someone turn to hatred over circumstances you blamed them for? How has this study affected your perspective of that person or circumstance?

7. Did you experience any other personal conviction as you read this chapter and answered the questions presented? What were you convicted about? (Conviction is meant to lead us to prayers of repentance, wherein we receive YHVH's grace, mercy, and forgiveness.)

8. How has this chapter's study encouraged you to greater love for YHVH and your neighbor?

9
THE GAVEL FALLS

"Though the mills of God grind slowly, yet they grind exceeding small; though with patience he stands waiting, with exactness grinds He all."[1] This quote is often heard in legal circles today as, "The wheels of justice turn slowly, but they grind thoroughly." Having worked alongside the criminal justice system, I can testify that sometimes the administration of law takes an exceedingly long time. In the process, it can seem as if nothing is being done at all. The wait can be agonizing for the one who has suffered the injustice. Yet we can be sure of this: in the courtroom of heaven, a just judgment will one day come, just as we will see that it finally came to Saul.

Live or Die by the Sword

In 1 Samuel 30, the Philistine armies had gathered together against Israel, but now, in Chapter 31, the Philistines were whooping on Israel big time! Saul's three sons, including David's covenant friend Jonathan, were killed. Saul took an arrow through the weak spot in his armor. He asked his armor-bearer to end his life so that he would not be tortured and killed by the heathen Philistines. Because his armor-bearer was too afraid to kill him, Saul took his own sword and fell on it (1 Sam. 31:1-4 KJV, 1 Chron. 10:1-4 KJV).

When Saul fell upon his own sword, his physical act had prophetic significance for what took place in the spiritual realm. We would be wise to take note. Ultimately, Saul rejected YHVH's sword—His Word (Eph. 6:17). Instead, Saul chose to live by his own word. In so doing, he was committing spiritual suicide. The chronicler reported this truth as he penned, "So Saul died for his transgression which he committed against the LORD, even against the word of the LORD, which he kept not, and also for asking counsel of one that had a familiar spirit, to enquire of it" (1 Chron. 10:13-14). We can choose to live by YHVH's sword (His Word) or die by our own. If our free will is not submitted to YHVH's will, it could lead to the same end as Saul's. As long as we still have breath, we have an opportunity to sincerely repent, receive forgiveness, and live.

Saul's armor-bearer was so distraught over Saul's death, that he also committed suicide by his own sword (1 Sam. 31:5, 1 Chron. 10:5). The armor-bearer was simply following his leader's example. This should challenge us to be careful what we do as leaders (as parents, grandparents, teachers, pastors, government officials, etc.). There are people who follow us so closely they will mimic our every move. If we want those under our watch to prosper and have life more abundant in the Spirit, then we would do well to live that out before them and behind closed doors.

A Fountain of Violent Emotion or Living Water

Saul, his sons, and an immeasurable number of Israelites laid slain at *Gilboa* (the fountain of violent outburst of emotions).[2] Their deaths have become a stark warning to us that living in the flesh without self-control can destroy us and those we love dearly. Saul's outbursts were ultimately driven by an evil spirit whose aim was to steal, kill, and destroy as many as possible in Israel. The evil spirit took an incredible victory in this battle.

As born-again disciples of *Yeshua*, we should live in complete contrast to Saul. Instead, we must have a fountain of living water within us (symbolic of the *Ruach ha-Kodesh*) "springing up unto eternal life" that will overflow to everyone around us (John 4:14, 7:37-39). How well have we mastered the fruit of self-control over our emotions, proving that the *Ruach ha-Kodesh* reigns over our flesh? I am a mother who sometimes loses her cool when her four youngest children respond to each other in violent outbursts of emotions; I am deeply convicted by these revelations to be diligent to ever increase the fruit of self-control in my life. We should always desire to be a fountain of living water that gives life to others.

Fear is Wildly Contagious

At the sight of all the slain, the remainder of Israel's army fled from the enemy. After seeing the army flee, the people in the nearby towns became so afraid of the Philistines that they deserted their towns. The Philistines came into their deserted towns and inhabited them (1 Sam. 31:6-7, 1 Chron. 10:6-7). The spirit of fear that ruled in Saul was wildly contagious. Fear infected the people he was chosen to shepherd and deliver from the oppression of the Philistines. Fear always leads to oppression by the enemy.

What the Israelites did speaks loudly of an important spiritual truth. When we become fearful and retreat because of the dire circumstances around us, we desert our promised inheritance and leave it for the enemy to trample. In those moments, we have forgotten who YHVH is. He can be a shield to us and save us from our enemies if only we will call on Him and repent for any rebellion against His ways (2 Chron. 7:14).

After a good night's sleep in the nearby deserted towns, the Philistines returned to the battlefield to strip the slain of all their armor, weapons, and any other spoils they could find. They found Saul's body, beheaded him, and absconded with his armor. They paraded his head and armor throughout the Philistine land to show their prowess over Israel. Saul's armor ended up in the house of Ashteroth, and his head hung in the temple of Dagon. The rest of Saul's body was fastened to the wall of Beth Shan so that everyone could see he was dead and as a reminder to fear the mighty Philistines (1 Sam. 31:8-10, 1 Chron. 10:8-10).

It is interesting that Saul's armor ended up in the house of one of Israel's most worshipped false goddesses. This is especially notable considering that Saul may have had household idols, as Michal used one to hide David's escape (1 Sam. 19:3). From Scripture, we do not know which idols Saul may have had specifically. However, we do know that Baal and Ashteroth worship was very prevalent in the land, so it is quite possible that Saul was worshipping Ashteroth. "YHVH is not mocked;" we reap what we sow (Gal. 6:7 KJV). I believe YHVH used the Philistine's act as a big neon sign to drive home a point to Israel (and to all of us consequentially). Our armor will not protect us from the arrows of the enemy if we commit idolatry!

Faith in the one true and living *Elohim* of Israel is the only shield against which no flaming arrow of the enemy can penetrate (Eph. 6:10-18). "Under His wings you shall take refuge" and not fear "the arrow that flies by day" (Ps. 91:4-5 NKJV). The Hebrew word for wings is *kanaph*. It is the same word used in Numbers 15:38 and Deuteronomy 22:12 to describe the corners of the garment where the *tzitzit* or tassels hang as a reminder to keep

YHVH's commandments (H3671).[3] This gives more perspective to *Yeshua's* lament over Jerusalem, "How often would I have gathered thy children together, as a hen doth gather her brood under her *wings*, but ye would not" (Luke 13:34 KJV).

The Greek word for wings in *Yeshua's* lament is *pterux*. Its derivative was used in the Septuagint (the Greek version of the Old Testament) in Numbers 15:38 (LXX) in place of the Hebrew word *kanaph* (G4419-G4420).[4] *Yeshua* wanted to gather His people under the refuge of His *kanaph*—His commandments—but they would not. YHVH has always been the same, and He has always cried out to His wayward people through the prophetic. As I read about Saul's armor hanging in the house of Ashteroth, I could hear the echoes of the Heavenly Father's heart lamenting over Saul and rebellious Israel, "How I longed to gather your children together, as a hen gathers her chicks under her wings. If only you had worshipped Me only and obeyed My commandments, but you would not."

Dry Bones

There were valiant men of *Jabesh-Gilead* who could not stand to see Saul's body exposed and hung so dishonorably by the enemy. So, under cover of night, they stealthily entered enemy territory and retrieved his body and those of his three sons. The men of *Jabesh-Gilead* burned the four bodies because they had been so defiled by the Philistines. They tried to honor their fallen leader by burying his bones under a tamarisk tree in *Jabesh* (1 Sam. 31:11-13, 1 Chron. 10:11-12). The root of *Jabesh* means "dry, dried, and withered" (H3002).[5]

Prophetically, *Jabesh* is an intriguing burial place for Saul's bones. Saul had become dry bones because his rebellion resulted in the removal of the *Ruach ha-Kodesh*, causing him to be spiritually withered and dry. Likewise, according to Ezekiel's prophecy, anyone who lives in rebellion to YHVH's word, and who does not have the Spirit of YHVH in them, is like dry bones (Ezek. 37:1-14).

David Learns of Saul and Jonathan's Death

David had only been back in *Ziklag* with his wives for a few days when a young man from Saul's camp approached him. The young man, who looked like a mourner with torn clothes and a dust-covered head, prostrated himself in humility and submission before David. He relayed to David and his men the tragic news of the death of Saul and Jonathan, as well as the defeat of Israel's armies by the Philistines.

David asked the young man how he knew of Saul's death, and the young man informed him that he happened to find Saul dying on Mount *Gilboa* (2 Sam. 1:1-6). Saul had called out to the young man and asked him to put him out of his misery. He had identified himself to Saul as an Amalekite (2 Sam. 1:7-9). It is a bit ironic that the very people Saul was supposed to utterly extinguish from the earth ended up putting the nail in his coffin, so to speak. Our disobedience to YHVH's instructions can likewise be our demise.

The young man told David that he did not believe there was any way that Saul could have recovered from his wounds and so he did as Saul requested. He then offered David Saul's crown and bracelet as a gift. David and his men rent their garments, "mourned, wept, and fasted" the remainder of the day (2 Sam. 1:10-12).

David and his men represented the remnant of Israel. Their actions set the example of godliness and brotherly love as they mourned, wept, and fasted over the devastation of the rest of their brothers in Israel. That devastation occurred because Saul rejected YHVH's Word. From all that we have previously seen of David's men, it is obvious their hearts had been refined; they were not judgmentally celebrating Saul's death as just rewards for his dastardly deeds, as we might have come to expect from them. Rather, they grieved together with David over the loss of the Heavenly Father's sheep. Will we follow their godly example to lay aside our judgment and mourn, weep, and fast for those whose lives are devastated because they have rejected YHVH's Word?

Judgment for Touching YHVH's Anointed

At the end of his weeping, David's curiosity was suddenly sparked. He inquired of the young man, "Where are you from?" The young man identified himself as "the son of an alien, an Amalekite" (2 Sam. 1:13 NKJV). It is possible that this young man was one of the four hundred Amalekites that had fled from David's assault on the Amalekite raiders only a few days prior. They were likely pilfering Saul's camp for spoils.

The young man was probably thinking this was his chance to make peace with David; no doubt the Amalekites expected that once David became the king of Israel he would seek to destroy them just as YHVH had commanded Saul to do. The young man was undoubtedly looking for kudos. To the young man's surprise, David was anything but happy to learn that he had killed YHVH's anointed. David commanded his valiant warriors to rise up and slay the young Amalekite (2 Sam. 1:14-16). David was only concerned with the transgression against YHVH that this young man committed.

Surely, as prudent as David was, he must have considered that this young Amalekite was likely part of the raiding party that had burned *Ziklag* to the ground. Yet David did not mention any of the hurt and turmoil that that situation had caused. And he didn't bring that into any part of his reasoning for having this young man killed. This was David's first act of righteous judgment as anointed king of Israel. According to the law of YHVH, touching His anointed is a serious offense!

An Honorable Memorial

After justice was served, David resumed his lamentations over Saul and Jonathan. He ordered the sons of Judah to learn his memorial song for them, "Song of the Bow." The words of David's memorial song are extraordinary! He referred to Saul and his slain sons as "mighty" and called them "the beauty of Israel." David declared they were "lovely and pleasant," "swifter than eagles," and "stronger than lions." He further instructed the "Daughters of Israel" to "weep over Saul" (2 Sam. 1:19-27).

Ordinarily, such laments do not originate from a man who is rejoicing over YHVH's judgment upon his enemy. Saul was the man who had relentlessly pursued David's life, kept him from his family, his best friend, and the homeland that he loved. And yet, this memorial song reflects a man whose heart was totally broken for the loss of someone he dearly loved. With it, David had honored Saul's memory by calling out what was good in Saul.

Clearly, David recognized the real source of Saul's actions toward him. Therefore, he ascribed none of that evil to Saul. David recognized the powers and principalities at work behind Saul's behaviors and ascribed the evil to them (Eph. 6:12). He had nothing but tender-hearted mercy and love for Saul in the words of his song (Col. 3:12-17). This was a shining example of a man after YHVH's own heart! Are we ready to follow such an extraordinary example?

Can you imagine lamenting in the same way as David over the person who had taken everything you loved from you? Can you imagine singing such an honorable song for the one who sought, for years, to destroy you and never brought restitution? I think this would be a very hard thing for most people to do, myself included.

Yet this was David's godly leadership example. It was why he was chosen to be Israel's king.

His Name is Love

David consistently lived up to his name in how he related to Saul. Most of us understand that the name David means "beloved." Strong's Concordance gives the name meaning as *"perhaps* 'beloved one.'" The Brown-Driver-Briggs Hebrew and English Lexicon indicates that "beloved one" is followed by a question mark (H1732),[6] which indicates it is not a solid meaning. Therefore, we need to drill down to the root of the name David for more information. At the heart of this name is love (H1730).[7]

If you recall from this book's introduction, I told of how our family's local congregation went through a major crisis. We had lost our head pastor, and it was a very emotionally and spiritually painful and challenging experience for our entire congregation. At the same time, my husband and I were also in the midst of working our way through a significant marital crisis. Any time we experience traumatic events it can be a wonderful opportunity for YHVH to facilitate healing. Yet such times can present an opportunity for *ha-Satan* to manipulate our emotions to sow division in relationships. Whether the door is opened to healing or division is determined by the choices that each person makes as they navigate the traumatic experience.

In my distress over all that was transpiring around me, I sought understanding from the Heavenly Father through prayer and fasting. My desire was to remain in submission to the *Ruach ha-Kodesh* while navigating through both crises so that the end result would ***not*** be division. At the time, our congregation had two teachers named David. I discerned strongly in my spirit that YHVH was trying to communicate something by having two men named David take the stage. Whether it be in Scripture, in a prophetic dream or vision, or in a situation in our lives, repetition of a theme usually means that YHVH is pointing to something. For example, in Genesis 41, Pharaoh had two similarly themed dreams that symbolized seven years of plenty followed by seven years of overwhelming famine. YHVH gave Pharaoh two dreams in a row because He had established the matter and was about to bring it to pass. With that in mind, I diligently inquired of YHVH about what He was trying to say through my vision.

Later that same week the Heavenly Father gave me a figurative prophetic vision and a word of understanding about the name David that has been foundational to facilitating total healing and restoration to my marriage. I believe the vision was also meant to encourage brotherly love, unity, healing, and restoration in our congregation as well as the entire body of Messiah. The vision has served as the catalyst that ultimately led to the overall message of this book series. What YHVH showed me drew attention to the fullness of the meaning of the name David. The following pictures come from a PowerPoint presentation I made in late 2015 to try to communicate the vision and word to the leadership of my congregation:

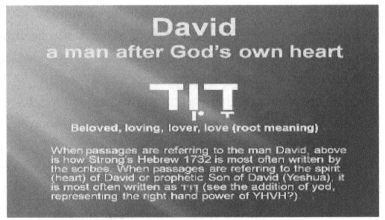

We can clearly see that the name David is all about love, being loved, and loving. The meaning of this name gets more interesting when we take into consideration the ancient Paleo-Hebrew pictograph meanings of each letter of his name. *Dalet* represents an open door,[8] the door of the tabernacle or temple (which is a human heart according to 1 Cor. 3:16). The *vav* in the middle of the two *dalets* in the name David means a nail or tent-peg.[9] A nail or tent-peg connects or secures one thing to another. *Yeshua* took the nails for us, so He is representative of the *vav* or the prophesied tent peg of Judah (Zech. 10:4). Therefore, the Paleo-Hebrew pictograph[10] meaning of the name David is:

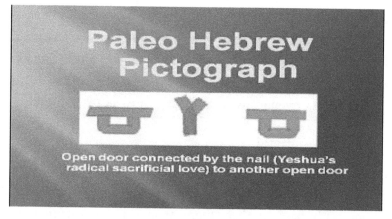

We will go into more detail about the deeper meaning of the Paleo-Hebrew letters in just a moment. It is important to set the backdrop for their meanings by first communicating what the Heavenly Father showed me in relation to what these two open doors point to. Again, in Hebrew thought, when something is repeated twice—or there are two consistent witnesses—it should always bring us to attention. Two witnesses always establish a matter (Deut. 19:15). In the midst of the 2015 vision, YHVH showed me that these two open doors in the name David, which are connected by the nail, point to the two greatest commandments (Matt. 22:37-40):

Love God with all your heart, soul, and mind
(the open door of a person's temple connects through
Yeshua's love to the open door of YHVH's temple)

Love your neighbor as yourself
(the open door of a person's temple connects through
Yeshua's love to the open door of another person's temple)

However, it is not enough to simply look at the *dalet* as an open door. We need to look more closely at the Paleo Hebrew pictograph with the understanding of the ancient Middle Eastern door. The ancient *dalet* may not look much like our modern understanding of a door, but it does resemble the basin at the threshold of an ancient Middle Eastern door. This basin is where the blood for a covenant was collected, most notably the blood of the Passover Lamb.

In the ancient Middle East, a door was flanked by the lintel and doorposts, often with a basin at the threshold of the door (see the basin on the front cover of this volume). When people made a covenant with one another, there would be a sacrifice at the threshold, wherein the blood of the sacrifice would drain into the basin. The parties of the covenant would cross over the threshold, crossing over the blood of the covenant they were entering into.[11] Do you recognize the imagery of the first Passover in the land of Goshen (Exod. 12)?

At the deepest level, all three letters of the name David speak of the blood and the atoning sacrifice of the Passover Lamb. Isn't that phenomenal? That is what true love for YHVH and our neighbor is all about: entering into covenant with YHVH and with each other through the blood of the sacrificed Passover Lamb, *Yeshua*. We effectively do this by following our Messiah's example two ways. First, we must take up our cross (Matt. 16:24) and lay our lives down as a living sacrifice (Rom. 12:1). And second, we must be willing to freely forgive one another as *Yeshua* freely forgave us (Eph. 4:32, Col. 3:13). He demonstrated this during his crucifixion when He said, "Father forgive them, for they do not know what they are doing" (Luke 23:34 BSB).

Love is an Action

The Heavenly Father further confirmed the message of His vision through an object lesson. He revealed to me how we can practically love our neighbor as we love ourselves while in the midst of conflict. If you look at the modern Hebrew letter *dalet*, it looks like something that is bent forward or bowed. In my vision, the two *dalets* of the name David were both bent over or bowed toward *Yeshua*, the *vav* who stood between them. It looked as though the two *dalets* in the name David appeared to form a double door or gate, like that of a sheepfold, with *Yeshua* in the center.

Yeshua stands like a doorkeeper in the midst of the double door formed by the two *dalets*. Whoever holds the key of David is a doorkeeper with the power to open what no one can shut and shut what no one can open (Isa. 22:22, Rev. 3:7). In the second volume of this series, we will confirm that *Yeshua* holds the key of David, which we already learned is love for YHVH and neighbor. As I pondered the image of the name David, *Yeshua's* words in John 10 came to my mind. He identified Himself as "the door of the sheep" and "the good shepherd" whose "sheep follow him: for they know his voice" (John 10:4, 7, 11).

Within the vision itself, YHVH used the two teachers named David from my congregation to symbolize the two *dalets* in the name David. Symbolically, the *Ruach ha-Kodesh* gave me an understanding that there was a conflict or offense creating division in the relationship between the two men. What followed was an object lesson on how to resolve conflict between two disciples of *Yeshua* who are called to be people after YHVH's heart (just as the biblical David was). I understood that the object lesson applies to all relationships, whether in marriage, family, friendships, workplace relationships, or in our congregations.

First, one of the men bowed the knee in submission; he took on the yoke of humility before both *Yeshua* (the *vav*) and his brother, repenting for his own wrongdoing in the conflict. Then, the other man also humbled his own position in the offense. He openly accepted and forgave his repentant brother, and their fellowship was restored. YHVH showed me that when any two people reconcile their offenses in the covenant bond of unity and brotherly love, they prove themselves to be YHVH's sheep, and *Yeshua* is elevated and glorified between them. I understood that the opposite is also true. When two people fail to reconcile their offenses because they are unwilling to humble themselves to repentance and/or freely forgive one another, they fail to represent themselves as YHVH's sheep, and *Yeshua* is not elevated. The following illustration is the best representation I can give you of what I saw and understood the Father wanted from all parties involved in the crises:

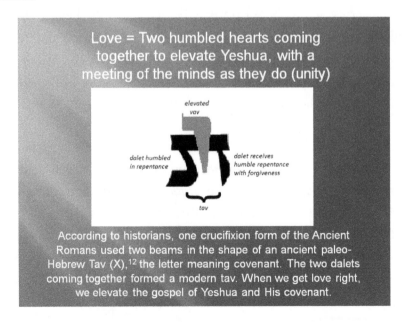

Love = Two humbled hearts coming together to elevate Yeshua, with a meeting of the minds as they do (unity)

elevated
vav

dalet humbled
in repentance

dalet receives
humble repentance
with forgiveness

tav

According to historians, one crucifixion form of the Ancient Romans used two beams in the shape of an ancient paleo-Hebrew Tav (X),[12] the letter meaning covenant. The two dalets coming together formed a modern tav. When we get love right, we elevate the gospel of Yeshua and His covenant.

What I witnessed in my vision, was essentially what we saw David continually do toward Saul. David took on the yoke of humility before YHVH and Saul. David's heart and mindset toward Saul, typified in his words in "Song of the Bow," was the fulfillment of the second greatest commandment to love his neighbor as himself. David was also walking in humility out of love and reverence for YHVH. By serving as a reflection of the Father's heart, David ultimately fulfilled the first great commandment at the same time.

David treated Saul the way he wanted to be treated in both life and death. I believe the love that David displayed, and which our Messiah displayed as well, is the key of David that is spoken of in the Scriptures (Isa. 22:22, Rev. 3:7). *Yeshua* spoke of this key to only one of the seven churches mentioned in Revelation. Is it any wonder that it was the church of *Philadelphia*, a word that has a root meaning of brotherly love (G5361)?[13] Our King does nothing by coincidence!

Divinely Empowered Love

At the bottom of the first picture of the name David a few pages back, there was a note describing two different ways this name is written in the Torah scrolls. When referencing the spirit of David or the prophesied Son of David, a *yod* is typically inserted in David's name. The addition of the *yod* in David's name symbolizes the hand or power of YHVH in the Paleo-Hebrew pictograph,[14] which is the *Ruach ha-Kodesh*. This *yod* hints that divinely-sourced, brotherly love, like what was displayed in my vision and by David to Saul, only comes from the power which resides in our spirit man, not our flesh man. We are not capable of producing this kind of love without YHVH's power. Divine love opens doors in our relationships with YHVH and our neighbor (all of humanity).

Divine love also closes the door on the enemy's schemes to sow division and strife in our relationships.[15]

At this point in David's journey, his heart of love was now fully aligned to who YHVH had created and called him to be. His time had finally come to physically step into the anointing that YHVH had promised him all those years ago. David was about to finally receive his crown. Likewise, YHVH has created and called each one of us by name, anointed us, and promised us a place in His kingdom. When our hearts and minds are fully aligned with YHVH's heart, we will walk in a supernatural kind of love. Equipped with this divine love, we will then be ready to fully step into our destiny as the kings and priests YHVH has called us to be (Rev. 1:6, 5:10). Are we ready?

"Put on therefore, as the elect of God, holy and beloved, bowels of mercies, kindness, humbleness of mind, meekness, longsuffering; Forbearing one another, and forgiving one another, if any man have a quarrel against any: even as Christ forgave you, so also do ye. And above all these things put on charity, which is the bond of perfectness. And let the peace of God rule in your hearts, to the which also ye are called in one body; and be ye thankful. Let the word of Christ dwell in you richly in all wisdom; teaching and admonishing one another in psalms and hymns and spiritual songs, singing with grace in your hearts to the Lord. And whatsoever ye do in word or deed, do all in the name of the Lord Jesus, giving thanks to God and the Father by him." (Col. 3:12-17)

"And to the angel of the church in Philadelphia write; These things saith he that is holy, he that is true, he that hath the key of David, he that openeth, and no man shutteth; and shutteth, and no man openeth; I know thy works: behold, I have set before thee an open door, and no man can shut it:

for thou hast a little strength, and hast kept my word, and hast not denied my name. Because thou hast kept the word of my patience, I also will keep thee from the hour of temptation, which shall come upon all the world, to try them that dwell upon the earth. Behold, I come quickly: hold that fast which thou hast, that no man take thy crown. Him that overcometh will I make a pillar in the temple of my God, and he shall go no more out: and I will write upon him the name of my God, and the name of the city of my God, which is new Jerusalem, which cometh down out of heaven from my God: and I will write upon him my new name. He that hath an ear, let him hear what the Spirit saith unto the churches." (Rev. 3:7-8, 10-13)

JOURNEY JOURNAL

1. Do you personally identify with any of David's characteristics or experiences? If so, which one(s)?

2. Have you ever felt as though YHVH's judgment would never come for wrongs committed against you? How has this chapter's study changed your perspective of justice for wrongs?

3. How has this chapter's study affected your perspective on the actions of your human "enemy?" How will that perspective affect the way you respond to them in the future?

4. How has this chapter's study affected your perspective on love and unity as they relate to the two greatest commandments?

5. Did you experience any personal conviction as you read this chapter and answered the questions presented? What were you convicted about? (Conviction is meant to lead us to prayers of repentance, wherein we receive YHVH's grace, mercy, and forgiveness.)

6. How has this chapter's study encouraged you to greater love for YHVH and your neighbor?

10
RECEIVING A CROWN

We spend most of our lives waiting for something. We wait in traffic. We wait in line to purchase groceries. We wait to see the doctor. But there is one wait that is most agonizing to every human being, and that is the wait for the fulfillment of a dream. David certainly experienced a long wait for his dream, the dream of one day being the king of Israel. He had received this promise of kingship many years ago as a youth, and his wait was finally over. It was finally time for David to receive his crown.

Father May I?

After David completed his time of mourning for Saul and Jonathan, he inquired of YHVH asking, "Shall I go up into any of the cities of Judah?" YHVH said, "Go up." David inquired further, "Whither shall I go up?" And YHVH answered, "Unto Hebron" (2 Sam. 2:1 KJV). I love how David had learned to leave nothing to assumption and to inquire about every situation before he took a step. He did not assume that his anointing and promise from YHVH automatically qualified him to waltz into the land and take over Saul's old throne and the palace. Anyone else in the culture of his day would probably have done just that. However, David first asked his Heavenly Father, "May I?" What a godly leadership example to follow!

Upon the Father's instruction, David took his people, moved to Hebron, and simply started living there. He did not come to Hebron parading himself as the next anointed leader, expecting everyone to line up behind him. Instead, he merely lived humbly among the people, and let them come to him and set him up as king (2 Sam. 2:2-3).

David was willing to wait to let the people recognize, acknowledge, and agree with YHVH's choice for their new king. He did not impose his calling and anointing upon them. He did not demand that they recognize and promote him into his calling and anointing, even though he knew he had it. His conduct is another godly leadership example that is almost unheard of!

The humility that David displayed is the character of people who whole-heartedly pursue YHVH's heart—priestly kings. Such people may know their calling, anointing, and promises from YHVH, but they are content to live their lives out in meekness among the people. They are satisfied to sit back and wait upon YHVH to fulfill His plans for them in His way and His time. Priestly kings, like David, focus on faithfully following YHVH's specific instructions of where to be at any given time, giving the people around them time to recognize their calling and anointing and come into agreement with YHVH's plans. Leaders of this nature walk humbly before YHVH and man and wait for the people to lift them up, rather than trying to lift themselves up.

David's Counter-Culture Kindness

The men of Judah did come to recognize and acknowledge David's calling, and they anointed him as their new king. Immediately thereafter, they informed him that the men of *Jabesh-Gilead* had rescued the bodies of Saul and his sons and gave them an honorable burial. David's first act as crowned king of Judah was to reach out to the men of *Jabesh-Gilead*, commending them for showing kindness to Saul. He pronounced the blessing of YHVH's kindness and faithfulness over them (2 Sam. 2:4-6).

The Hebrew word used for the kindness that the men of *Jabesh-Gilead* showed is the same word for YHVH's kindness that David blessed them with—*checed*. *Checed* means "goodness, loving favor, mercy, and covenant loyalty" (H2617).[1] David informed the men that, as the new king, he would always show them goodness, or *towb* (2 Sam. 2:4-6). *Towb* is a Hebrew word that can also mean "beauty, kindness, favor, love, graciousness" (H2896).[2] David's first judgment as crowned king was to give the men of *Jabesh-Gilead* measure for measure (Luke 6:36-38).

David was going out of his way to allay any fears of those who showed loyalty to Saul. He did this by showing that he would not be like other ascending kings of the ancient Middle Eastern culture. He would not root out and destroy those who were loyal to his predecessor in an effort to protect himself and his position from a potential revolt. David's behavior was counter-culture and counter-human nature. He was going out of his way to show his honor and kindness toward those loyal to Saul, those who would have been considered David's enemies by the culture of his day. David had perfect love and did not live in fear. He continued to publicly honor Saul, a man who had hurt him deeply, repeatedly attempted to kill him, and never sought to bring restitution. Over and over, David proved to be a man after YHVH's own heart.

Rebellion Divides the Kingdom

While David was being crowned as king of Judah, Saul's army commander, Abner, took Saul's son Ish-bosheth to *Mahanaim* to establish him as king over the rest of the tribes of Israel (2 Sam. 2:8). *Mahanaim* was a place that was known as "God's camp." It was named such by Jacob because the angels of YHVH met him there as he prepared to go home and face his brother, Esau (Gen. 32:2). Perhaps Abner was thinking he had the true anointed king of Israel and was looking for YHVH's help to take the throne from David. Abner did not recognize the calling and anointing that YHVH had placed on David's life. Instead, Abner only recognized how the world culture determined kingly succession.

Abner declared Ish-bosheth king over all Israel. Interestingly, *Ish-bosheth* means "man of shame" (H378).[3] Ish-bosheth's name should have been a big red flag for the people of Israel, but they ignored it. Judah and Israel were a divided kingdom. Judah recognized YHVH's anointed leader, while Israel recognized the world culture's appointed leader. Ish-bosheth had the majority opinion, but Israel was still dead-wrong and outside of YHVH's perfect will.

The story of Abner and Ish-bosheth is highly reminiscent of another time in Israel's history. Generations prior, a majority of Israel followed after Korah, a leader who challenged YHVH's chosen anointed leader, Moses (Num. 16). Had this new generation forgotten the account of Korah's rebellion and how badly it had ended? We will see that things also did not end well for Abner and Ish-bosheth, just as it did not end well for Korah, Dathan, and Abiram.

Division Ends in Bloodshed

One day, Abner took Ish-bosheth's army out to Gibeon, and Joab brought David's army out to meet them there. Each army arrayed itself on opposite sides of the pool that was there (2 Sam.

2:12-13). From a prophetic perspective, a pool of water instantly speaks of the water of the Word of YHVH (Eph. 5:26). Once again, what was happening in the physical was reflecting what was happening in the spiritual. The armies of Israel were divided on opposite sides of the Word of YHVH concerning who was king of Israel.

As they sat poolside, Abner challenged Joab to let the young men "play" and Joab agreed. What was happening here? This word translated as "play" means "to laugh (in jest, to scorn), to mock, to make sport or contest, and to deride" (H7832).[4] Twelve young men were chosen from each side to contest each other (2 Sam. 2:14-15). In Scripture, twelve is always symbolic of the tribes of Israel. In essence, the young men were having a contest to determine who best represented Israel. Their competition was meant to prove who had the correct interpretation of the Word of YHVH and who was following the legitimate shepherd or king of Israel.

As twelve men from each side came together against one another, "they caught every one his fellow by the head, and thrust his sword in his fellow's side." All twenty-four men fell dead! In the end, no one proved to be better (2 Sam. 2:16). This is such a picture of what happens when there is division among YHVH's people. When we try to prove who is better, no one really ever wins, and everyone gets hurt in the process. Yet this type of contest continues to happen among YHVH's people all the time!

We mock, scorn, deride, and challenge each other. We try to go for the head by debating higher reasoning and logic. And then we pull out the sword of the Spirit (the Word of YHVH) and thrust it into each other's side as we staunchly defend our positions on interpretation and doctrine. Everyone falls dead to offense, and lives end up destroyed.

Have you ever been through a congregational division? I have been through more than one, and all were exactly like this.

Everyone got hurt, and some people walked away from the faith altogether, which is spiritual death. It was horrific! We need to repent and make restitution if we have ever been party to this type of contest against other children of YHVH.

A Civil War Begins

Needless to say, things between Judah and Israel descended into all-out war (2 Sam. 2:17). These fellow countrymen were once brothers who had rallied together in battle against their true enemies. Now, they had become bitter enemies, divided by the men or ideals they had chosen to follow. They were now ready and willing to go to war and destroy each other. Sadly, this is the very thing happening all over YHVH's body of believers.

Our enemies can sit back and laugh at us because we are destroying ourselves from within. All the while, our Father in Heaven watches with tear-stained eyes and a broken heart. His children are killing one another with the sword that is meant to slay the true enemy, *ha-Satan* and his demons. Our Bridegroom, *Yeshua,* also watches in horror as His bride mutilates herself. His bride is supposed to be a body of many members knit together as one (1 Cor. 12:12-26), but the right hand is thrusting the sword into the left. The current state of the body of Messiah is just as heartbreaking as what transpired at Gibeon.

As the battle between Ish-bosheth's army and David's army raged on, Ish-bosheth's army recognized they were being defeated. Abner began to flee, but Joab's swift-footed brother Asahel pursued him. Abner sternly warned Asahel to stop his pursuit; he did not want to kill Asahel in self-defense and then have to face Joab's revenge. However, in his zeal, Asahel was determined to destroy Abner and would not listen to his warnings (2 Sam. 2:17-23).

Ultimately, this decision cost Asahel his life. When his brothers, Joab and Abishai, learned of his death at the hands of Abner, they were enraged and determined to avenge his blood. The brothers pursued Abner to the hill of *Ammah* as the sun set (2 Sam. 2:24). *Ammah* has a root meaning of "an ell, a cubit, or a measure" (H520).[5] Joab and Abishai were quite literally letting the sun go down on their anger (Eph. 4:26-27). They were determined to bring measure for measure upon Abner—a life for a life (Luke 6:27-38).

Shall the Sword Devour Forever?

As Joab and Abishai closed in on Abner, the men of Benjamin rallied behind Abner, united in their stand with him. Finally, someone spoke some sense in an attempt to diffuse this whole mess, and ironically it was the very person who started the whole battle. Abner said, "Shall the sword devour for ever? Knowest thou not that it will be bitterness in the latter end? How long shall it be then, er thou bid the people return from following their brethren?" (2 Sam. 2:25-26)

These are words of wisdom for all who call themselves children of YHVH. How long will we continue to pursue and devour each other with the sword? Do we realize how bitter it will be in the end if we continue to war over our interpretations, doctrines, differences, or the leaders we have chosen? Ultimately, we have one King, *Yeshua,* who is to be the leader of us all (Matt. 23:10). We are all supposed to be on the same team fighting against the true enemy of our souls, *ha-Satan*, not each other.

Thankfully, Joab was not blinded by his anger and lust for vengeance over losing his brother; he recognized the wisdom in Abner's words, and immediately agreed to stand down and end the battle. Joab blew the shofar signaling his army to stand down (2 Sam. 2:27-28). I am likewise blowing the shofar for all who have an ear to hear and a heart of discernment. It is time for this battle amongst the body of YHVH's people to end! Can I get an "Amen!"?

The Father's Love for His Children

At the blast of the shofar, both sides of Israel's contest-turned-war backed off from their positions and retreated to their respective places. All told, three hundred eighty people lost their lives that day over a competition to see who was better (2 Sam. 2:28-31). David's army only suffered a loss of twenty (including the original twelve of the "contest") out of those three hundred eighty casualties. Our human temptation may be to look at the numbers and declare that David's army was clearly superior and favored by YHVH. However, as I understand the Heavenly Father's heart, He did not see it that way. Rather, He saw all three hundred eighty of these casualties equally. Three hundred and eighty of His children were destroyed by division and infighting.

Even if the men who followed Ish-bosheth were considered to be "wicked," YHVH revealed through Ezekiel the prophet that He has no pleasure in the death of the wicked but desires they repent and live. YHVH said, "When the wicked man turneth away from his wickedness that he hath committed, and doeth that which is lawful and right, he shall save his soul alive." He then reiterated, "For I have no pleasure in the death of him that dieth, wherefore turn yourselves and live ye!" (Ezek. 18:23-32, *condensed*)

There is no better part of YHVH's team. We are all His children who have been created in His image. He loved every one of us so much that He sent His only beloved Son, *Yeshua,* to die in our place (John 3:16). His will is that none should perish, but that all would repent and live with Him eternally, united as one (John 17:20-26).

YHVH desires us all to return to walking in the Garden of Eden together with Him, dwelling in His presence as one big happy family. It is His good and perfect will that we stop contesting each other for who is better in His kingdom. We must put away judgment and condemnation. We must forsake our need to argue, fight, and mock one another. And our habit of slandering our brethren on the internet, television, and radio must come to an end. *Yeshua* once corrected His disciples for these very behaviors, and we would all do well to remember His words (Luke 9:46-48). He said, "The one who is least among all of you is the one who is great." The position of humility—considering ourselves to be the least—is the way to become the greatest in YHVH's kingdom.

David's Full House

I wish I could say that Judah and Israel came into unity after this war ended. But as we see in 2 Samuel 3, the war between Ish-bosheth (Israel) and David (Judah) lasted a very long time, seven and a half years in fact. Over the course of time, YHVH's anointed king, David, grew stronger while the majority leader, Ish-bosheth, steadily grew weaker. David's house was certainly increasing—busting at the seams actually; his many wives bore him six bouncing baby boys (2 Sam. 3:1-2).

The names for each of David's sons spoke to all that YHVH had been to him over the years: Amnon (H550: "faithful"),[6] Chileab (H3609: root "restraint of his father")[7], Absalom (H53: "My father is peace"),[8] Adonijah (H138: "My Lord is YHVH"),[9] Shephatiah (H8203: "Yah has judged"),[10] and Ithream (H3507: root "abundant, remnant, excellence of people").[11] With the name of David's last son, was David subtly declaring that he had an abundance of sons and did not need anymore? Having three energetic boys myself, I can only imagine he was trying to communicate, "Enough is enough already!"

Abner's Allegiance Turns in Offense

While David was busy managing his full house, Abner was strengthening his position in the house of Saul. Abner regarded himself so highly that he felt he could take one of Saul's concubines. Ish-bosheth learned of the matter and confronted Abner. Ish-bosheth's objection royally ticked Abner off, and Abner staunchly defended himself on the basis of all the good he had done for Saul's house. He resorted to emotional blackmail and reminded Ish-bosheth that he had not handed him over to David (2 Sam. 3:6-8). Abner was offended that Ish-bosheth would dare call him on the carpet or judge him for such a thing.

If someone holds us accountable for sin, do we resort to staunchly defending ourselves based on all the good we have done, like Abner? Do we take offense and respond, "How dare you judge me?" As believers, we should avoid such defensive posturing and, instead, thank YHVH for giving us someone who loves us enough to hold us accountable to a higher standard. When we adhere to YHVH's standard it is pleasing to Him; the result is that, at the end of our lives, we will hear, "Well done good and faithful servant" (Matt. 25:23).

Abner certainly had no appreciation for being held accountable. In his offense, he immediately switched his allegiance (2 Sam. 3:9-10). The man, who was once staunchly loyal to Saul's house, was now only loyal to his own house. As a result, Ish-bosheth was afraid to even speak to Abner again (2 Sam. 2:11). Negative reactions to accountability, like Abner's, potentially place a stumbling block of fear of man before our brothers and sisters in Messiah. As believers, we should avoid reactions that could hinder another believer from making spirit-led decisions, such as holding us accountable.

Clearly, Abner had come to the conclusion that David would ultimately win the war due to YHVH's promise and favor. In his selfish-ambition, Abner wanted to ensure that he was on the right side when the war came to an end. He was not motivated to honor YHVH or David, but Abner was only motivated to honor himself.

People like Abner are incredibly fickle and will follow whoever seems to be the most personally advantageous to them. Such individuals will change sides on a dime of offense. Their loyalty is not real, because their true loyalty is to self. We would all do well *not* to follow Abner's ungodly example!

Michal as a Condition of Peace

In his quest for peace with David, Abner sent messengers to David and offered to bring all of Israel to him. David agreed to Abner's request for a covenant of peace on one condition: Abner had to bring David his first wife, Michal, the daughter of Saul. Additionally, David sent a message to Ish-bosheth demanding his wife and reminding Ish-bosheth that he had paid one hundred Philistine foreskins to Saul for Michal's hand in marriage. Ish-bosheth agreed to David's demand and sent Abner to retrieve Michal for David (2 Sam. 3:12-15).

Michal had been given by Saul to a new husband named Paltiel, son of Laish, not long after David had gone into hiding seven years prior. It is obvious that Paltiel cherished Michal; he followed her weeping all the way to *Bahurim*, where Abner finally got fed up and commanded him to leave off and return home (2 Sam. 3:15-16). In a later chapter, we are going to confirm that this was a bitter departure for Michal as well. She really did love David when they were first married. However, after he never returned for her or sent for her, her father gave her to Paltiel, whose name means "deliverance of God" (H6409).[12] Surely, Paltiel's intense love for Michal must have delivered her from the bitter loss of her first love, David, all those years ago. Fully aware of David's many wives, now Michal knew she would just be one of many to compete for her husband's time, attention, and affections; returning to David would be a far cry from her experience with Paltiel.

Israel Persuaded to Choose YHVH's Anointed

After Abner delivered Michal to David, he called a meeting together with all the elders of Israel and reminded them that they once desired David as their king (2 Sam. 3:17). When did this happen? Was it prior to Saul's death, perhaps when David was leading Israel's army into victory? Or was it after Saul's death, before Abner convinced Israel that Ish-bosheth would be a better king? The Scriptures do not make this clear. All we know is that, at some point, the elders of Israel actually wanted David as their king but allowed themselves to follow the "man of shame" instead. How easily were the people of Israel swayed? Very easily, as we will continue to see throughout the remainder of David's life.

Abner encouraged the elders of Israel that it was now their chance to have David as their king. He reminded them of YHVH's covenant promise that, through David, He would "save His people Israel out of the hand of the Philistines" and "out of the hand of all their enemies." The elders agreed to make David their king, so Abner traveled to Hebron bringing David the news. David held a banquet for Abner and his men. In the middle of the feast, Abner requested leave of David, so that he might go and gather all Israel into covenant with David. Of course, David's desire was after YHVH's own heart and to see Israel united under one king, so he sent Abner on his quest "in peace" (2 Sam. 3:18-20).

Joab's Vengeance

Meanwhile, Joab and David's army returned from a raid and learned of the banquet they missed. Joab was unhappy to learn that David had thrown a banquet for Abner, and the elders of Israel. Joab still had an old bone to pick with Abner for killing his brother

Asahel. Joab thought David had just missed his golden opportunity to put an end to Abner's treasonous ways. He assumed that Abner's true intentions toward David were deceptive and that Abner was only planning to spy on David so that he might destroy him (2 Sam. 3:22-25). Joab had become an accuser of the brethren.

Based on his false assumptions, Joab decided to usurp David's authority by secretly sending David's messengers to bring Abner back. The messengers made Abner believe that he was coming back in peace when they were actually setting a trap to kill him (2 Sam. 3:26). Isn't it a bit ironic how Joab, who accused Abner of being deceitful to set a trap for David, was now doing that very thing himself? How often does this happen with us? Do we make assumptions about people's intentions and accuse them of something, only to turn around and do that very thing ourselves? This is what *Yeshua* refers to as needing to remove "the beam out of thine own eye" (Matt. 7:3-5).

As Abner entered the city gate of Hebron, Joab waltzed out pretending to be friendly and looking to speak with him. However, he took Abner aside and stabbed him to death, as vengeance for killing his brother Asahel (2 Sam. 3:27). Joab must have figured that he was acting within the scope of YHVH's law to avenge the blood of his brother (Num. 35, Deut. 19, Josh. 20). However, Joab had missed the mark of the law concerning the avenger of blood.

First of all, Abner tried to warn Asahel twice. He did not want to kill him, but because Asahel persisted in trying to kill Abner, Abner acted in self-defense in the midst of war (2 Sam. 2:21-23). Additionally, Hebron is one of the named cities of refuge, where the avenger of blood is not allowed to overtake the manslayer. Finally, the manslayer was to stand trial before the assembly or congregation, and they were to judge between the manslayer and the avenger of blood.[13]

Joab had taken Abner's judgment and vengeance into his own hands and sinned against the law of YHVH, which would bring a curse upon him. In fact, when David learned what Joab had done, he invoked a curse upon Joab and all of his descendants. This is prophetically significant for all believers. If we do as Joab, going behind the back of our leaders, taking judgment and vengeance into our own hands (Deut. 32:35, Rom. 12:19), we will invoke a curse upon ourselves and our descendants. Furthermore, we may cause our King (*Yeshua*) to utter the same words as David uttered over Joab and Abishai, that we are just "too hard for him" (2 Sam. 3:29-39). Do we *ever* want our King to feel that way about us? I certainly do not!

Navigating a Politically Sensitive Situation

David went on record before all Israel that he had no part in what Joab had done to Abner. David was furious that Joab had gone behind his back and done this shameful act! Joab's actions created a very sensitive political situation for David. The Scriptural record seems to indicate that David immediately went into fasting and prayer to inquire of YHVH's wisdom to handle this situation (2 Sam. 3:28-35).

David must have received supernatural wisdom to diffuse this situation, though we have no biblical record that YHVH spoke to him. David commanded everyone, including Joab and Abishai, "rend your clothes, and gird you with sackcloth, and mourn before Abner." David wept and "lamented over Abner" in the sight of all Israel (2 Sam. 3:31-33). In this, David served as a prophetic foreshadow of the true King of Israel, YHVH, who weeps and laments over the death of His precious children at the hands of their brethren.

The people noticed David had been fasting and urged him to eat. However, he refused to take any food until the sun set on the day of Abner's burial. All of his actions were taken into account by the people of Israel, and they sincerely believed that David had nothing to do with Abner's death. At the end of the day of Abner's burial, all of Israel was pleased with everything that the king had done. However, King David was anything but pleased with Joab and Abishai (2 Sam. 3:34-39).

Off with Their Heads

Meanwhile, when Ish-bosheth learned of Abner's death, "he lost courage." This is the sad state of anyone whose courage is in a mortal human being, rather than in YHVH. Ish-bosheth was so weak that he went to lay down in his bed for a midday nap. While he was sleeping, two of Saul's servants, Baanah and Rechab, snuck into his room, brutally assassinated him, and beheaded him (2 Sam. 4:1-7 NIV). Interestingly, Ish-bosheth is not the only illegitimate leader who rose up in place of David as king whose final fate was beheading. We will see this happen to another individual in a future chapter (in Volume Two). Abner and Ish-bosheth, the two leaders who had risen up against YHVH's anointed leader of Israel, David, were dead. They had met the same fate as Korah and the leaders who followed him against Moses (Num. 16).

Baanah and Rechab thought they had done a praiseworthy favor for David and believed they would be richly rewarded for their actions. They swiftly carried Ish-bosheth's head to David in Hebron. Apparently, they had never heard about what happened to the young Amalekite who brought David the news that he had slain Saul. So, David enlightened Baanah and Rechab about the events surrounding the young Amalekite. David asked them why he should not do more so to them, who rose up and took the life of "an innocent man in his own house and on his own bed" (2 Sam. 4:8-11 KJV). David called Ish-bosheth innocent, even though most everyone else did not see him that way. David seemed to have a favorable opinion of everyone, except those who took the life a leader—even if that leader was illegitimate.

Baanah and Rechab were slain and beheaded at David's command. They received measure for measure for what they had done to Ish-bosheth. As an ensign to all of the people, their bodies were hung beside the pool in Hebron (2 Sam. 4:12).

David wanted to make it crystal clear that he would not look favorably upon anyone who ruthlessly killed his opponents. He was establishing himself as a righteous king and judge, not partial to himself or to those who sought his favor. It was surely an example to follow, for it ultimately led to all of Israel and Judah being united under one righteous king and judge. Likewise, YHVH is calling all disciples of *Yeshua* to be righteous and impartial to ourselves and those seeking our favor. Such conduct will lead to all of Israel and Judah being united under one King.

"But I say unto you which hear, Love your enemies, do good to them which hate you, Bless them that curse you, and pray for them which despitefully use you. And unto him that smiteth thee on the one cheek offer also the other; and him that taketh away thy cloak forbid not to take thy coat also. Give to every man that asketh of thee; and of him that taketh away thy goods ask them not again. And as ye would that men should do to you, do ye also to them likewise. For if ye love them which love you, what thank have ye? for sinners also love those that love them. And if ye do good to them which do good to you, what thank have ye? for sinners also do even the same. And if ye lend to them of whom ye hope to receive, what thank have ye? for sinners also lend to sinners, to receive as much again. But love ye your enemies, and do good, and lend, hoping for nothing again; and your reward

shall be great, and ye shall be the children of the Highest: for he is kind unto the unthankful and to the evil. Be ye therefore merciful, as your Father also is merciful. Judge not, and ye shall not be judged: condemn not, and ye shall not be condemned: forgive, and ye shall be forgiven: Give, and it shall be given unto you; good measure, pressed down, and shaken together, and running over, shall men give into your bosom. For with the same measure that ye mete withal it shall be measured to you again." (Luke 6:27-38)

JOURNEY JOURNAL

1. Do you personally identify with any of David's characteristics or experiences? If so, which one(s)?

2. Do you personally identify with any of Abner's characteristics or experiences? If so, which one(s)?

3. Do you personally identify with any of Joab's characteristics or experiences? If so, which one(s)?

4. What is your attitude toward accountability? How do you respond toward those who try to hold you accountable to a higher standard? How should you respond?

5. How loyal have you been toward the leaders that YHVH has set over you? Have you allowed yourself to be swayed by anything other than the *Ruach ha-Kodesh* moving you under new leadership?

6. Have you ever taken judgment into your own hands, believing you were doing what was right only to learn later that you had erred?

7. Did you experience any other personal conviction as you read this chapter and answered the questions presented? What were you convicted about? (Conviction is meant to lead us to prayers of repentance, wherein we receive YHVH's grace, mercy, and forgiveness.)

8. How has this chapter's study encouraged you to greater love for YHVH and your neighbor?

11
UNITED UNDER ONE KING

Division and warfare are born of principalities and powers who take advantage of the fact that humanity insists on their own ideals and the furtherance of their own agendas. The disunity of Israel began with one man who wanted to follow the ways of his culture. He persuaded the majority of his nation that his agenda was the right one. Because the majority allowed themselves to be persuaded by this man, they lived in a constant state of brutal civil warfare for seven and a half years.

Many people perished believing they were on the right side. Ultimately, Abner, the man who started it all, along with Ish-bosheth, the man he supported to be ruler over Israel, died. Sadly, it took their deaths for the whole nation to unite and recognize the one true agenda—YHVH's agenda through His anointed leader, David.

Unity: the Precious Anointing Oil of the High Priest

Seven and half years of division and civil war were finally brought to an end. All of the remaining tribes of Israel finally unified with Judah by cutting a covenant with David and anointing him as the king of all Israel (2 Sam. 5:1-3 KJV, 1 Chron. 11:1-3 KJV). Psalms 21, 60, 93, 95 through 99, 103, and 133 likely recorded David's emotions and declarations of praise over this glorious event.[1] David proclaimed, "The king shall joy in thy strength, O LORD. Thou settest a crown of pure gold on his head. Honour and majesty hast thou laid upon him" (Ps. 21:1, 3, 5, *condensed*).

In fact, David was so exuberant about Israel's reunification that he sang, "Behold how good and how pleasant it is for brethren to dwell together in unity! It is like the precious ointment upon the head, that ran down upon the beard, even Aaron's beard: that went down to the skirts of his garments; As the dew of Hermon, and as the dew that descended upon the mountains of Zion: for there the LORD commanded the blessing, even life for evermore" (Ps. 133:1-3).

David might not have known it at the time, but his song is also a deeply meaningful prophecy. The reunification of all Israel under David is such a beautiful prophetic foreshadow of what Ezekiel and the Apostle Paul prophesied (Ezek. 37:15-28, Rom. 11:25-27). All of Israel, including those who have been grafted into Israel (Rom. 11:17), will be united in covenant under the one true king, *Yeshua*, the Son of David.[2]

When David compared Israel's unity under him to the anointing oil upon Aaron, the High Priest, he was hinting at another aspect of unity in the body of Messiah. In addition to being King of kings, *Yeshua* also serves in the role of High Priest after the order of Melchizedek (Heb. 5:10, 6:20, 7:21-22). Our unity is like precious ointment on the head of our High Priest *Yeshua!* All the more reason we should strive to dwell in unity, rather than striving against one another in division.

The Cutting of Covenant

There is a recurrent theme that appears in the reunification of Israel, both in the 2 Samuel 5 account under David and in Ezekiel's prophecy (Ezek. 37:26) under David (or the Son of David). In both accounts, a covenant is cut between the people of Israel and David (or the Son of David). Covenant is something that is important to YHVH. This practice was quite prevalent in ancient Middle Eastern culture as well.[3] Covenant was never reserved solely for the marriage relationship. Covenants between friends, such as David and Jonathan's three covenants, were commonplace. Clearly, covenants between a nation and its leaders were also common. We saw this occur between Abner and David and again in 2 Sam. 5:3 between the people of Israel and David.

Cutting covenant often involved the sacrifice of an animal. A common ancient Middle Eastern covenant practice[4] can be seen in the account of YHVH's covenant with Abraham (Gen. 15); the animals were cut in halves and the parties to the covenant walked between them. Such actions indicated a mutual agreement that, if either party failed to keep the covenant, it would result in the transgressor ending up like one of the animals. For this reason, people of the ancient Middle East did not enter into covenants lightly, nor did they break them lightly. Their very life depended on keeping covenant!

In our modern world, we could seriously use a little more of the type of covenant loyalty and commitment of the ancient Middle East. It is rare for people to sincerely honor covenants anymore, especially the covenant of marriage. This is sadly evident in our current statistics of the church. There are astonishingly high rates of divorce, adultery, and pornography (among those married, as well as pastors) taking place among those who call themselves followers of the *Elohim* of the Bible.[5]

It astounds me that an incredibly high percentage of Christian women in my sphere have marriages that have been impacted by adultery and/or pornography. I can only imagine how it grieves our Heavenly Father that so many of his daughters are being deeply wounded by the sons He has anointed and called to cover them (Eph. 5:25-31). He takes the wounding of His daughters very seriously, as indicated by the prophet Malachi (Mal. 2:13-16). Sadly, the statistics also reveal an increasing trend for women who view pornography and commit adultery. The Father's heart is also broken for the deep wounding of His sons by the women He has called and anointed to be their helper (Gen. 2:18).

What has also been disturbing is what I have observed in my personal experience in various congregations across many denominational backgrounds. There have been many who have committed themselves into covenant agreements with a congregation and its leadership and then not adhered to their end of the agreement. Or these individuals were willing to excuse themselves from the covenant altogether over offense or some belief that it no longer applied to them anymore. I am thankful that our Heavenly Father takes His covenant commitments to us a lot more seriously than we take them with each other, otherwise, we would all be in a heap of trouble!

When we enter into covenant vows of marriage or covenants with our congregations, we must have the fear of YHVH. YHVH takes covenant vows *very* seriously and requires that we follow through and perform them (Num. 30, Deut. 23:22-24, Eccles. 5:4-6). *Yeshua* and the Apostle James said that it is better not to swear, but to "let your 'yes' be 'yes,' and your 'no,' 'no;'" "lest you fall into judgment" (Matt. 5:34-37 NKJV, James 5:12 NKJV). In other words, we are called to say what we mean, mean what we say, and follow it up with action, otherwise we will fall into judgment.

Yeshua and James were referring to those who make grandiose statements, swearing falsely by Heaven, by YHVH, or something else in order to somehow make their word more trustworthy. The context was that such people were not really swearing because they sincerely intended to keep their word. If keeping our word was no longer important to YHVH, why would someone fall into judgment for breaking their vows or covenant agreements? YHVH is "the same yesterday, today, and forever" (Heb. 13:8 BSB), and there is "no variation or shadow of turning" in Him (James 1:17 YLT). Therefore, we must strive to be people of our word, reflecting the image and likeness of the One who always keeps His word.

Israel most likely intended to honor the new covenant they made with David. Unfortunately, as we will see in future chapters of Volume Two, Israel would prove to be fickle and break their covenant with David twice. Sadly, both times were due to offenses that Israel perceived David had committed against them. These misperceptions caused Israel to judge David as an inept or inadequate leader, and they ultimately chose a new leader in his place.

Spoiler alert! Both of those leaders ended up dead for their treason and Israel quickly returned to following David thereafter. After the second rebellion, Israel finally learned that the grass was not greener on the other side of the fence and remained loyal to David for the remainder of his life.

A Promise Worth the Wait

Getting back to the present narrative, David was about thirty-years-old[6] when all of Israel united under him as their king (2 Sam. 5:4 KJV). Most scholars agree that he was anointed somewhere around the age of fifteen; David was most likely under twenty years of age since he was considered too young to join his brothers in the battle against the Philistines.[7] This means that David spent upwards of fifteen years waiting for the complete fulfillment of YHVH's promise. Much of that time was spent in the wilderness being hunted like prey. Halfway through those years, he enjoyed a partial fulfillment by becoming king over Judah, but those remaining years were filled with division and warfare within the kingdom.

David was not unlike every other highly esteemed leader of the Bible. Abraham had to wait just as long for his promise of a son to be fulfilled. Moses experienced a forty-year wilderness preparation as a shepherd before his promise to be Israel's deliverer was fulfilled. Though Moses was raised in the world system, and highly educated while living in Pharaoh's household, this did not qualify him to lead Israel. Forty years of shepherding sheep trained and qualified Moses as the shepherd and deliverer of Israel.

Likewise, Joshua received forty years of wilderness preparation before leading the people of Israel into the Promised Land. Joseph spent roughly ten to fifteen years in slavery and in prison before his promise was fulfilled.[8] It seems that long waits and rough wilderness experiences were the norm for YHVH's most noteworthy anointed leaders.

However, in our instant gratification, microwave modern culture, YHVH's people seem to believe and act as though a calling and anointing must be recognized by everyone in the church immediately and put into use. However, this is not consistent with how YHVH has always worked with His people. Before entering their promised position, YHVH's people have always had to endure a long season of hard training to purge their flaws and develop spiritual maturity. Therefore, we must be willing to wait on YHVH for as long as it takes. In the waiting process, we can find contentment to minister at whatever capacity He deems appropriate for us, just as Joseph did while he was in prison.

I have personally been (and witnessed many others who were) the type of believer who expected to use my gifts and talents in a certain way and at a certain time. When it did not happen according to my expectations, I became bitter and angry, taking offense toward anyone who I perceived to be holding me back from fulfilling my calling. What my Heavenly Father taught me is that He is *always* in sovereign control of every situation. He is able to turn the hearts of our spiritual leaders (Prov. 21:1). Therefore, YHVH is ultimately the One holding us back with a good purpose and plan (Jer. 29:11, Rom. 8:28). Just like David, if we find ourselves waiting to come into our calling, then we can trust that YHVH is still preparing, training, and equipping us to be used in our foremost capacity.

The Heavenly Father also taught me that we can actually delay the process of stepping into our calling. This can happen if we take up offense against our spiritual leaders for not giving us the opportunities that we feel we deserve. David, the man after YHVH's own heart, never took offense when his kingship seemed to be delayed. For fifteen years, David patiently waited on YHVH's timing and plan to get him to where He had promised! David refused to take the advice of others and remove the hindrance that Saul was to his promised throne. How long have we been waiting? Let us be as patient as David was. YHVH's plan *will* come together at the right time and in the right way, *if* we let go and let God.

Jerusalem Delivered

Now that David had the entire army of Israel united under His leadership, he decided it was time to go and secure Jerusalem as his capital. Is the Son of David (*Yeshua*) likewise waiting for all of Israel (including those who are grafted-in) and Judah to be united under His leadership before He will take up His throne in Jerusalem? That is a question I seriously ponder as I see just how many prophetic pointers to *Yeshua* there were in David's life. Perhaps this is why we have been waiting for the Messiah's return for so long.

We know from 2 Peter 3:3-9 that *Yeshua* is not slow concerning His coming, but patiently waiting for all "to come to repentance" (NIV). The effect of perfected unity among all believers is that the whole world comes to know *Yeshua* is the Messiah and comes to repentance (John 17:20-23). What are we waiting for brothers and sisters? Let's get united already, so our King can take up His throne in Zion!

In order for David to take his throne to Jerusalem, he had to defeat the Jebusites who had maintained their stronghold there throughout Israel's history in the Promised Land. The root of *Jebusite* means "to tread down or trample" (H947).[9] The Jebusites were very prideful concerning their strength to keep control of the city. They told David that he would never be successful in conquering the city. They even mocked and insulted him and his army by saying, "You will not get in here; even the blind and the lame could ward you off" (2 Sam. 5:6 NIV, 1 Chron. 11:5 NIV).

The Jebusites were a prophetic foreshadow of a Gentile people, prophesied by the Apostle John, who will "tread the Holy city underfoot" (Rev. 11:2 NKJV). For many centuries, Jerusalem was under the control of the Ottomans and Muslims. Sultan Suleiman sought to prevent the Son of David (*Yeshua*) from entering Jerusalem through the eastern gate (Golden Gate), as prophesied by Ezekiel (Ezek. 43), by sealing the eastern gate. Additionally, the Ottomans buried their dead between the gate and the Mount of Olives as if to mock the Son of David, "Even our dead can ward you off."[10]

Just as their efforts will prove to be futile against the Son of David, the Jebusites insults were nothing but futility. David took the insults as a challenge. He offered a commander-in-chief position to the first man in his army to go and strike the Jebusites. He further ordered the strike be done by going through the water shaft to the pool of Siloam; in *Yeshua's* time, this pool was the very place where the blind and lame gathered to seek their healing (John 9:6-7 KJV). In essence, David's response to the Jebusites was, "I will show you!" (2 Sam. 5:7-8, 1 Chron. 11:6).

After his big faux-pas with Abner, David's nephew Joab needed to get back in David's good graces again. So, Joab took up the challenge, climbed up the foreboding water shaft, and sacked the city by storm. David made good on his word and appointed Joab commander-in-chief of Israel's army. David moved his headquarters from Hebron to Jerusalem, renamed it the City of David, and began fortifying the walls (2 Sam. 5:9, 1 Chron. 11:6-8). Joab also worked to repair the city. Scripture states that "David went on, and grew great, and the LORD God of Hosts was with him" (2 Sam. 5:10, 1 Chron. 11:8-9). Growth is a positive sign that YHVH is with you. Psalm 118 commemorates this momentous occasion.

A House Fit for a King

As David built up Jerusalem, the neighboring king of Tyre showed unparalleled kindness and favor toward David by sending him cedar logs, skilled carpenters, and masons to build a palace for David (2 Sam. 5:11, 1 Chron. 14:1). In the ancient Middle East, when did a king ever celebrate the victory of a neighboring king by supplying him with everything he needed, including the labor to build his palace? Truly YHVH glorifies those whom He has called. "If God be for us, who can be against us" (Rom. 8:31)? He makes those who would be our natural enemy to be at peace with us (Prov. 16:7).

Following this marvelous provision, "David perceived that the LORD had established him king over Israel and that He had exalted his kingdom *for His people Israel's sake*" (2 Sam. 5:12, 1 Chron. 14:2, *emphasis mine*). It was not when Saul died that David realized that his kingdom had been established, nor was it when Judah crowned him as king. One would think that the pivotal moment would have come when Israel cut their covenant with David and anointed him as king, but it was not. However, when YHVH provided the resources and labor for his palace, David realized that YHVH's promises to him had fully manifested. Even more, David had the humility to recognize that his kingdom had not been established for his own sake. Psalm 101 communicates his sentiments at this realization.

Such incredible provision is how we truly know that YHVH has elevated us to our calling and anointing. He will do all the work to position and provide for us and we will not have to labor for it. This type of favor and provisioning is how YHVH elevated Joseph into his majestic position. Joseph had nothing more to do than to consistently live out his faith. He served YHVH in whatever way he could, even while imprisoned for a crime he did not commit. Through that trial, YHVH positioned Joseph and provided for him to become the second most powerful leader in the world. Joseph did not have to try to attain that position in any way. It was simply done for him as a reward for being content and faithful in prison (Gen. 41).

To see his kingdom established, David was now experiencing the reward of being content and faithful during his trials in the Judean wilderness. Let us likewise be content and faithfully serve YHVH wherever He has us and for as long as He has us there. Let us never fight and scratch our own way into our calling and anointing. If we have to work hard for something we feel called to, it might be a work of our own hands and not His. YHVH will exalt us in due time *if* we let Him (1 Pet. 5:6). Otherwise, we may be settling for less than His best, if we insist on exalting or building ourselves up in our own way and time.

YHVH's Law Neglected

Unfortunately, as David was being glorified, it seemed to go to his head a little; he started multiplying more wives for himself (2 Sam. 5:13, 1 Chron. 14:3-7). Perhaps, he had yet to write a copy of YHVH's laws for himself, as it was commanded for the kings of Israel to do (Deut. 17:18). Did he not know that it was a big no-no for the king of Israel to multiply wives to himself (Deut. 17:17)? If David had known this, he would have been guilty of intentional rebellion against YHVH. Therefore, he must not have known because YHVH did not appear to rebuke him for this trespass or acknowledge it as sin to his descendants (1 Kings 15:5).

Why didn't David know YHVH's law by this time in his life? Samuel the prophet anointed him and later spent time with him in Ramah and Naioth. Abiathar, the priest, also served David for over ten years before this time. Either one of them should have been reading YHVH's law in the ears of the king and all of the people of Israel every seven years during the Feast of Tabernacles (Deut. 31:9-13).

Even more, Samuel should have communicated YHVH's legal requirements for the king of Israel to David at his anointing. Yet based on the scriptural record, Samuel seemed to have rushed home after anointing David (1 Sam. 16:13). Samuel had taught Saul, and all the Israelites present at Saul's anointing, what the rules of kingship were, and wrote them in a scroll for their remembrance (1 Sam. 10:25). However, it does not appear that the scroll Samuel wrote for Saul or YHVH's rules for kingship were ever passed on to David. Nor does it appear that Samuel communicated these rules to David while he was under Samuel's protection in Naioth.

Unfortunately, somewhere along the line, there was a colossal failure by those who were entrusted with making YHVH's laws known to all the people of Israel; it resulted in people like David unknowingly doing things that were against YHVH's law, things that would hurt them and those around them. In future chapters (in both volumes), we are going to see just how much this ignorance of YHVH's laws would hurt David, his family, and the entire nation of Israel under his rule. In particular, David's multiplicity of wives and their children would prove to be a detriment to his reign.

Sadly, the same failure to teach YHVH's law has been plaguing the body of Messiah for generations. Our congregations are full of people who do not know the Word of YHVH as well as they should. Much sin and pain exists among YHVH's people today because we do not know His Word and follow it. Our young people are walking away from faith in YHVH and His Messiah, *Yeshua*, because they lack the foundation of knowledge and faith in His Word. Without this spiritual equipping, young people are unable to overcome the opposing world views that they are being taught through the public education system.[11] With the unhindered access we have to YHVH's Word, this should not be so!

It is the solemn duty of every parent to make sure that our children hear the whole Word of YHVH so they will prosper in His ways (Deut. 6:4-9, Prov. 29:18, Hos. 4:6). It is not merely our pastors, Christian school teachers, or rabbis who have this duty to teach the Word of YHVH to our children. One does not have to be a seminary graduate to teach and train their children in the ways of YHVH.

Scripture tells us that "faith cometh by hearing, and hearing by the Word of God" (Rom. 10:17). Therefore, we simply need to read YHVH's Word to our children cover-to-cover and encourage them to do the same when they are old enough to read. YHVH's Word is the single most *crucial* thing we can teach our future generations. The Word will bring both temporal and eternal rewards *if* we align our lives with it! America's founding fathers understood this principle as the early American education system primarily taught children to read using the Bible.[12]

In the Land of the Giants

After David unknowingly sinned by multiplying wives to himself, the Philistines encamped at Rephaim against David (2 Sam. 5:17-18, 1 Chron. 14:8-9). Israel's enemy had one mission: take out the king and scatter Israel. As we saw in 1 Samuel 30, this was exactly what the Philistines accomplished when they took out King Saul. Israel's enemy understood that unity of a nation under one leader was too powerful against them, so they were compelled to fight against that unity by destroying their leader. Our spiritual enemy, *Ha-Satan*, knows the same truth and is likewise compelled. For this reason, it is imperative that we cover our leaders in prayer (1 Tim. 2:1-2).

Rephaim was known as the land of the giants. Though David had experienced YHVH's victory over a Philistine giant and the Philistine army before, he did not assume that this enemy encampment against him automatically demanded that he engage in battle. He did not even assume that YHVH would be on his side to give him victory as He had done in the past. Rather, David inquired of YHVH whether he was even to engage in battle and whether YHVH would be on his side (2 Sam. 5:19, 1 Chron. 14:10). We have much to learn and gain from David's example. How often do we jump into and engage our adversary without even consulting YHVH?

David was certainly not lacking in faith by asking whether YHVH would be on his side. This was not a sign of disbelief, but rather a sign of spiritual maturity and godly leadership. David had learned through his wilderness training that YHVH sometimes has a purpose in bringing the adversary against us, and it is not always our responsibility to destroy that enemy. Therefore, David understood the importance of stopping to ask the real King what He knew, saw, and desired in this particular situation. David drew no inferences from past situations or victories into the present without YHVH telling him to do so. Are we following David's godly example before we engage with the enemy? At David's inquiry, YHVH informed David that he was to go to battle against the Philistines and that He would give him victory over them.

A Drink Offering Poured Out

In 2 Samuel 23, we learn of an interesting backstory that occurred at this time. As soon as David heard that the Philistines were planning to attack, Scripture says that he "went down to the hold" (2 Sam. 5:17). We later learn David was in the cave of Adullam (2 Sam. 23:13), located southwest of the Valley of Rephaim where the Philistines were setting up their encampment. If you recall from our discussion in Chapter Five, the cave of Adullam also overlooked the Valley of Elah, the location of Goliath's defeat. David was not unlike us. How often do we return to a place where we once experienced great victory with YHVH's help when we are faced with a new battle involving similar circumstances? It is a very effective prayer strategy to prepare our hearts and renew our identity as mighty warriors in YHVH before stepping out to face our enemy.

As David camped out and waited for YHVH's permission to strike his enemy, three of his chief mighty men came to his side. The arid wilderness had created a deep thirst in David for the refreshing water near the gate of Bethlehem where a garrison of Philistines happened to be. To David's three most loyal chiefs, that was no threat! Without hesitation, the three broke through the

Philistine army, apprehended the water their king desired, and brought it back to him. David was so humbled that his men would risk their very lives to bring him a drink of water that he felt unworthy to drink it (2 Sam. 23:13-17).

Can you imagine what those three might have been feeling? The Scriptures do not give any indication that they became offended at David pouring the water on the ground. They appear to have simply brushed it off and gone on with being his faithful chiefs. I think most of us have to admit that we would be pretty flabbergasted if we had just gone to all that trouble to bring water to our king, and he poured it on the dust.

Admittedly, we would probably be royally incensed over it. I can hear someone saying, "Are you kidding me? Do you have any idea what we just went through to get that water for you! You could have at least allowed one of us to drink it if you did not want it. What a waste! Seriously… I'm out of here! I'm not doing this for you anymore." From what I have observed (and fought against in my own flesh) is that, in this day and age, humans can get easily offended and give up on people way too quickly. I am glad for David that his mighty men had unfeigned loyalty and patience with him to overlook this offense.

Victory Over the Enemy

At some point after the water incident, David and his troops attacked the Philistines. YHVH was faithful to His word, and Israel defeated them. David gave praise, honor, and glory to YHVH because He had "broken forth upon his enemies…as the breach of waters." To commemorate the victory YHVH had given them there, David named that location Baal-Perazim which means "possessor of breaches" (H1188)[13] (2 Sam. 5:19-20, 1 Chron. 14:11). David may also have written Psalms 124 and 139 around this time to memorialize the victory in song.[14]

The Philistines fled from David's slaughter in such haste that they abandoned their idols. David burned the abandoned Philistine idols in what seems to be his attempt to fulfill the commandment of Deuteronomy 7:5. It is ironic how the Philistines had to abandon their idols, which had clearly been worthless to cover them in battle (2 Sam. 5:21, 1 Chron. 14:12)!

Déjà-vu in the Land of the Giants

It did not take long for the defeated Philistines to regroup and return to Rephaim for round two. Perhaps they hoped to retrieve their useless idols unaware they had been burned. When David heard that the Philistines had returned, he made no assumption based on his recent breakthrough. He also did not assume that just because this situation looked and felt like déjà-vu that YHVH's answer or strategy would be the same. David paused again to inquire of YHVH as to whether he should go to battle. It is a good thing that he did this because, even though the battle looked identical to the one David had just overcome, YHVH gave him a whole different strategy (2 Sam. 5:22-23, 1 Chron. 14:13-15).

YHVH instructed David to circle around behind the Philistines and wait for the sound of marching coming from the tops of the balsam (mulberry) trees. YHVH revealed that it was He who would be marching ahead of Israel's army and striking the Philistine camp. David and his army obeyed the word of YHVH and were victorious over the Philistines (2 Sam. 5:24-25, 1 Chron. 14:16-17).

What might have happened if David had assumed that, since everything looked and felt the same as the previous battle, that YHVH would bless him with victory again? If David had jumped into battle headlong it could have been disastrous for him and the army of Israel. Instead of David and the army of Israel pursuing the Philistines from Geba to Gezer, the Philistines might have been pursuing them.

We can glean a great deal from David's godly leadership example. It is crucial that inquiring of YHVH be our only strategy in every situation we face, regardless of how similar it is to a previous experience. No two battles are the same. YHVH is the only One who sees all and knows all. We must constantly stay in tune with His *Ruach ha-Kodesh* to ensure that we successfully navigate every battle so that it ends in victory.

What battles are we facing today? Is *ha-Satan* encamped against a united people under YHVH's anointed leader? Does our enemy seek to take out that leader and those loyal to him? Is the enemy hoping to scatter the flocks of YHVH in division by taking out their spiritual leadership in the same way the Philistines scattered Israel by taking out King Saul?

We would be wise to seek the *Ruach ha-Kodesh* for direction in how to navigate such battles against the enemy. Israel stayed loyal to YHVH and His anointed leader, and perfectly obeyed YHVH's instructions to remain unified and victorious under the one true king. We also need to remain loyal to YHVH and obey His greatest commandments of love to remain unified and victorious under the one true King *Yeshua*.

> *"And say unto them, Thus saith the Lord GOD; Behold, I will take the children of Israel from among the heathen, whither they be gone, and will gather them on every side, and bring them into their own land: And I will make them one nation in the land upon the mountains of Israel; and one king shall be king to them all: and they shall be no more two nations, neither shall they be divided into two kingdoms any more at all. Neither shall they defile themselves any more with their idols, nor with their detestable things, nor with any of their*

transgressions: but I will save them out of all their dwellingplaces, wherein they have sinned, and will cleanse them: so shall they be my people, and I will be their God. And David my servant shall be king over them; and they all shall have one shepherd: they shall also walk in my judgments, and observe my statutes, and do them. And they shall dwell in the land that I have given unto Jacob my servant, wherein your fathers have dwelt; and they shall dwell therein, even they, and their children, and their children's children for ever: and my servant David shall be their prince for ever. Moreover I will make a covenant of peace with them; it shall be an everlasting covenant with them: and I will place them, and multiply them, and will set my sanctuary in the midst of them for evermore. My tabernacle also shall be with them: yea, I will be their God, and they shall be my people. And the heathen shall know that I the LORD do sanctify Israel, when my sanctuary shall be in the midst of them for evermore." (Ezek. 37:21-28)

"For I would not, brethren, that ye should be ignorant of this mystery, lest ye should be wise in your own conceits; that blindness in part is happened to Israel, until the fulness of the Gentiles be come in. And so all Israel shall be saved: as it is written, There shall come out of Sion the Deliverer, and shall turn away ungodliness from Jacob: For this is my covenant unto them, when I shall take away their sins. As concerning the gospel, they are enemies for your sakes: but as touching the election, they are beloved for the father's sakes. For the gifts and calling of God are without repentance. For as ye in times past have not believed God, yet have now obtained mercy through their unbelief: Even so

have these also now not believed, that through your mercy they also may obtain mercy. For God hath concluded them all in unbelief, that he might have mercy upon all." (Rom. 11:25-32)

JOURNEY JOURNAL

1. Do you personally identify with any of David's characteristics or experiences? If so, which one(s)?

2. How does your personal experience with covenants compare to how they were treated in the ancient Middle East? Do you think there is value in how they honored covenant? Why or why not?

3. How has this chapter's study affected your perspective about waiting for your anointing and calling to be fulfilled?

4. How has this chapter's study affected your perspective about the importance of inquiring of YHVH in each and every situation?

5. How well do you personally know the whole counsel of YHVH (His Word)? How well have you passed on the knowledge of His Word to future generations?

6. Did you experience any personal conviction as you read this chapter and answered the questions presented? What were you convicted about? (Conviction is meant to lead us to prayers of repentance, wherein we receive YHVH's grace, mercy, and forgiveness.)

7. How has this chapter's study encouraged you to greater love for YHVH and your neighbor?

12
HIS GLORY RETURNS

Abraham Lincoln is still remembered as one of the most celebrated presidents of the United States of America. In his most famous speech, "House Divided," he said, "A house divided against itself cannot stand."[1] He was quoting *Yeshua* from Matthew 12:25 and Mark 3:25. In Lincoln's day, America had faced a brutal loss of approximately 600,000 lives through division and civil war. But because President Lincoln followed the principles of his personal Savior, he was instrumental in beginning the process of reuniting and healing our divided nation and bringing it into further glory.

As we saw in our previous chapter, David followed the leading and instructions of the *Ruach ha-Kodesh* and became instrumental in reuniting a deeply divided Israel. Like Lincoln, David saw many people perish during seven and a half years of civil war. David's reunited Israel was also about to see YHVH's glory return to the land.

How the Glory Departed

To recap briefly, the glory of YHVH, which rested above the mercy seat of the Ark of the Covenant, had departed out of the land of Israel over twenty years earlier. This occurred because of the corrupt priesthood under Eli and his sons. They were rebellious against YHVH's laws, unrepentant to His rebukes through the prophets He sent and had created division amongst the people as a result of their unrepentant sins. Due to the priests' corruption, two religious factions were created in Israel: those who continued to follow the corrupt and rebellious Levitical priesthood of Eli's family, and those who followed Samuel the prophet, a man who exemplified obedience to YHVH's instructions. This division lasted until after Samuel's death.

In 1 Samuel 4, Israel was facing defeat at the hands of the Philistines. The elders of Israel, acting in unity with the priesthood, brought the Ark of the Covenant into the battle in an attempt to secure their victory. Eli's sons, Hophni and Phineas, the most corrupt of all the priesthood, led this charge. They removed the Ark from its prescribed place in the Holy of Holies and took it out to a battlefield against the heathen Philistines. With much ceremony, triumphal shouting, and fanfare, they brought the mercy seat—the holy throne of YHVH—into a profane place of corruption and death. They did this for their own personal benefit, actually believing that YHVH would rally in support of them.

Needless to say, this action only emboldened the enemy against Israel; the Philistines fought even more fiercely. As a result, the Israelites were shamefully defeated, and the Ark was taken into the enemy's territory. At the news of the Ark's capture and the deaths of his sons, Eli toppled over dead. Eli's daughter-in-law was so distraught over these events that, when she gave birth to a son, she named him *Ichabod*, which means "there is no glory" (H350).[2] She said, "The glory is departed from Israel" (1 Sam. 4:21). There truly was no glory in the presence of corrupt leadership who rebelled against YHVH's law, refused to heed His rebuke, and thereby created division among His people. As it was then, so it is in our modern time.

Ignorance Leads to Death

It had been nearly twenty years since the loss of the Ark. But now that Israel and the religious factions were finally reunited under King David, David felt it was time for the Ark of the Covenant to finally come home to Jerusalem. He may certainly have been led by the Spirit in his desire. However, David consulted with the captains, leaders, and all of Israel about bringing up the Ark. There is no mention that he or anyone else consulted with YHVH or His Word about the matter in order that he be led in Spirit and in Truth. In fact, 1 Chronicles 15:13 confirms they never sought YHVH's Word concerning the decision.

David said to his human counselors, "If it seem good unto you," and described his proposal to fetch the Ark, which "was right in the eyes of all the people." They were united in a desire that seemed good, perhaps even born of the Spirit. They considered everything they were doing to be led with good intentions (1 Chron. 13:1-6). Nonetheless, everything they did was out of alignment with YHVH's instructions for handling the Ark of the Covenant. In full unity, David, the leaders, and all the people departed from Baalah (or Baale-Judah according to the interlinear Hebrew text), which was the center of Baal worship in Judah (H1184).[3] They went with much ceremony, praise, and worship (possibly reciting Psalm 15 or 24)[4] to retrieve the Ark from

Abinadab's house in Kirjath-Jearim, using a new cart pulled by oxen (2 Sam. 6:1-3, 1 Chron. 13:4-7).

Where did they get this idea to use a new cart pulled by cattle or oxen? Is it possible they were just copying what the Philistines did when they returned the Ark to the land of Israel? They put the Ark on a new cart pulled by two milk cows and nothing bad seemed to happen until common Israelites touched it to look inside (1 Sam. 6:19). They probably thought, "So long as nobody tries to look inside, we should all be ok, right?"

David and the people should have known better. They should have known the Torah requirement that only Levites of Kohathite descent carry the Ark on poles after the High Priest and his sons have covered it (Num. 4). David was supposed to write a copy of the Torah for himself (Deut. 17:18), and the Torah was supposed to be read in the ears of the people by the priesthood (Deut. 31:9-13). David also had Abiathar, the remnant priest, in his close circle.

Clearly, there had been a miserable failure of the priesthood of Israel to teach YHVH's instructions. No one, not even the priests, stood up to speak the truth and direct things to be done the appropriate way. Perhaps the main thrust of the problem can be seen in the fact that they all departed from Baale-Judah, the center of Baal worship. Perhaps the amount of Baal worship going on in Judah was choking out the Word of YHVH.

Most of us have heard this chronicle many times and know its classical elements well. David's celebrating entourage arrived at the home of Abinadab. The Ark had remained with Abinadab for twenty years after YHVH had struck down seventy men of Beth-Shemesh for looking inside of it (1 Sam. 6-7). Now Abinadab's sons Uzzah and Ahio took the Ark out on its new cart. The oxen pulling the cart stumbled, Uzzah reached out to stabilize the Ark and *wham-o*! Uzzah died as judgment from YHVH for touching the Ark. The Bible says, "The anger of the LORD was kindled [*charah*] [H2734][5] against Uzzah; and God smote him there for his error" (2 Sam. 6:3-7, 1 Chron. 13:7-10, *brackets mine*). YHVH's "people perish for lack of knowledge" (Hos. 4:6).

David's Displeasure in YHVH's Judgment

David became displeased (*charah*) (H2734)[5] with YHVH for killing Uzzah. The same word used to describe YHVH's anger being kindled was used in this verse to describe David's displeasure against YHVH. David, a mere man, was allowing his displeasure to burn against YHVH in the same way that YHVH's anger burned against Uzzah (2 Sam. 6:8, 1 Chron. 13:11). That is a problem!

David judged YHVH for making a breach against Uzzah by calling the place Perez (Breach)-Uzzah (H6556).[6] David failed to realize that he was ultimately the one who had made a breach. He had led Uzzah into making a breach against YHVH by handling the Ark of the Covenant in a way that was outside of YHVH's commandments (2 Sam. 6:8, 1 Chron. 13:11). As king, David should have known better. How often have we likewise allowed our displeasure to burn and misjudged YHVH for tragic circumstances in our own lives? At the time, we may not have understood that those circumstances came about as a result of choices we were ultimately responsible for.

David was totally out of alignment in his heart. He had failed to fulfill YHVH's instructions to write his own copy of the Torah. The priesthood and leadership around David had failed to teach the people YHVH's instructions, and so there was no one to hold David accountable. Ultimately, David had failed to inquire of YHVH and get His input for moving the Ark. Instead, David trusted in what seemed good to the people. He had sought many counselors instead of YHVH.

Doesn't Scripture state that there is safety in many counselors? Not if their counsel is out of alignment with YHVH's Word. This is why it is so important to test everything we hear against the written Word of YHVH and through prayer. This misaligned counsel that was given to David led to death in the midst of a passionate worship service. It also led to David having unrighteous feelings and judgments against YHVH. Ultimately, David was too afraid to further handle the Ark. It was set in Obed-Edom's nearby threshing floor until David could figure out what to do from there (2 Sam. 6:9-10, 1 Chron. 13:12-13).

Obed-Edom: Caretaker of the Ark

Obed-Edom was called a "Gittite" (2 Sam. 6:10, 1 Chron. 13:13). Some scholars argue that a Gittite is a Philistine from Gath[7] Others suggest that people from the city of Gittaim (Gath), in the land of Benjamin, were also called Gittites.[8] Gittaim was not far from the Levitical city of Gibeon[9] (Josh. 21:17-18) where the tabernacle stood at this time in history.[10] 1 Chronicles 26 listed Obed-Edom as a Levite gatekeeper of Kohathite descent.

Obed-Edom was also named in 1 Chronicles 15, 16, and 26 as a singer, a porter, a gatekeeper for the Ark, and a doorkeeper for the temple storehouse. Therefore, it would make sense that his threshing floor would be located near a Levitical city. Kirjath-Jearim was not far from Gibeon.[11] Some scholars believe this Levitical assignment is an assumption rather than a fact; they ascribe Obed-Edom's mention as a Gittite only to Gath of the land of the Philistines,[12] rather than the ancient Benjamite city of Gittaim. Reviewing maps of ancient Israel for these two cities reveals they are different places with the same name.

After the mishap with the Ark, would it make sense for David to turn the Ark aside into the house of a Philistine? YHVH struck poor Uzzah dead simply for touching the Ark. Would the same

Elohim that had afflicted the Philistines with tumors and mice for having the Ark in their possession (1 Sam. 5) now bless the socks off a Philistine for keeping the Ark in his home? It makes more sense to me that YHVH orchestrated this stumble to take place right in front of the house of a Levite of Kohathite descent, the very family of Levites charged with carrying the Ark (Num. 4). This was likely an act of mercy to prevent something more serious from happening had David and the people continued in their disobedience by carrying the Ark the improper way.

One Man Dies for Sin

You may wonder how I can possibly view the judgment leading to Uzzah's death as an act of mercy. However, his death is a prophetic foreshadowing of the gospel message: one man dying for the sins of the people (Rom. 5:6-11, 2 Cor. 5:14). Sin is defined as "the transgression of the law" (1 John 3:4). Essentially, everyone in Israel was guilty of sin for carrying the Ark in the wrong way. They were copying the way that the pagan Philistines did it instead of looking into YHVH's "perfect law of liberty" for His prescribed way of doing it (James 1:25).

Numbers 4 tells us that even if the Kohathites tried to see or handle the Ark before the Aaronic priests covered it, they would die. So clearly, mishandling of the Ark was a sin worthy of death. King David was ultimately responsible and should have been the one worthy of the death penalty for this sin. However, since Messiah was destined to come from his line, YHVH made atonement for David through Uzzah's death. With this perspective in mind, we can see that the *Elohim* of the Old Testament really is the same merciful and compassionate *Elohim* of the New Testament.

Repentance and Submission Restores the Glory

After the death of Uzzah, the Ark remained in Obed-Edom's house for three months. YHVH increased Obed-Edom's blessings the entire time the Ark was with him. 2 Samuel 6:12 gives us the impression that when David heard how blessed Obed-Edom's house was, he just decided to go get the Ark because of the blessings. However, 1 Chronicles 15 gives further detail that indicates that David must have inquired of YHVH and His Word during this time. David came to the realization that he had been the one to breach against YHVH for the way he had tried to retrieve the Ark the first time. It is clear that David studied the Torah, repented, and was now ready to do things according to YHVH's instructions. David acknowledged to the priests and Levites, "Because ye did not do it at the first, the LORD our God made a breach upon us, for that we sought him not after the due order" (2 Sam. 6:11-12, 1 Chron. 13:14, 15:12-13).

This time, David enlisted the priests and Levites to carry the Ark and lead the worship. He and all the people set out a second time with much celebration, dancing, and praise, just like before. David reverenced YHVH so greatly he had the Levites stop every six paces and make sacrifices to YHVH. Because things were done in their proper order, this scenario ended much happier for everyone. Psalms 15, 20, 24, 68, 96, 105, 106, or 136 may record the praises that were a part of the celebration as some ascribe these psalms to this event.[13]

1 Chronicles 16:7-36 definitively records the psalms that David provided to Asaph, the head of his worship team, for the special occasion. Verses 8-22 of 1 Chronicles 16 matches Psalm 105:1-15, verses 23-33 match Psalm 96:1-13, and verses 34-36 match Psalm 106:1, 47-48. The Ark entered Jerusalem with shouts of joy, shofar blasts, and joyful dancing by David.

David had prepared a tent in Jerusalem specifically for the Ark (2 Sam. 6:12-15, 1 Chron. 15:1-28). Certainly, David had looked into YHVH's law concerning the proper handling of the Ark, but had he also read that the Holy of Holies in Moses' tabernacle was the rightful place for the Ark, according to YHVH's law? Why didn't he take the Ark to the tabernacle that had been moved from Nob to Gibeon and still resided in Gibeon? 1 Chronicles 16:39 and 1 Chronicles 21:29 state that the tabernacle of Moses remained in Gibeon and was not moved to Jerusalem by David. With stopping every six paces to sacrifice, Gibeon would have been a much easier trip, since it was closer to Obed-Edom's than Jerusalem.

The biblical text gives us no record of what caused David to build a tent for the Ark in Jerusalem rather than putting it in the tabernacle or moving the tabernacle to Jerusalem. I am very curious if he heard a word from YHVH about it. Based on YHVH's word to Nathan the prophet in 2 Samuel 7, it is possible that David was supposed to move the Tabernacle of Moses to Jerusalem. This would have kept all the priesthood together instead of splitting them between the tent for the Ark in Jerusalem and the Tabernacle of Moses in Gibeon (1 Chron. 16:37-40).

Ultimately, we know that Mount Moriah in Jerusalem is the place where YHVH chose to put His name, so His house was to be set up there (Deut. 12:11, Ps. 132:13, Ezra 6:12). This entire narrative of YHVH's glory residing in Jerusalem clearly served as another prophetic foreshadowing. David is symbolic of things to come concerning the Son of David (*Yeshua*). We are currently waiting for the restoration of YHVH's glory to Jerusalem. This is dependent on the leaders and people of Israel (both native-born and grafted-in) consulting and obeying YHVH's Word in unity. In particular, we must be united concerning the proper handling of YHVH's judgment and mercy toward one another, which are both represented in the Ark of the Covenant.

The Levites and priests brought the Ark into the tent David prepared for it, and they offered burnt offerings, peace offerings, and fellowship offerings before YHVH. David appointed ministers, singers, musicians, and shofar blowers before the Ark to continually thank, praise, and petition YHVH. Then David gave gifts of food, bread, and raisin cakes to all the people of Israel to celebrate the return of YHVH's glory to the land (2 Sam. 6:17-19, 1 Chron. 16).

David was a good shepherd king who fed the united sheep of Israel. Here we see yet another prophetic foreshadowing of the Good Shepherd, King *Yeshua*, who will restore YHVH's glory to its rightful place when all are united under Him. The Ark has been missing from the earth for over 2,500 years. Scripture says that the next time we will see it is in Revelation 11:15-19 when the last trumpet is blown, and the kingdoms of this earth become the kingdoms of YHVH and His Anointed One. This time coincides with Ezekiel's prophecy of all Israel uniting under one King (the Son of David) when YHVH restores His sanctuary on earth (Ezek. 37:21-28).

A Glorious Day Ends in Division

After the fanfare of this glorious celebration ended, David returned home in cheerfulness of heart desiring to bless his own household with the same gifts he had shared with the assembly. His judgmental and jealous wife, Michal, met him at the door. She had seen David dancing before YHVH and exposing his thighs, his garments flapping open in front of the maidens of Israel. As she watched David's joyous display, Michal "despised him in her heart." In her jealousy and judgmental attitude towards him, Michal shamed David for his actions and likened him to a "vulgar fellow" (2 Sam. 6:16, 20 NIV, 1 Chron. 15:29 KJV). David must have thought, "*What?* Seriously! I cannot believe she just said that to me!"

Many students of Scripture are often quick to judge Michal, but have we judged her righteously? Was her hatred simply because David exposed himself as he joyfully danced? Or was there another underlying reason? Michal once admired and loved David very much, so much that she covered for him to escape from her father's murderous pursuit. How could such admiration and love turn to hatred over one little dance? Is her assessment of his behavior as vulgar based on this one little incident? Not likely.

Women do not generally despise their husbands in their hearts for one little transgression like this. If a woman lacks good communication with her husband, her anger and frustration usually build up over time until she just cannot bottle it anymore, and she snaps. Is it possible that a young Michal, the wife of David's youth and his first love, hoped that David would send for her or come back for her? Perhaps, Michal's deep disdain was rooted in the hurt she experienced due to their separation. It took fifteen years for their reunion, after David had finally become king of all Israel. He had not even sought for her in the seven and a half years that he was king of Judah. Even more, he had already taken many other wives.

Shortly after David had run from Saul, Saul gave Michal to another man named Paltiel. Paltiel clearly loved her and wanted to be with her. Remember how he followed her weeping for many miles when Abner came to take her back to David (2 Sam. 3:15-16 KJV)? Perhaps, after all those years, Michal had grown to deeply love Paltiel just as deeply as he loved her. I believe she was truly happy again with Paltiel, delivered by his deep love and affection from the emotional trauma of separation from David, her first love.

Is it possible that Michal resented David for taking her away from Paltiel when he already had many wives? Imagine how she must have felt going from being the one and only beloved wife of a tenderhearted man to just being one of David's many wives. Surely, she must have felt unloved because he didn't reach out to her for fifteen years, only after he became king and felt entitled to have her back. I can only imagine that Michal must have felt like a possession to David, someone that he only came to when it pleased him. It is very likely she never got the chance to express her feelings in a healthy way and this created a bitter root in her.

I believe Michal was likely suffering for a long time with feeling rejected by David. And because she never resolved this emotional offense, it may have been the underlying issue that caused Michal to despise David in her heart. I believe that was not just something that came up all of a sudden that day, but rather the way that she had been feeling about him for a long time. That feeling was so strong that she could not see all the good in him and the fact that he was there to bless her. Bitterness and unforgiveness can make one emotionally and spiritually blind.

Michal probably thought David was pretty disgusting the way he had abandoned her and had taken many other wives. I would venture to say that his thigh exposure while dancing was just the straw that broke the camel's back, and it caused all of her bottled up emotions to manifest on the surface. She had been feeling rejected by David, so Michal rejected him through her disrespectful and judgmental response. This is how rejection operates in and through us if we are not careful. This is spiritual warfare that purposes to destroy our relationships. And because Michal reacted to David in this way, it actually sealed his complete rejection of her. Michal lived the rest of her life barren and alone in David's house as a result of her bitterness, judgment, and disrespectful release of emotion (2 Sam. 6:23).

I have personally heard many teachers who felt that this was a just judgment from YHVH for the way that Michal judged and shamed her husband. However, the text does not give us the indication that this was YHVH's judgment upon her, but rather a result of David's judgment of her. This doesn't absolve Michal—she was clearly wrong in the way that she reacted toward David. But perhaps this situation could have ended happily if David attempted to understand Michal's heart rather than defending himself and being angry at her reaction. All David seemed to be concerned with was defending his pride. He was thinking he was basically a good man and could not even fathom any reasonable explanation for why Michal viewed him with disgust. This was very evident in his response to her (2 Sam. 6:21-23).

If David had truly loved Michal as he loved himself, he might have pursued her heart behind this matter a little more instead of taking up offense and rejecting her completely. It would have helped if he had slowed down in that moment to inquire of YHVH *before* responding. This would have given him the opportunity to hear Michal's heart and learn how much it likely hurt due to his past actions. As a result, he might have been more patient, compassionate, and forgiving towards Michal. Perhaps, he might have even sought to restore her.

Because David did not take the opportunity to inquire with YHVH before reacting, is it possible that he missed a golden opportunity to foreshadow YHVH's heart for His bride? Unfortunately, both David and Michal handled this situation in emotional reaction and offense (the flesh). They operated out of rejection instead of operating under the influence of the *Ruach ha-Kodesh*. As a result, their relationship was forever broken and fruitless, and Michal died in utter loneliness. Such division in a marriage was a tragic way to end an otherwise glorious day of celebration in unity.

A Better Way to Handle Marital Conflict

Unfortunately, this kind of tragic ending happens all too often in the marriages of disciples of *Yeshua* today. It is something that should never take place in one who is after YHVH's own heart. YHVH is a King who is willing to lay His life down for His bride, even in her sin and disobedience (Rom. 5:8). This is the kind of response that all husbands (even David) are called by the *Ruach ha-Kodesh* to follow. The *Ruach ha-Kodesh* inspired the words of Paul in Ephesians 5:25-33 when he called upon husbands to love their "wives, even as Christ also loved the church and gave himself for it."

Certainly, Michal should have submitted to, honored, and respected her husband and king. She should have taken her thoughts captive (2 Cor. 10:5), focused on what was pure, lovely, noble, virtuous, and praiseworthy about David (Phil. 4:8), and affirmed those things in him. However, David also should have given himself up for Michal. They both failed the test of a godly marriage.

Ladies, let us be careful not to let feelings of rejection, bitterness, unforgiveness, or any other negative emotion fester in us. We must stand firm and resist the temptation to judge our husbands and dishonor them in our hearts. We must also be careful not to judge and dishonor them with our words and actions towards them or about them to others. We might be missing information about their thoughts and intentions. In the midst of conflict, we would be wise to give our husbands the benefit of the doubt; they could also be missing information and may not know what they are doing to hurt or offend us.

We also need to consider the possibility that the actions of our husbands might be driven by their own hurt feelings. We may need to seek to understand their hearts every bit as much as we want them to understand ours. Love always "believes the best in every person," and seeks the needs of others above its own (1 Cor. 13:4-8 AMPC). We need to communicate our feelings to our husbands as quickly as possible, in a healthy and respectful way (1 Pet. 3:1-6). They will respond better if we do.

Gentlemen, when your wives fail to control their emotions and blurt out disrespectful words towards you, please "be quick to hear [a ready listener], slow to speak, slow to take offense *and* to get angry" (James 1:19-21 AMPC). I implore you, seek to hear past her disrespect and try to understand that there is a hurting heart underlying it. Seek to understand her heart before you seek to defend yourself and your honor or before you judge her harshly for not honoring you.

The husband is the stronger vessel and "joint heir of the grace" of YHVH through *Yeshua* the Messiah (1 Pet. 3:7 AMPC). *Yeshua* died for your wife's sin of dishonoring you in the same way that he died for your sins that dishonored Him. He has called you to love her in the same way He has loved all of us—He laid His life down for us while we were yet sinners (Eph. 5:21-33). "Love does not seek its own and takes no account of the evil done to it" (1 Cor. 13:5 AMPC). When you choose to overlook an offense, it will be to your glory and the glory of the Bridegroom you were created to reflect (Prov. 19:11 NIV). A wife will honor and respect the husband who responds to her in this way, guaranteed!

The message of submitting to one another, loving others as we love ourselves, and seeking to understand one another's hearts is not just for our marriages. We can apply this message in all of our relationships, even in our congregations and the greater body of Messiah. Just as the unity of a nation brought YHVH's glory back to the land, unity in our marriages will bring His glory back to our families. Unity among the body of Messiah will bring back YHVH's glory to our congregations and the greater body as a whole, which will ultimately bring His glory to the whole world (John 17).

All of these lessons are ones that my husband and I have had to learn over the course of our marriage because neither of us had a godly example of marriage to follow. During the first decade of our marriage, we both played either Michal's or David's role, following after the dysfunctional family model we saw in our previous generations. The spiritual warfare of rejection, pride, unforgiveness, bitterness, jealousy, and resentment nearly separated our family. Thankfully, YHVH came to our help through a pastoral couple. They had the patience, compassion, understanding, experience, and spiritual discernment to help my husband and I walk out deliverance from the generational patterns that had us bound. Since we started putting into practice the principles I've shared in this chapter and throughout this book, our marriage and family have done a complete one-eighty. We are walking in beautiful unity, returning the glory of YHVH that has been missing for generations.

Sadly, this chapter that began with kingdom unity and resulted in the return of YHVH's glory, ended with division of relationship. Spiritual warfare always seeks to destroy unity in an attempt to destroy YHVH's glory. We must know and fully understand that this is *ha-Satan's* scheme and stand firm against it. We must steadfastly maintain unity through brotherly love, compassion, mercy, and pardon (Luke 6:36-38) to give YHVH glory. "United we stand, divided we fall."[14] Are we ready to stand firm in unity, my brothers and sisters, and see His glory return to Jerusalem?

"And the seventh angel sounded; and there were great voices in heaven, saying, The kingdoms of this world are become the kingdoms of our Lord, and of his Christ; and he shall reign for ever and ever. And the four and twenty elders,

which sat before God on their seats, fell upon their faces, and worshipped God, Saying, We give thee thanks, O LORD God Almighty, which art, and wast, and art to come; because thou hast taken to thee thy great power, and hast reigned. And the nations were angry, and thy wrath is come, and the time of the dead, that they should be judged, and that thou shouldest give reward unto thy servants the prophets, and to the saints, and them that fear thy name, small and great; and shouldest destroy them which destroy the earth. And the temple of God was opened in heaven, and there was seen in his temple the ark of his testament: and there were lightnings, and voices, and thunderings, and an earthquake, and great hail." (Rev. 11:15-19)

JOURNEY JOURNAL

1. Do you personally identify with any of David's characteristics or experiences? If so, which one(s)?

2. Do you personally identify with any of Michal's characteristics or experiences? If so, which one(s)?

3. Do you always test the counsel you receive against the Word of YHVH? Do you inquire of YHVH and His Word before every decision? Why or why not?

4. How have you been doing in your interpersonal relationships, especially in marriage, with fulfilling the Scriptural principles presented in this chapter?

5. Did you experience any personal conviction as you read this chapter and answered the questions presented? What were you convicted about? (Conviction is meant to lead us to prayers of repentance, wherein we receive YHVH's grace, mercy, and forgiveness.)

6. How has this chapter's study encouraged you to greater love for YHVH and your neighbor?

CONCLUSION

Welcome to midway camp on the Emmaus road journey through the annals of David's life. We have just traveled a long way from the sheepfolds of Jesse to the battlefields of Israel, from King Saul's palace to Philistine territory. We have trekked through miles of wandering wilderness peaks and valleys, back into Philistine territory again, and from Hebron to Jerusalem. This first leg of our journey took us from David's anointing to his crowning as king of Israel, culminating in the return of the Ark of the Covenant. The life lessons we have learned along the way have been abundant and rich. We learned how the key of David, spoken of by Isaiah the prophet (Isa. 22:22) and Messiah *Yeshua* (Rev. 3:7), is divinely-sourced, Spirit-empowered love for YHVH and our neighbor.

We are only halfway to the end of our journey and have a long and treacherous mountain trek ahead. So, we will camp out, catch our breath, and let the revelations we have garnered thus far sink deep into our hearts before moving on to Volume Two of David's saga. Hopefully, the beautiful views we soaked in along the trail are fresh in our minds, and we did plenty of memorable journey journaling along the way. I find there is nothing better to do at midway camp than to share my favorite memories of the journey so far. So, let us grab a cup of hot cocoa, cozy up in front of the fire, and recap our most memorable journey highlights.

When we first met David, he was just a young, faith-filled shepherd. He was a young man of no reputation, disregarded by his own family as no one extraordinary. However, in YHVH's eyes,

David was a superstar in the making because he took joy in knowing YHVH in a very personal and praise-filled relationship. David had a real heart of love and tenderness for his father's sheep, a love that made him willing to lay his life on the line for them.

His shepherd's heart was modeled after the heart of the Good Shepherd (*Yeshua*). Because of this, David was chosen and anointed with the *Ruach ha-Kodesh* to become the most notable priestly king of Israel. In YHVH's eyes, every faith-filled person— no matter their station in life or the opinion of others—has the same superstar potential to become a chosen and anointed leader in His kingdom. Such an individual must take joy in their personal relationship with YHVH, as well as learn and obey His instructions out of love and honor for Him as Father. Most importantly, they must love His sheep, just as David did.

Following David's anointing with the *Ruach ha-Kodesh*, we saw him face the most epic battle of his life, the one he is most celebrated for. Declining the protection of the physical armor of the world, David sported the spiritual armor of YHVH in his fight against Goliath. Because David's identity and security were one hundred percent rooted in YHVH, and were not codependent on his family identity or other people's assessments of him, David was victorious over his adversary. David also led others to rise up into their victorious warrior identities. We will likewise have victory over our adversary, *ha-Satan,* and lead others to do so when our identity and security rests solely in being beloved children of YHVH. The atoning sacrifice of *Yeshua*, the stone which the builders rejected, provides both our victory over the enemy and our identity as YHVH's beloved children.

After conquering Goliath, David entered into a multi-faceted covenant relationship with the son of the king of Israel. Jonathan loved David more than a brother. He stripped himself of his royal robes and garments of warfare and gave them to David. The two men exchanged the promise of protection and blessing over one another and their future generations. Their covenant relationship withstood the temptation of the evil one to betray the covenant and it remained an everlasting covenant. *Ha-Satan* could not destroy David no matter how hard he tried.

Likewise, every believer who has experienced eternal exile (through the law of sin and death) has also entered into a multi-faceted covenant relationship with the Son of the King of the Universe (*Yeshua*). Such a relationship is designed to withstand every temptation by the evil one to betray the covenant, and it remains an everlasting covenant. Additionally, because of our position in this relationship, we have been gifted *Yeshua's* royal robe of righteousness and spiritual garments of warfare. Through these gifts, no weapon formed by the enemy shall prosper!

Despite David's covenant relationship with Jonathan, David found himself exiled from Saul's kingdom under threat of death. David's first thought was to seek refuge only in YHVH's presence, in the tabernacle at Nob. At Nob, David was provisioned by the high priest with the consecrated bread of the presence and the most renowned sword in the land. Such provisions sustained David through the uncharted wilderness journey ahead. Although, this did not prevent David from succumbing to spiritual weaknesses (such as anxiety, fear, and possibly pride), which led him to a momentary diversion into enemy territory. YHVH still protected David through those weaknesses, and ultimately led him out of his mistakes, maturing David in the process.

Likewise, because of our covenant relationship with *Yeshua*, we may find ourselves exiled from the world system under threat of death. However, as long as we seek refuge in the presence of YHVH, we too will be provisioned by the High Priest *Yeshua.* He gives us the bread of His presence and sword of His Spirit to sustain and protect us as we continue our journey. YHVH even turns our weaknesses and mistakes into something good and useful in His purposes for us. It is the process by which we mature.

YHVH's mercy in David's distress led him out of enemy territory and into the refuge of YHVH's judgment at the cave of Adullam. The cave overlooked the valley of Elah, the place of David's awe-inspiring victory over Goliath. As David was experiencing a refreshing of his faith, security, and identity in YHVH, the entirety of his father's house came out to minister to him. They were followed by all the distressed, indebted, and discontented individuals of Israel, who rallied around David, and submitted themselves to his leadership. In the dry desert hills and valleys of the Judean wilderness, YHVH provided David with a prophet, a priest, and an army in preparation for his future kingdom rule.

Likewise, as we seek refuge in our Father's judgment, in who we are in Him, He will bring those who are of His house to minister to us. He will also draw those who are distressed, indebted, and discontented to rally around us; YHVH will use us to lead them into fuller understanding and relationship with Him and His Messiah. YHVH will also provide us with all that we need to be successful in the kingdom work He has called us to.

As David and his entourage traversed the Judean wilderness, Saul relentlessly hunted them. David continually inquired of YHVH and remained submitted to the *Ruach ha-Kodesh's* leading in every decision. Because David faithfully moved in the Spirit, YHVH faithfully covered and protected David and his servants from all of Saul's advances. YHVH even created timely divine diversions to distract Saul away from David and his men. David learned that, as long as he took refuge in YHVH's shelter, YHVH would protect him by creating a separation between him and his enemy.

Most importantly, David learned that YHVH did not lead Saul into his presence so that David could take advantage of the opportunity to destroy him; instead, it became an opportunity for David to take on a yoke of humility before his enemy. In humility, David sought peace and reconciliation in his relationship with Saul rather than justice and restitution for himself. In so doing, David learned that his act of kindness led his enemy to repentance. However, it was not a sincere and lasting repentance the first time around. In the same way, we will see YHVH's protection and covering over us as we remain fully submitted to the *Ruach ha-Kodesh*. We may also see our enemy brought to repentance when we display humility and kindness toward them.

After David learned these valuable lessons with Saul, he was tested by a whole new "enemy" who was carrying the same "evil" spirit as Saul—Nabal. Such testing was meant to ascertain how well David would apply the lessons he had learned in every aspect of his life. David nearly ended up with a failing grade due to his knee-jerk emotional response to Nabal's actions. However, YHVH's Spirit of wisdom came to the rescue through Abigail, a woman of outstanding inner and outer beauty and wisdom; she was willing to lay her life down as a ransom for her undeserving and foolish husband, Nabal. Her righteous actions led David to remember that he was a man after YHVH's own heart.

After David repented and released judgment of Nabal to YHVH alone, YHVH tested him once again through his archenemy, Saul. Saul betrayed his covenant of peace with David and resumed his relentless hunt to destroy him. David overcame all temptation to arouse his emotional defense system. He displayed the first fruit of humility, which led Saul to genuinely repent for his actions. This time, David passed his test with flying colors. David had managed to submit himself to the beautification and adornment process of the bride of Messiah. Through this process, the *Ruach ha-Kodesh* conformed David so that he could show forth the glory of the Bridegroom. Likewise, YHVH continually tests us to ascertain how well we will resist emotional offense and display kindness and humility to our offenders. We must submit ourselves to the beautification and adornment process as the *Ruach ha-Kodesh* conforms us into *Yeshua's* glorious image.

After his honorable examples of humble submission toward Saul and Nabal, David was a beautiful reflection of the Good Shepherd. However, he was far from perfect. He still had weaknesses and imperfections (spots and wrinkles) that needed to be ironed out. Despite all the glorious manifestations of YHVH's protection, an irrational thought arose within David's heart. He feared that Saul would continue to pursue him and eventually destroy him. David allowed this fear to drive him into the throngs of enemy territory—the land of the Philistines.

In the midst of David's weakness, YHVH gave him intense favor. David lived out his faith and integrity in such a way that a pagan enemy ruler, King Achish, declared, "YHVH lives."Although there was blessing and favor, YHVH did allow David and his men to experience tremendous loss and defeat while camped out in the enemy's territory. And yet they also experienced YHVH's awesome power and might in a victorious battle; everything they lost and more was restored to David, his men, and their Israelite brothers. After that victory, David and his men would no longer be a slave to fear. We can take heart that YHVH can do the same for us. He can turn our weaknesses, imperfections, and mistaken steps into blessings for us and for our brothers and sisters in Messiah. May He likewise deliver us from being slaves to the spirit of fear!

After what must have seemed like an eternal wait, YHVH brought judgment upon Saul through the hands of the Philistines. Although Saul's judgment was just and long overdue, David refused to rejoice at his destruction. David honored and memorialized what was virtuous and praiseworthy in Saul through the "Song of the Bow." He commanded all the men of Israel to recite this song with him in honor of Saul and Jonathan's memory.

David's response to Saul's judgment and death proved that he was a living testimony to the meaning of his name—love. David successfully displayed love for both YHVH and his neighbor (Saul). He showed love for an enemy who had acted out of jealousy and selfish ambition. Saul had taken away everything that was dear in David's life, except for his relationship with YHVH. Even more, Saul never restored what he had taken from David. The love that David displayed toward such an enemy had to have come from his spirit man.

David's spirit man was empowered to overcome his flesh man by the *Ruach ha-Kodesh*. The flesh man naturally desires justice and restitution or vengeance. Like David, we all have access to the same power of the *Ruach ha-Kodesh* to overcome our flesh man. Through Him, we are equipped to be a living testimony of what it means to love YHVH and our neighbors—even when our neighbors are our worst enemies.

Upon completing the time of mourning for Saul and Jonathan's deaths, David did not assume YHVH's promise to him would be immediately fulfilled. Rather, David asked YHVH to direct every step into his anointing as king. David obediently went to Hebron and humbly lived out his life among his people. David waited for the people to recognize his anointing and appoint him as their king.

Even after the tribe of Judah crowned David as their king, David continued to honor his covenants of peace with Saul and Jonathan by showing kindness and favor to the house of Saul. Even so, those remaining of Saul's house (Abner and Ish-bosheth) waged a brutal civil war against David for seven and a half years, resulting in many deaths in Israel. David remained submitted to the

Ruach ha-Kodesh, and faithfully sought to honor his covenant with Saul's house. As a result, all of Israel finally desired to make David their king as well. A similar parallel can be drawn for those who are disciples of *Yeshua*. As we seek to honor and show kindness to the house of YHVH's chosen people, all of Israel and Judah will desire to make the Son of David, *Yeshua*, their King as well.

After nearly fifteen years of waiting, and seven and a half years of brutal division and civil war, David finally entered into the fullness of his anointing. A reunited Israel entered into a covenant with David and anointed him as their king. With Israel's army backing him, David overthrew the Jebusite stronghold and moved his capital to Jerusalem. The neighboring king of Tyre built David a brand-new palace at his own expense.

At this point, we began to see that David lacked a thorough knowledge of the Word of YHVH because the religious establishment of his day had failed to teach it. Despite his lack of knowledge in the Word, David continually inquired and submitted to the counsel of the *Ruach ha-Kodesh* in battle. As a result, David continued to overcome all attempts of the enemy to destroy him and divide his kingdom. In the same way, in our modern age, we are beginning to see that many disciples of *Yeshua* lack a thorough knowledge of the Word of YHVH. This tragedy is due to failure on the part of our religious establishment to teach the whole counsel of YHVH. Therefore, it is crucial for each disciple of *Yeshua* to continually inquire and submit to the counsel of the *Ruach ha-Kodesh*. As we do, we will likewise overcome all attempts of the enemy to destroy us and divide *Yeshua's* Kingdom.

Once David had been established as king over all Israel, he sought to restore YHVH's glory to the land by bringing the Ark of the Covenant to Jerusalem. Unfortunately, David lacked knowledge of the Torah and failed to test the counsel of the people against YHVH's Word. This led to the mishandling of the Ark of the Covenant and a man died as a result. The incident made room for fear, anger, and false judgment against YHVH to enter David's heart.

After taking the time to consult and obey the Torah, David brought the Ark into Jerusalem with glorious celebration and dancing. YHVH's glory was restored to the land of Israel after an absence of two decades. Unfortunately, the glorious celebration was cut short as unresolved emotional conflict arose within David and Michal's marriage. The conflict was handled in the flesh and ended tragically in the permanent separation of their relationship. In this moment, David may have missed an opportunity to live out YHVH's image of love for His bride.

One day, perhaps when all the disciples of *Yeshua* consult and obey YHVH's Torah, we will see YHVH's glory returned to Jerusalem with much joy and glorious celebration. We must do our part to keep His glory evident in our world by making a concerted effort to promptly resolve our conflicts with one another. We must be led by the *Ruach ha-Kodesh* and according to the instructions in YHVH's Word, instead of being led by our flesh and unhealthy negative emotional reactions. Such unhealthy reactions create division in our relationships and dampen the light of YHVH's glory in our lives.

When we maintain brotherly love and unity in our relationships, our behavior points directly to the key of David. The key is love. We must love YHVH with all our heart, mind, soul, and strength by being diligent to obey His instructions for life. We must also love our neighbor as we love ourselves by refusing to take up offense and being quick to forgive our fellow man. Through David's journey to the throne in Jerusalem, we have seen that the greatest two commandments of love are the ultimate instructions for life. Love will lead us into greater glory in the Kingdom of YHVH. And we will continue to see how love leads to glory throughout the rest of David's saga as we move into Volume Two. Until next time…

> *"Jesus said unto him, Thou shalt love the Lord thy God with all thy heart, and with all thy soul, and with all thy mind. This is the first and great commandment. And the second is like unto it, Thou shalt love thy neighbour as thyself. On these two commandments hang all the law and the prophets." (Matt. 22:37-40)*

JOURNEY JOURNAL
CONCLUDING INSIGHTS

1. How has your own life journey mirrored David's so far? In what ways has it differed?

2. What have you learned from the other biblical figures and stories that shaped David's world?

3. What are the most valuable lessons you have taken away from the first volume of this study?

4. What practical and/or spiritual changes has the *Ruach ha-Kodesh* prompted you to make in your walk with YHVH and with your neighbor as a result of this study?

5. How has the first volume of this study deepened your understanding of what is happening behind the scenes in the spiritual realm in your relationships? How has this encouraged you to overcome the enemy's schemes to divide and conquer our unity in the body of Messiah?

6. How has the first volume of this study given you a deeper revelation and intimate knowledge of who *Yeshua* is in your life?

BIBLIOGRAPHY

Introduction

1. Parsons, J. J. *The Hebrew Name For God-YHVH*. Hebrew for Christians. Retrieved from http://www.hebrew4christians.com/Names_of_G-d/YHVH/yhvh.html

2. Isaiah 42:1. (2001, 2003, 2005, 2006, 2011). In *Pulpit Commentary for Isaiah 42:1*. Biblesoft, Inc. Biblehub.com. Retrieved from http://biblehub.com/isaiah/42-1.htm
   Gill, J. (1746-63). In *Gill's Exposition of the Entire Bible for Isaiah 42:1*. Internet Sacred Texts Archive. Biblehub.com. Retrieved from http://biblehub.com/isaiah/42-1.htm

3. The Rock. *Solid Life "Whole Bible" Reading Plan*. (Primarily read in Tree of Life Version) YouVersion Bible App. Retrieved from https://www.bible.com/reading-plans/214-solid-life

4. The Blue Letter Bible *"Chronological" Plan*. (Primarily read in King James Version) YouVersion Bible App. Retrieved from https://www.bible.com/reading-plans/5#!

5. Tyrrell, M. S. *Wholetones: The Healing Music Frequency Project*. Wholetones. Retrieved from www.wholetones.com

6. Howgego, J. (July 15, 2013). *Sound waves Levitate and Move Objects*. Scientific American. Retrieved from https://www.scientificamerican.com/article/sounds-waves-levitate-and-move-objects/
   Bland, E. (April 6, 2010). *'Sound Bullets' Blast Cancer*. ABC Science. Retrieved from http://www.abc.net.au/science/articles/2010/04/06/2865165.htm

7. Wikipedia contributors. (2018, May 27). Satan. In *Wikipedia, The Free Encyclopedia*. Retrieved 15:34, May 30, 2018, from https://en.wikipedia.org/w/index.php?title=Satan&oldid=843230999

8. Parsons, J. J. *Hebrew Name For God – The Holy Spirit*. Hebrew for Christians. Retrieved from http://www.hebrew4christians.com/Names_of_G-d/ Holy_Spirit/holy_spirit.html

Chapter 1

1. Malick, D. (June 17, 2004). *An Introduction to the Book of 2 Samuel*. Bible.org. Retrieved from https://bible.org/article/introduction-book-second-samuel

   Malick, D. (June 14, 2004) *An Introduction to First and Second Chronicles*. Bible.org. Retrieved from https://bible.org/article/introduction-first-and-second-chronicles

2. Parsons, J. J. *The Hebrew Name For God-Elohim*. Hebrew for Christians. Retrieved from http://www.hebrew4christians.com/Names_of_G-d/Elohim/ elohim.html

3. Hirsch, E. G., Schechter, S., & Seligsohn, M. (2002-2011). *Haman the Agagite*. Jewish Encyclopedia.com. Retrieved from http:// jewishencyclopedia.com/articles/7124-haman-the-agagite

4. *ibid*

5. Wikipedia contributors. (2018, May 16). Edom. In *Wikipedia, The Free Encyclopedia*. Retrieved 18:56, May 21, 2018, from https:// en.wikipedia.org/w/index.php?title=Edom&oldid=841507251

6. Dawn, A. (2017). *My Testimony*. Passion For Yeshua. Retrieved from https://passionforyeshua.wordpress.com/my-testimony/

7. Brown, F., Driver, S. R., & Briggs, C. A. (2002, 2003, 2006). Strong's H7451. In *Brown-Driver-Briggs Hebrew and English Lexicon*. Biblesoft, Inc. Biblehub.com Retrieved from http://biblehub.com/hebrew/7451.htm

   Strong, J. (1890, 1986). Strong's H7451. In *Strong's Exhaustive Concordance*. Abingdon Press. Biblehub.com. Retrieved from http://biblehub.com/ hebrew/7451.htm

8. Inductive Bible Study. *1 Samuel*. Indubiblia.org. Retrieved from
https://sites.google.com/a/indubiblia.org/inductive-bible-study/1-
samuel-1
Chronology of David's Psalms. Retrieved from https://docs.google.com/document/
d/1ytq4O-8AsXgXBiqkuln6EtggED6YiTx75GEljT5xbnc/edit#!

9. Watchman Bible Study. (2005-2018). *Biblical Astronomy: The Hebrew Mazzaroth*.
Watchmanbiblestudy.com. Retrieved from http://
www.watchmanbiblestudy.com/BibleStudies/BiblicalAstronomy.html

Chapter 2

1. Brown, F., Driver, S. R., & Briggs, C. A. (2002, 2003, 2006). Strong's H658. In
Brown-Driver-Briggs Hebrew and English Lexicon. Biblesoft, Inc.
Biblehub.com Retrieved from http://biblehub.com/hebrew/658.htm
Strong, J. (1890, 1986). Strong's H658. In *Strong's Exhaustive Concordance*.
Abingdon Press. Biblehub.com Retrieved from http://biblehub.com/
hebrew/658.htm

2. Strong, J. (1890, 1986). Strong's H7754. In *Strong's Exhaustive Concordance*.
Abingdon Press. Biblehub.com. Retrieved from http://biblehub.com/
strongs/hebrew/7754.htm

3. Brown, F., Driver, S. R., & Briggs, C. A (2002, 2003, 2006). Strong's H5825 and
H5823. In *Brown-Driver-Briggs Hebrew and English Lexicon*. Biblesoft, Inc.
Biblehub.com Retrieved from http://biblehub.com/hebrew/5825.htm
Strong, J. (1890, 1986). Strong's H5825 and H5823. In *Strong's Exhaustive
Concordance*. Abingdon Press. Biblehub.com. Retrieved from http://
biblehub.com/hebrew/5825.htm

4. Strong, J. (1890). Strong's H425. In *Strong's Concordance*. Biblehub.com. Retrieved
from http://biblehub.com/hebrew/425.htm
Strong's H425. (1997). In *NAS Exhaustive Concordance*. Foundation Publications
Inc. Biblehub.com. Retrieved from http://biblehub.com/hebrew/
425.htm

5. Orr, J. (1939). *Terebinth*. In *International Standard Bible Encyclopedia*. Wm. B.
Eerdman's Publishing Co. Biblehub.com. Retrieved from http://
biblehub.com/topical/t/terebinth.htm

6. The Bible Study Site. *The Meaning of Numbers in the Bible: The Number Forty.* Biblestudy.org. Retrieved from http://www.biblestudy.org/bibleref/meaning-of-numbers-in-bible/40.html

7. Strong, J. (1890, 1986). Strong's H1540. In *Strong's Concordance* and *Strong's Exhaustive Concordance.* Abingdon Press. Biblehub.com. Retrieved from http://biblehub.com/hebrew/1540.htm
   Strong's H1540. (1997). In *NAS Exhaustive Concordance.* Foundation Publications Inc. Biblehub.com. Retrieved from http://biblehub.com/hebrew/1540.htm
   Brown, F., Driver, S. R., & Briggs, C. A (2002, 2003, 2006). Strong's H1540. In *Brown-Driver-Briggs Hebrew and English Lexicon.* Biblesoft, Inc. Biblehub.com. Retrieved from http://biblehub.com/hebrew/1540.htm

8. Strong, J. (1890, 1986). Strong's H6138. In *Strong's Exhaustive Concordance.* Abingdon Press. Biblehub.com. Retrieved from http://biblehub.com/hebrew/6138.htm

9. Strong, J. (1890, 1986). Strong's H8189. In *Strong's Exhaustive Concordance.* Abingdon Press. Biblehub.com. Retrieved from http://biblehub.com/hebrew/8189.htm

10. Strong, J. (1890). Strong's H1661. In *Strong's Concordance.* Biblehub.com. Retrieved from http://biblehub.com/hebrew/1661.htm
    Strong's H1661. (1997). In *NAS Exhaustive Concordance.* Foundation Publication Inc. Biblehub.com. Retrieved from http://biblehub.com/hebrew/1661.htm

11. Inductive Bible Study. *1 Samuel.* Indubiblia.org. Retrieved from https://sites.google.com/a/indubiblia.org/inductive-bible-study/1-samuel-1
    Chronology of David's Psalms. Retrieved from https://docs.google.com/document/d/1ytq4O-8AsXgXBiqkuln6EtggED6YiTx75GEljT5xbnc/edit#!

Chapter 3

1. Strong, J. (1890). Strong's H3083. In *Strong's Concordance.* Biblehub.com. Retrieved from http://biblehub.com/hebrew/3083.htm

1. (con't) Strong's H3083. (1997). In *NAS Exhaustive Concordance* . Foundation
Publication Inc. Biblehub.com. Retrieved from http://biblehub.com/
hebrew/3083.htm

2. Brown, F., Driver, S. R., & Briggs, C. A (2002, 2003, 2006). Strong's H7451. In
Brown-Driver-Briggs Hebrew and English Lexicon. Biblesoft, Inc.
Biblehub.com. Retrieved from http://biblehub.com/hebrew/7451.htm
Strong, J. (1890, 1986). Strong's H7451. In *Strong's Exhaustive Concordance*.
Abingdon Press. Biblehub.com. Retrieved from http://biblehub.com/
hebrew/7451.htm

3. **Verses pertaining to Satan's fall:** Isaiah 14:12-15, Revelation 12:7-9,
Isaiah 14:12, Luke 10:18, Ezekiel 28:14, 1 Peter 5:8, Jude 1:6,
Ezekiel 28:15, Revelation 12:9, Genesis 3:1-24, Ezekiel 28:16,
Ezekiel 28:13, Hebrews 2:14, Matthew 4:3, Revelation 12:4,
1 Timothy 3:6, Job 1:6, Revelation 20:10

4. Brown, F., Driver, S. R., & Briggs, C. A (2002, 2003, 2006). Strong's H8655. In
Brown-Driver-Briggs Hebrew and English Lexicon. Biblesoft, Inc.
Biblehub.com. Retrieved from http://biblehub.com/hebrew/8655.htm
Prince, J. D., Bacher, W., Seligsohn, M., (2002-2011). *Teraphim*. Jewish
Encyclopedia.com. Retrieved from http://jewishencyclopedia.com/
article/14331-teraphim
Bible Hub. (2004-2018). *1 Samuel 19:13 Commentaries*. Biblesoft, Inc.
Biblehub.com. Retrieved from https://biblehub.com/commentaries/
1_samuel/19-13.htm

5. Gill, J. (1746-63). In *Gill's Exposition of the Entire Bible for 1 Samuel 19:13*. Internet
Sacred Texts Archive. Biblehub.com. Retrieved from https://
biblehub.com/commentaries/1_samuel/19-13.htm

6. Inductive Bible Study. *1 Samuel*. Indubiblia.org. Retrieved from
https://sites.google.com/a/indubiblia.org/inductive-bible-study/1-
samuel-1
Chronology of David's Psalms. Retrieved from https://docs.google.com/
document/d/1ytq4O-8AsXgXBiqkuln6EtggED6YiTx75GEljT5xbnc/
edit#!=

7. Brown, F., Driver, S. R., & Briggs, C. A (2002, 2003, 2006). Strong's H5116. In *Brown-Driver-Briggs Hebrew and English Lexicon*. Biblesoft, Inc. Biblehub.com. Retrieved from http://biblehub.com/hebrew/5116.htm
   Strong, J. (1890, 1986). Strong's H5116. In *Strong's Exhaustive Concordance*. Abingdon Press. Biblehub.com. Retrieved from http://biblehub.com/hebrew/5116.htm

8. Spurgeon, C. H. (1869-1885). *Psalm 91*. The Treasury of David. Biblestudytools.com. Retrieved from https://www.biblestudytools.com/commentaries/treasury-of-david/psalms-91-1.html
   Jamieson, R., Fausset, A. R., & Brown, D. (1871). In *Jamieson-Fausset-Brown Bible Commentary on Psalm 91*. Biblehub.com. Retrieved from http://biblehub.com/commentaries/psalms/91-1.htm

9. Popik, B. (Nov. 24, 2008). *Insanity is doing the same thing and expecting different results*. Barrypopik.com. Retrieved from https://www.barrypopik.com/index.php/new_york_city/entry/insanity_is_doing_the_same_thing_and_expecting_different_results/

10. Strong's G4728. (1987, 2011). In *HELPS Word-studies*. Helps Ministries, Inc. Biblehub.com. Retrieved from http://biblehub.com/greek/4728.htm

11. Strong, J. (1890, 1986). Strong's G2346. In *Strong's Concordance* and *Strong's Exhaustive Concordance*. Abingdon Press. Biblehub.com. Retrieved from http://biblehub.com/greek/2346.htm
   Strong's G2346. (1987, 2011). In *HELPS Word-studies*. Helps Ministries, Inc. Biblehub.com. Retrieved from http://biblehub.com/greek/2346.htm
   Strong's G2346. (1997). In *NAS Exhaustive Concordance*. Foundation Publications Inc. Biblehub.com. Retrieved from http://biblehub.com/greek/2346.htm
   Strong's G2346. (2002, 2003, 2006, 2011). In *Thayer's Greek Lexicon*. Biblesoft, Inc. Biblehub.com. Retrieved from http://biblehub.com/greek/2346.htm

12. Strong, J. (1890, 1986). Strong's H237 In *Strong's Concordance* and *Strong's Exhaustive Concordance*. Abingdon Press. Biblehub.com. Retrieved from http://biblehub.com/hebrew/237.htm

13. 1 Sam. 20:5-7. (2001, 2003, 2005, 2006, 2011). In *Pulpit Commentary for 1 Samuel 20:5-7*. Biblesoft, Inc. Biblehub.com. Retrieved from http://biblehub.com/1_samuel/20-5.htm

14. Gordon, N. *New Moon*. Karaite-Korner.org. Retrieved from http://www.karaite-korner.org/new_moon.shtml

15. **Verses pertaining to unity**: Philippians 2:2, 1 Peter 3:8, 1 Corinthians 1:10, Colossians 3:14, 2 Corinthians 13:11, Ephesians 4:1-6, Romans 15:6, Romans 12:4-5, Ephesians 4:3, Psalms 133:1, Romans 12:16, Romans 15:5, Romans 14:19, Acts 4:32, John 17:11-23

16. Inductive Bible Study. *1 Samuel*. Indubiblia.org. Retrieved from https://sites.google.com/a/indubiblia.org/inductive-bible-study/1-samuel-1
    Chronology of David's Psalms. Retrieved from https://docs.google.com/document/d/1ytq4O-8AsXgXBiqkuln6EtggED6YiTx75GEljT5xbnc/edit#!

Chapter 4

1. Wikipedia contributors. (2018, April 18). Tabernacle. In *Wikipedia, The Free Encyclopedia*. Retrieved 12:48, May 23, 2018, from https://en.wikipedia.org/w/index.php?title=Tabernacle&oldid=837074669

2. Brown, F., Driver, S. R., & Briggs, C. A (2002, 2003, 2006). Strong's H5011. In *Brown-Driver-Briggs Hebrew and English Lexicon*. Biblesoft, Inc. Biblehub.com. Retrieved from http://biblehub.com/hebrew/5011.htm

3. Strong, J. (1890). Strong's H5108. In *Strong's Concordance*. Biblehub.com. Retrieved from http://biblehub.com/hebrew/5108.htm
    Strong's H5108 (1997). In *NAS Exhaustive Concordance*. Foundation Publications Inc. Biblehub.com. Retrieved from http://biblehub.com/hebrew/5108.htm
    Brown, F., Driver, S. R., & Briggs, C. A (2002, 2003, 2006). Strong's H5108. In *Brown-Driver-Briggs Hebrew and English Lexicon*. Biblesoft, Inc. Biblehub.com. Retrieved from http://biblehub.com/hebrew/5108.htm

4. Strong, J. (1890, 1986). Strong's H5110. In *Strong's Concordance* and *Strong's Exhaustive Concordance*. Abingdon Press. Biblehub.com. Retrieved from http://biblehub.com/hebrew/5010.htm

Strong's H5110 (1997). In *NAS Exhaustive Concordance*. Foundation Publications Inc. Biblehub.com. Retrieved from http://biblehub.com/hebrew/5010.htm

Brown, F., Driver, S. R., & Briggs, C. A (2002, 2003, 2006). Strong's H5110. In *Brown-Driver-Briggs Hebrew and English Lexicon*. Biblesoft, Inc. Biblehub.com. Retrieved from http://biblehub.com/hebrew/5010.htm

5. Strong's H1672. (1997). In *NAS Exhaustive Concordance*. Foundation Publications Inc. Biblehub.com. Retrieved from http://biblehub.com/hebrew/1672.htm

6. Spurgeon, C. H. (1869-1885). *Psalm 27*. The Treasury of David. Biblestudytools.com. Retrieved from https://www.biblestudytools.com/commentaries/treasury-of-david/psalms-27-1.html

Chapter 5

1. *Adullam*. Biblewalks.com. Retrieved from https://biblewalks.com/Sites/Adullam.html

2. Brown, F., Driver, S. R., & Briggs, C. A (2002, 2003, 2006). Strong's H4631. In *Brown-Driver-Briggs Hebrew and English Lexicon*. Biblesoft, Inc. Biblehub.com. Retrieved from http://biblehub.com/hebrew/4631.htm

3. Brown, F., Driver, S. R., & Briggs, C. A (2002, 2003, 2006). Strong's H5783. In *Brown-Driver-Briggs Hebrew and English Lexicon*. Biblesoft, Inc. Biblehub.com. Retrieved from http://biblehub.com/hebrew/5783.htm

Strong, J. (1890, 1986). Strong's H5783 In *Strong's Concordance* and *Strong's Exhaustive Concordance*. Abingdon Press. Biblehub.com. Retrieved from http://biblehub.com/hebrew/5783.htm

4. Strong, J. (1890). Strong's H5724. In *Strong's Concordance*. Biblehub.com. Retrieved from http://biblehub.com/hebrew/5724.htm

Brown, F., Driver, S. R., & Briggs, C. A (2002, 2003, 2006). Strong's H5724. In *Brown-Driver-Briggs Hebrew and English Lexicon*. Biblesoft, Inc. Biblehub.com. Retrieved from http://biblehub.com/hebrew/5724.htm

5. Strong, J. (1890, 1986). Strong's H8199. In *Strong's Concordance* and *Strong's Exhaustive Concordance.* Abingdon Press. Biblehub.com. Retrieved from http://biblehub.com/hebrew/8199.htm

Strong's H8199. (1997). In *NAS Exhaustive Concordance.* Foundation Publications Inc. Biblehub.com. Retrieved from http://biblehub.com/hebrew/8199.htm

Brown, F., Driver, S. R., & Briggs, C. A (2002, 2003, 2006). Strong's H8199. In *Brown-Driver-Briggs Hebrew and English Lexicon.* Biblesoft, Inc. Biblehub.com. Retrieved from http://biblehub.com/hebrew/8199.htm

6. Inductive Bible Study. *1 Samuel.* Indubiblia.org. Retrieved from https://sites.google.com/a/indubiblia.org/inductive-bible-study/1-samuel-1

Chronology of David's Psalms. Retrieved from https://docs.google.com/document/d/1ytq4O-8AsXgXBiqkuln6EtggED6YiTx75GEljT5xbnc/edit#!

7. Strong's G3875. (1987, 2011). In *HELPS Word-studies.* Helps Ministries, Inc. Biblehub.com. Retrieved from http://biblehub.com/greek/3875.htm

8. Sell, H. T. (1904). *Bible Studies in the life of Paul - Second Missionary Journey.* Fleming H. Revell Company. Biblehub.com. Retrieved from http://Biblehub.com/library/sell/Bible_studies_in_the_life_of_paul/study_iv_second_missionary_journey.htm

9. Dawn. A. (2017). *Love Covers All Transgressions.* Passion For Yeshua YouTube. Retrieved from https://youtu.be/MdQPKjum1OQ

10. Strong, J. (1890, 1986). Strong's H4689. In *Strong's Exhaustive Concordance.* Abingdon Press. Biblehub.com. Retrieved from http://biblehub.com/hebrew/4689.htm

11. Strong, J. (1890, 1986). Strong's H5378. In *Strong's Exhaustive Concordance.* Abingdon Press. Biblehub.com. Retrieved from http://biblehub.com/hebrew/5378.htm

Strong's H5378. (1997). In *NAS Exhaustive Concordance.* Foundation Publications Inc. Biblehub.com. Retrieved from http://biblehub.com/hebrew/5378.htm

11. (con't) Brown, F., Driver, S. R., & Briggs, C. A (2002, 2003, 2006). Strong's H5378. In *Brown-Driver-Briggs Hebrew and English Lexicon*. Biblesoft, Inc. Biblehub.com. Retrieved from http://biblehub.com/hebrew/5378.htm

12. Strong, J. (1890, 1986). Strong's H4751. In *Strong's Exhaustive Concordance*. Abingdon Press. Biblehub.com. Retrieved from http://biblehub.com/hebrew/4751.htm

    Strong's H4751. (1997). In *NAS Exhaustive Concordance*. Foundation Publications Inc. Biblehub.com. Retrieved from http://biblehub.com/hebrew/4751.htm

    Brown, F., Driver, S. R., & Briggs, C. A (2002, 2003, 2006). Strong's H4751. In *Brown-Driver-Briggs Hebrew and English Lexicon*. Biblesoft, Inc. Biblehub.com. Retrieved from http://biblehub.com/hebrew/4751.htm

13. Strong, J. (1890, 1986). Strong's H4707-4708 In *Strong's Concordance* and *Strong's Exhaustive Concordance*. Abingdon Press. Biblehub.com. Retrieved from http://biblehub.com/hebrew/4707.htm and http://biblehub.com/hebrew/4708.htm

    Strong's H4707-4708. (1997). In *NAS Exhaustive Concordance*. Foundation Publications Inc. Biblehub.com. Retrieved from http://biblehub.com/hebrew/4707.htm and http://biblehub.com/hebrew/4708.htm

    Brown, F., Driver, S. R., & Briggs, C. A (2002, 2003, 2006). Strong's H4707-4708. In *Brown-Driver-Briggs Hebrew and English Lexicon*. Biblesoft, Inc. Biblehub.com. Retrieved from http://biblehub.com/hebrew/4707.htm and http://biblehub.com/hebrew/4708.htm

14. Brown, F., Driver, S. R., & Briggs, C. A (2002, 2003, 2006). Strong's H4686. In *Brown-Driver-Briggs Hebrew and English Lexicon*. Biblesoft, Inc. Biblehub.com. Retrieved from http://biblehub.com/hebrew/4686.htm

    Strong, J. (1890, 1986). Strong's H4686. In *Strong's Exhaustive Concordance*. Abingdon Press. Biblehub.com. Retrieved from http://biblehub.com/hebrew/4686.htm

15. Strong's H2801. (1997). In *NAS Exhaustive Concordance*. Foundation Publications Inc. Biblehub.com. Retrieved from http://biblehub.com/hebrew/2801.htm

    Brown, F., Driver, S. R., & Briggs, C. A (2002, 2003, 2006). Strong's H2801. In *Brown-Driver-Briggs Hebrew and English Lexicon*. Biblesoft, Inc. Biblehub.com. Retrieved from http://biblehub.com/hebrew/2801.htm

16. Strong, J. (1890). Strong's H2318. In *Strong's Concordance*. Biblehub.com. Retrieved from http://biblehub.com/hebrew/2318.htm

17. Strong's H1672(1997). In *NAS Exhaustive Concordance*. Foundation Publications Inc. Biblehub.com. Retrieved from http://biblehub.com/hebrew/1672.htm

18. Strong, J. (1890, 1986). Strong's H1121 & H1100. In *Strong's Concordance* and *Strong's Exhaustive Concordance*. Abingdon Press. Biblehub.com. Retrieved from http://biblehub.com/hebrew/1121.htm and http://biblehub.com/hebrew/1100.htm

19. Strong, J. (1890). Strong's H54. In *Strong's Concordance*. Biblehub.com. Retrieved from http://biblehub.com/hebrew/54.htm

Chapter 6

1. Strong, J. (1890). Strong's H7049. In *Strong's Concordance*. Biblehub.com. Retrieved from http://biblehub.com/hebrew/7049.htm
    Brown, F., Driver, S. R., & Briggs, C. A (2002, 2003, 2006). Strong's H7049. In *Brown-Driver-Briggs Hebrew and English Lexicon*. Biblesoft, Inc. Biblehub.com. Retrieved from http://biblehub.com/hebrew/7049.htm

2. Inductive Bible Study. *1 Samuel*. Indubiblia.org. Retrieved from https://sites.google.com/a/indubiblia.org/inductive-bible-study/1-samuel-1
    Chronology of David's Psalms. Retrieved from https://docs.google.com/document/d/1ytq4O-8AsXgXBiqkuln6EtggED6YiTx75GEljT5xbnc/edit#!

3. Strong, J. (1890, 1986). Strong's H2793. In *Strong's Concordance* and *Strong's Exhaustive Concordance*. Abingdon Press. Biblehub.com. Retrieved from http://biblehub.com/hebrew/2793.htm
    Brown, F., Driver, S. R., & Briggs, C. A (2002, 2003, 2006). Strong's H2793. In *Brown-Driver-Briggs Hebrew and English Lexicon*. Biblesoft, Inc. Biblehub.com. Retrieved from http://biblehub.com/hebrew/2793.htm

4. *Shroud*. (2018). Oxford Dictionaries. Oxford University Press. Oxforddictionaries.com. Retrieved from https://en.oxforddictionaries.com/definition/shroud

5. Inductive Bible Study. *1 Samuel.* Indubiblia.org. Retrieved from
   https://sites.google.com/a/indubiblia.org/inductive-bible-study/1-
   samuel-1
   Chronology of David's Psalms. Retrieved from https://docs.google.com/document/
   d/1ytq4O-8AsXgXBiqkuln6EtggED6YiTx75GEljT5xbnc/edit#!

6. Strong, J. (1890). Strong's H2444. In *Strong's Concordance.* Biblehub.com.
   Retrieved from http://biblehub.com/hebrew/2444.htm

7. Bible Atlas. *Hill of Hachilah.* (estimated mileage based on scale).
   Bibleatlas.org. Retrieved from http://bibleatlas.org/hachilah.htm

8. Strong, J. (1890, 1986). Strong's H4583-4584. In *Strong's Concordance* and *Strong's
   Exhaustive Concordance.* Abingdon Press. Biblehub.com. Retrieved from
   http://biblehub.com/hebrew/4583.htm and http://biblehub.com/
   hebrew/4584.htm

9. Wikipedia contributors. (2018, May 30). Psalm 91. In *Wikipedia, The Free
   Encyclopedia.* Retrieved 18:57, May 30, 2018, from https://
   en.wikipedia.org/w/index.php?title=Psalm_91&oldid=843671744
   Jamieson, R., Fausset, A. R., & Brown, D. (1871). In *Jamieson-Fausset-Brown Bible
   Commentary on Psalm 91.* Biblehub.com. Retrieved from http://
   biblehub.com/commentaries/psalms/91-1.htm

10. Strong's H5553. (1997). In *NAS Exhaustive Concordance.* Foundation
    Publications Inc. Biblehub.com. Retrieved from http://biblehub.com/
    hebrew/5553.htm
    Brown, F., Driver, S. R., & Briggs, C. A (2002, 2003, 2006). Strong's
    H5553. In *Brown-Driver-Briggs Hebrew and English Lexicon.* Biblesoft, Inc.
    Biblehub.com. Retrieved from http://biblehub.com/hebrew/5553.htm
    Strong, J. (1890, 1986). Strong's H5553. In *Strong's Exhaustive Concordance.*
    Abingdon Press. Biblehub.com. Retrieved from http://biblehub.com/
    hebrew/5553.htm

11. Strong, J. (1890, 1986). Strong's H5555. In *Strong's Exhaustive Concordance.*
    Abingdon Press. Biblehub.com. Retrieved from http://biblehub.com/
    hebrew/5555.htm

12. Strong, J. (1890). Strong's H5872. In *Strong's Concordance*. Biblehub.com. Retrieved from http://biblehub.com/hebrew/5872.htm
Strong's H5872. (1997). In *NAS Exhaustive Concordance*. Foundation Publications Inc. Biblehub.com. Retrieved from http://biblehub.com/hebrew/5872.htm

13. Parsons, J. J., *Ayin*. Hebrew for Christians. Retrieved from http://www.hebrew4christians.com/Grammar/Unit_One/Aleph-Bet/Ayin/ayin.html

14. Strong, J. (1890, 1986). Strong's H4256. In *Strong's Exhaustive Concordance*. Abingdon Press. Biblehub.com. Retrieved from http://biblehub.com/hebrew/4256.htm

15. Strong's H2505. In *Occurrences in text*. Biblehub.com. Retrieved from http://biblehub.com/hebrew/2505.htm

16. Dawn, A. (2017). *Love Covers All Transgressions*. Passion for Yeshua YouTube. Retrieved from https://youtu.be/MdQPKjum1OQ

17. Inductive Bible Study. *1 Samuel*. Indubiblia.org. Retrieved from https://sites.google.com/a/indubiblia.org/inductive-bible-study/1-samuel-1
Chronology of David's Psalms. Retrieved from https://docs.google.com/document/d/1ytq4O-8AsXgXBiqkuln6EtggED6YiTx75GEljT5xbnc/!

18. Strong's H3671. (1997). In *NAS Exhaustive Concordance*. (Occ. Num. 15:38 & Deut. 22:12). Foundation Publications Inc. Biblehub.com. Retrieved from http://biblehub.com/hebrew/strongs_3671.htm

19. Dawn, A. (2017). *Love Covers All Transgressions*. Passion for Yeshua YouTube. Retrieved from https://youtu.be/MdQPKjum1OQ

Chapter 7

1. Strong, J. (1890). Strong's H6286. In *Strong's Concordance*. Biblehub.com. Retrieved from http://biblehub.com/hebrew/6286.htm
Strong's H6286. (1997). In *NAS Exhaustive Concordance*. Foundation Publications Inc. Biblehub.com. Retrieved from http://biblehub.com/hebrew/6286.htm

2. Strong, J. (1890, 1986). Strong's H5036. In *Strong's Concordance* and *Strong's Exhaustive Concordance*. Abingdon Press. Biblehub.com. Retrieved from http://biblehub.com/hebrew/5036.htm

Strong's H5036. (1997). In *NAS Exhaustive Concordance*. Foundation Publications Inc. Biblehub.com. Retrieved from http://biblehub.com/hebrew/5036.htm

Brown, F., Driver, S. R., & Briggs, C. A (2002, 2003, 2006). Strong's H5036. In *Brown-Driver-Briggs Hebrew and English Lexicon*. Biblesoft, Inc. Biblehub.com. Retrieved from http://biblehub.com/hebrew/5036.htm

3. Strong, J. (1890, 1986). Strong's H7186. In *Strong's Concordance* and *Strong's Exhaustive Concordance*. Abingdon Press. Biblehub.com. Retrieved from http://biblehub.com/hebrew/7186.htm

Strong's H7186. (1997). In *NAS Exhaustive Concordance*. Foundation Publications Inc. Biblehub.com. Retrieved from http://biblehub.com/hebrew/7186.htm

Brown, F., Driver, S. R., & Briggs, C. A (2002, 2003, 2006). Strong's H7186. In *Brown-Driver-Briggs Hebrew and English Lexicon*. Biblesoft, Inc. Biblehub.com. Retrieved from http://biblehub.com/hebrew/7186.htm

4. Brown, F., Driver, S. R., & Briggs, C. A. (2002, 2003, 2006). Strong's H7451. In *Brown-Driver-Briggs Hebrew and English Lexicon*. Biblesoft, Inc. Biblehub.com Retrieved from http://biblehub.com/hebrew/7451.htm

Strong, J. (1890, 1986). Strong's H7451. In *Strong's Exhaustive Concordance*. Abingdon Press. Biblehub.com. Retrieved from http://biblehub.com/hebrew/7451.htm

5. Strong, J. (1890). Strong's H7922. In *Strong's Concordance*. Biblehub.com. Retrieved from http://biblehub.com/hebrew/7922.htm

Strong's H7922. (1997). In *NAS Exhaustive Concordance*. Foundation Publications Inc. Biblehub.com. Retrieved from http://biblehub.com/hebrew/7922.htm

6. Got Questions Ministries. (2002-2018). *What Does it Mean to Take the Lord's Name in Vain?* gotquestions.org. Retrieved from https://www.gotquestions.org/Lords-name-vain.html

7. Strong, J. (1890, 1986). Strong's H1121 and H1100. In *Strong's Concordance* and *Strong's Exhaustive Concordance*. Abingdon Press. Biblehub.com. Retrieved from http://biblehub.com/hebrew/1121.htm and http://biblehub.com/hebrew/1100.htm

8. Strong, J. (1890). Strong's H26. In *Strong's Concordance*. Biblehub.com. Retrieved from http://biblehub.com/hebrew/26.htm

Chapter 8

1. Strong, J. (1890). Strong's H1661. In *Strong's Concordance*. Biblehub.com. Retrieved from http://biblehub.com/hebrew/1661.htm

2. Strong, J. (1890, 1986). Strong's H4600. In *Strong's Concordance* and *Strong's Exhaustive Concordance*. Abingdon Press. Biblehub.com. Retrieved from http://biblehub.com/hebrew/4600.htm
   Strong's H4600. (1997). In *NAS Exhaustive Concordance*. Foundation Publications Inc. Biblehub.com. Retrieved from http://biblehub.com/hebrew/4600.htm
   Brown, F., Driver, S. R., & Briggs, C. A (2002, 2003, 2006). Strong's H4600. In *Brown-Driver-Briggs Hebrew and English Lexicon*. Biblesoft, Inc. Biblehub.com. Retrieved from http://biblehub.com/hebrew/4600.htm

3. Strong, J. (1890, 1986). Strong's H7766. In *Strong's Exhaustive Concordance*. (from root word). Abingdon Press. Biblehub.com. Retrieved from http://biblehub.com/hebrew/7766.htm

4. Strong, J. (1890, 1986). Strong's H1533. In *Strong's Exhaustive Concordance*. (from both root words). Abingdon Press. Biblehub.com. Retrieved from http://biblehub.com/hebrew/1533.htm

5. *Ebullition*. (2018). Oxford Dictionaries. Oxford University Press. Oxforddictionaries.com. Retrieved from https://en.oxforddictionaries.com/definition/ebullition

6. Strong's H5493. (1997). In *NAS Exhaustive Concordance*. Foundation Publications Inc. Biblehub.com. Retrieved from http://biblehub.com/hebrew/5493.htm

6. (con't) Strong, J. (1890, 1986). Strong's H5493. In *Strong's Exhaustive Concordance*. Abingdon Press. Biblehub.com. Retrieved from http://biblehub.com/hebrew/5493.htm

7. Strong, J. (1890, 1986). Strong's H5869. In *Strong's Concordance* and *Strong's Exhaustive Concordance*. Abingdon Press. Biblehub.com. Retrieved from http://biblehub.com/hebrew/5869.htm
   Strong's H5869. (1997). In *NAS Exhaustive Concordance*. Foundation Publications Inc. Biblehub.com. Retrieved from http://biblehub.com/hebrew/5869.htm
   Brown, F., Driver, S. R., & Briggs, C. A (2002, 2003, 2006). Strong's H5869. In *Brown-Driver-Briggs Hebrew and English Lexicon*. Biblesoft, Inc. Biblehub.com. Retrieved from http://biblehub.com/hebrew/5869.htm

8. Strong, J. (1890). Strong's H3157. In *Strong's Concordance*. Biblehub.com. Retrieved from http://biblehub.com/hebrew/3157.htm

9. Strong, J. (1890, 1986). Strong's H4397. In *Strong's Concordance* and *Strong's Exhaustive Concordance*. Abingdon Press. Biblehub.com. Retrieved from http://biblehub.com/hebrew/4397.htm
   Strong's H4397. (1997). In *NAS Exhaustive Concordance*. Foundation Publications Inc. Biblehub.com. Retrieved from http://biblehub.com/hebrew/4397.htm
   Brown, F., Driver, S. R., & Briggs, C. A (2002, 2003, 2006). Strong's H4397. In *Brown-Driver-Briggs Hebrew and English Lexicon*. Biblesoft, Inc. Biblehub.com. Retrieved from http://biblehub.com/hebrew/4397.htm

10. Inductive Bible Study. *1 Samuel*. Indubiblia.org. Retrieved from https://sites.google.com/a/indubiblia.org/inductive-bible-study/1-samuel-1
    Chronology of David's Psalms. Retrieved from https://docs.google.com/document/d/1ytq4O-8AsXgXBiqkuln6EtggED6YiTx75GEljT5xbnc/edit#!

11. Strong's H1319. (1997). In *NAS Exhaustive Concordance*. Foundation Publications Inc. Biblehub.com. Retrieved from http://biblehub.com/hebrew/1319.htm

12. Strong, J. (1890, 1986). Strong's H1121 and H1100. In *Strong's Concordance* and *Strong's Exhaustive Concordance*. Abingdon Press. Biblehub.com. Retrieved from http://biblehub.com/hebrew/1121.htm and http://biblehub.com/hebrew/1100.htm

13. Brown, F., Driver, S. R., & Briggs, C. A. (2002, 2003, 2006). Strong's H7451. In *Brown-Driver-Briggs Hebrew and English Lexicon*. Biblesoft, Inc. Biblehub.com Retrieved from http://biblehub.com/hebrew/7451.htm Strong, J. (1890, 1986). Strong's H7451. In *Strong's Exhaustive Concordance*. Abingdon Press. Biblehub.com. Retrieved from http://biblehub.com/hebrew/7451.htm

Chapter 9

1. Wikipedia contributors. (2017, September 4). Mills of God. (Longfellow, H.W. (1846). *Retribution.*) In *Wikipedia, The Free Encyclopedia*. Retrieved 19:39, May 30, 2018, from https://en.wikipedia.org/w/index.php?title=Mills_of_God&oldid=798884646

2. Strong, J. (1890, 1986). Strong's H1533. In *Strong's Exhaustive Concordance*. Abingdon Press. Biblehub.com. Retrieved from http://biblehub.com/hebrew/1533.htm
   Ebullition. (2018). Oxford Dictionaries. Oxford University Press. Oxforddictionaries.com. Retrieved from https://en.oxforddictionaries.com/definition/ebullition

3. Strong, J. (1890). Strong's H3671. In *Strong's Concordance* and *Occurrences in Text* (Num. 15:38 & Deut. 22:12). Biblehub.com. Retrieved from http://biblehub.com/hebrew/3671.htm

4. Numbers 15:38 LXX. (Strong's G4419 derivative of G4420 and equivalent to H3671). Studybible.info. Retrieved from https://studybible.info/LXX_WH/Numbers%2015

5. Strong, J. (1890). Strong's H3002. In *Strong's Concordance*. Biblehub.com. Retrieved from http://biblehub.com/hebrew/3002.htm
   Strong's H3002. (1997). In *NAS Exhaustive Concordance*. Foundation Publications Inc. Biblehub.com. Retrieved from http://biblehub.com/hebrew/3002.htm

6. Strong, J. (1890). Strong's H1732. In *Strong's Concordance*. Biblehub.com.
Retrieved from http://biblehub.com/hebrew/1732.htm
  Brown, F., Driver, S. R., & Briggs, C. A (2002, 2003, 2006). Strong's
H1732. In *Brown-Driver-Briggs Hebrew and English Lexicon*. Biblesoft, Inc.
Biblehub.com. Retrieved from http://biblehub.com/hebrew/1732.htm

7. Strong, J. (1890, 1986). Strong's H1730. In *Strong's Concordance* and *Strong's
Exhaustive Concordance*. Abingdon Press. Biblehub.com. Retrieved from
http://biblehub.com/hebrew/1730.htm
  Strong's H1730. (1997). In *NAS Exhaustive Concordance*. Foundation
Publications Inc. Biblehub.com. Retrieved from http://biblehub.com/
hebrew/1730.htm
  Brown, F., Driver, S. R., & Briggs, C. A (2002, 2003, 2006). Strong's
H1730. In *Brown-Driver-Briggs Hebrew and English Lexicon*. Biblesoft, Inc.
Biblehub.com. Retrieved from http://biblehub.com/hebrew/1730.htm

8. Parsons, J. J. *The Letter Dalet*. Hebrew for Christians. Retrieved from
http://www.hebrew4christians.com/Grammar/Unit_One/Aleph-Bet/
Dalet/dalet.html

9. Parsons, J. J. *The Letter Vav*. Hebrew for Christians. Retrieved from
http://www.hebrew4christians.com/Grammar/Unit_One/Aleph-Bet/
Vav/vav.html

10. Undocumented author. *Paleo-Hebrew pictograph table*. Retrieved from
http://4.bp.blogspot.com/-EGEBmngsbrM/UopKZbluHnI/
AAAAAAAAAM4/4XT-KNrfxwI/s1600/hebrew+chart.png

11. Trumbull, H. C. (1896). *The Threshold Covenant*. (pg 203). New York, C.
Scribner's Sons. Internet Archive. Retrieved from https://archive.org/
details/thresholdcovenan00trum

12. Wallace, J. W. (January 8, 2018). *What was the shape of Jesus' Cross?* (see X – Cross
Decussata) coldcasechristianity.com. Retrieved from http://
coldcasechristianity.com/2018/what-was-the-shape-of-jesus-cross/

13. Strong, J. (1890). Strong's G5361. In *Strong's Concordance*. Biblehub.com.
Retrieved from http://biblehub.com/greek/5361.htm

14. Parsons, J. J. *The Letter Yod.* Hebrew for Christians. Retrieved from http://www.hebrew4christians.com/Grammar/Unit_One/Aleph-Bet/Yod/yod.html

15. Dawn, A. (2017). *Love Covers All Transgressions.* Passion for Yeshua YouTube. Retrieved from https://youtu.be/MdQPKjum1OQ

Chapter 10

1. Strong, J. (1890, 1986). Strong's H2617. In *Strong's Concordance* and *Strong's Exhaustive Concordance.* Abingdon Press. Biblehub.com. Retrieved from hhttp://biblehub.com/hebrew/2617.htm

   Strong's H2617. (1997). In *NAS Exhaustive Concordance.* Foundation Publications Inc. Biblehub.com. Retrieved from http://biblehub.com/hebrew/2617.htm

   Brown, F., Driver, S. R., & Briggs, C. A (2002, 2003, 2006). Strong's H2617. In *Brown-Driver-Briggs Hebrew and English Lexicon.* Biblesoft, Inc. Biblehub.com. Retrieved from http://biblehub.com/hebrew/2617.htm

2. Strong, J. (1890, 1986). Strong's H2896. In *Strong's Concordance* and *Strong's Exhaustive Concordance.* Abingdon Press. Biblehub.com. Retrieved from http://biblehub.com/hebrew/2896.htm

   Strong's H2896. (1997). In *NAS Exhaustive Concordance.* Foundation Publications Inc. Biblehub.com. Retrieved from http://biblehub.com/hebrew/2896.htm

   Brown, F., Driver, S. R., & Briggs, C. A (2002, 2003, 2006). Strong's H2896. In *Brown-Driver-Briggs Hebrew and English Lexicon.* Biblesoft, Inc. Biblehub.com. Retrieved from http://biblehub.com/hebrew/2896.htm

3. Strong, J. (1890). Strong's H7832. In *Strong's Concordance.* Biblehub.com. Retrieved from http://biblehub.com/hebrew/378.htm

4. Strong, J. (1890, 1986). Strong's H7832. In *Strong's Concordance* and *Strong's Exhaustive Concordance.* Abingdon Press. Biblehub.com. Retrieved from http://biblehub.com/hebrew/7832.htm

   Strong's H7832. (1997). In *NAS Exhaustive Concordance.* Foundation Publications Inc. Biblehub.com. Retrieved from http://biblehub.com/hebrew/7832.htm

4. (con't) Brown, F., Driver, S. R., & Briggs, C. A (2002, 2003, 2006). Strong's H7832. In *Brown-Driver-Briggs Hebrew and English Lexicon*. Biblesoft, Inc. Biblehub.com. Retrieved from http://biblehub.com/hebrew/7832.htm

5. Strong, J. (1890). Strong's H520. In *Strong's Concordance*. Biblehub.com. Retrieved from http://biblehub.com/hebrew/520.htm
   Strong's H520. (1997). In *NAS Exhaustive Concordance*. Foundation Publications Inc. Biblehub.com. Retrieved from http://biblehub.com/hebrew/520.htm

6. Strong, J. (1890). Strong's H550. In *Strong's Concordance*. Biblehub.com. Retrieved from http://biblehub.com/hebrew/550.htm

7. Strong, J. (1890). Strong's H3609. In *Strong's Concordance* (meanings of both root words). Biblehub.com. Retrieved from http://biblehub.com/hebrew/3609.htm

8. Strong, J. (1890). Strong's H53. In *Strong's Concordance*. Biblehub.com. Retrieved from http://biblehub.com/hebrew/53.htm

9. Strong, J. (1890). Strong's H138. In *Strong's Concordance*. Biblehub.com. Retrieved from http://biblehub.com/hebrew/138.htm

10. Strong, J. (1890). Strong's H8203. In *Strong's Concordance*. Biblehub.com. Retrieved from http://biblehub.com/hebrew/8203.htm

11. Strong, J. (1890, 1986). Strong's H3507, H3499 & H5971. In *Strong's Concordance* and *Strong's Exhaustive Concordance*. Abingdon Press. Biblehub.com. Retrieved from http://biblehub.com/hebrew/3507.htm, http://biblehub.com/hebrew/3499.htm, and http://biblehub.com/hebrew/5971.htm
    Strong's H3507, H3499 & H5971. (1997). In *NAS Exhaustive Concordance*. Foundation Publications Inc. Biblehub.com. Retrieved from http://biblehub.com/hebrew/3507.htm, http://biblehub.com/hebrew/3499.htm, and http://biblehub.com/hebrew/5971.htm
    Brown, F., Driver, S. R., & Briggs, C. A (2002, 2003, 2006). Strong's H3507, H3499 & H5971. In *Brown-Driver-Briggs Hebrew and English Lexicon*. Biblesoft, Inc. Biblehub.com. Retrieved from http://biblehub.com/hebrew/3507.htm, http://biblehub.com/hebrew/3499.htm, and http://biblehub.com/hebrew/5971.htm

12. Strong, J. (1890). Strong's H6409. In *Strong's Concordance*. Biblehub.com. Retrieved from http://biblehub.com/hebrew/6409.htm

13. Ginzberg, L., Jastrow, M. Jr., Kohler, K., & Prince, J. D., (2002-2011). *Avenger of Blood*. Jewish Encyclopedia.com. Retrieved from http://jewishencyclopedia.com/articles/2162-avenger-of-blood

Chapter 11

1. Inductive Bible Study. *1 Samuel*. Indubiblia.org. Retrieved from https://sites.google.com/a/indubiblia.org/inductive-bible-study/1-samuel-1
   Chronology of David's Psalms. Retrieved from https://docs.google.com/document/d/1ytq4O-8AsXgXBiqkuln6EtggED6YiTx75GEljT5xbnc/edit#!

2. **Verses relating to Yeshua as the Son of David**: Matthew 1:1, Matthew 12:23, Matthew 15:22, Matthew 21:9, Mark 10:48, Mark 12:35, John 7:42, Romans 1:3, 2 Timothy 2:8, Revelation 5:5

3. Trumbull, H. C. (1896). *The Threshold Covenant*. (pg 203). New York, C. Scribner's Sons. Internet Archive. Retrieved from https://archive.org/details/thresholdcovenan00trum
4. ibid

5. Stanton, G. (2011). *Divorce Rate in the Church – as High as the World?* Focus on the Family.com. Retrieved from https://www.focusonthefamily.com/about/focus-findings/marriage/divorce-rate-in-the-church-as-high-as-the-world,
   McCormick, M. *Pornography in the Church: A New Epidemic*. Global Christian Center.com. Retrieved from http://globalchristiancenter.com/mens/overcoming-temptations/16765-pornography-in-the-church-a-new-epidemic,
   Bonewell, Dr. K. J. (January 21, 2011) *Adultery: Just the Statistics*. Kelly Bonewell.com. Retrieved from http://www.kellybonewell.com/adultery-just-the-statistics/

6. Kraft, V. (July 16, 2007) *Lesson 6: David Anointed Israel's King*. Bible.org. Retrieved from https://Bible.org/seriespage/lesson-6-david-anointed-israel's-king

7. Jamieson, R., Fausset, A. R., & Brown, D. (1871). In *Jamieson-Fausset-Brown Bible Commentary on 1 Sam. 16.* (see #12) Biblehub.com. Retrieved from https://www.biblestudytools.com/commentaries/jamieson-fausset-brown/1-samuel/1-samuel-16.html

8. Gill, J. (1746-63). In *Gill's Exposition of the Entire Bible for Gen. 39:20.* (see 3rd paragraph): Internet Sacred Texts Archive. Biblehub.com. Retrieved from http://biblehub.com/genesis/39-20.htm

9. Strong, J. (1890). Strong's H947. In *Strong's Concordance.* Biblehub.com. Retrieved from http://biblehub.com/hebrew/947.htm

10. Wikipedia contributors. (2018, May 18). Golden Gate (Jerusalem). In *Wikipedia, The Free Encyclopedia.* Retrieved 20:28, May 30, 2018, from https://en.wikipedia.org/w/index.php?title=Golden_Gate_(Jerusalem)&oldid=841812735

11. Stetzer, Ed. (May 14, 2014). *Drop Outs and Disciples: How Many Students Are Really Leaving the Church?* Christianity Today.com. Retrieved from http://www.christianitytoday.com/edstetzer/2014/may/dropouts-and-disciples-how-many-students-are-really-leaving.html

12. Peterson, R. A. (Sept. 1, 1983). *Education in Colonial America.* Foundation for Economic Education, Retrieved from https://fee.org/articles/education-in-colonial-america/

13. Strong, J. (1890). Strong's H1188. In *Strong's Concordance.* Biblehub.com. Retrieved from http://biblehub.com/hebrew/1188.htm

14. Inductive Bible Study. *1 Samuel.* Indubiblia.org. Retrieved from https://sites.google.com/a/indubiblia.org/inductive-bible-study/1-samuel-1
    Chronology of David's Psalms. Retrieved from https://docs.google.com/document/d/1ytq4O-8AsXgXBiqkuln6EtggED6YiTx75GEljT5xbnc/edit#!

Chapter 12

1. Wikipedia contributors. (2018, May 21). Lincoln's House Divided Speech. In *Wikipedia, The Free Encyclopedia*. Retrieved 20:31, May 30, 2018, from https://en.wikipedia.org/w/index.php?title=Lincoln%27s_House_Divided_Speech&oldid=842223658

2. Strong, J. (1890, 1986). Strong's H350. In *Strong's Exhaustive Concordance*. (both root words) Abingdon Press. Biblehub.com. Retrieved from http://biblehub.com/hebrew/350.htm

3. Strong, J. (1890). Strong's H1184. In *Strong's Concordance*. Biblehub.com. Retrieved from http://biblehub.com/hebrew/1184.htm

4. The Blue Letter Bible *"Chronological" Plan*, YouVersion, retrieved from https://www.bible.com/reading-plans/5#!

5. Strong, J. (1890). Strong's H2734. In *Strong's Concordance*. Biblehub.com. Retrieved from http://biblehub.com/hebrew/2734.htm

6. Strong, J. (1890). Strong's H6556. In *Strong's Concordance*. Biblehub.com. Retrieved from http://biblehub.com/hebrew/6556.htm

7. Orr, J. (1939). *Gittites*. In *International Standard Bible Encyclopedia*. Wm. B. Eerdman's Publishing Co. Biblehub.com. Retrieved from http://biblehub.com/topical/g/gittites.htm
Wikipedia contributors. (2018, April 22). Obed-Edom. In *Wikipedia, The Free Encyclopedia*. Retrieved 20:36, May 30, 2018, from https://en.wikipedia.org/w/index.php?title=Obed-Edom&oldid=837737770

8. Smith, W. (1863). *Gittites*. In *Smith's Bible Dictionary*. Biblehub.com. Retrieved from http://biblehub.com/topical/g/gittites.htm

9. Bible Atlas. *Gibeon*. Bibleatlas.org. Retrieved from http://bibleatlas.org/gibeon.htm

10. Wikipedia contributors. (2018, May 29). Tabernacle. In *Wikipedia, The Free Encyclopedia*. Retrieved 20:44, May 30, 2018, from https://en.wikipedia.org/w/index.php?title=Tabernacle&oldid=843545258

11. Bible Atlas. *Kiriath-Jearim*. Bibleatlas.org. Retrieved from
   http://bibleatlas.org/kiriath-jearim.htm

12. Bible Atlas. *Philistine Gath*. Bibleatlas.org. Retrieved from
   http://bibleatlas.org/gath.htm

13. Inductive Bible Study. *1 Samuel*. Indubiblia.org. Retrieved from
   https://sites.google.com/a/indubiblia.org/inductive-bible-study/1-
   samuel-1
   Chronology of David's Psalms. Retrieved from https://docs.google.com/
   document/d/1ytq4O-8AsXgXBiqkuln6EtggED6YiTx75GEljT5xbnc/
   edit#!

14. Wikipedia contributors. (2018, April 26). United we stand, divided we fall. In
   Wikipedia, The Free Encyclopedia. Retrieved 18:03, May 29, 2018, from
   https://en.wikipedia.org/w/index.php?
   title=United_we_stand,_dividedwe_fall&oldid=838389653

ABOUT THE AUTHOR

In addition to being author of this inaugural book, Angela Dawn is the recent founder, author, and poet of Passion For Yeshua blog and YouTube channel. An avid student and researcher of the Scriptures and ancient Middle East culture for over two decades, she occasionally leads Bible study and children's ministry for the home fellowship she and her family are regular members of near their home town of St. Louis, MO. Angela has also been an occasional conference presenter in the Pacific Northwest, where she was born and raised. She is a proud homeschooling mother of five and soon-to-be grandmother of two.

For Angela's complete testimony, please visit:
https://passionforyeshua.wordpress.com/my-testimony/

You can also follow Angela at https://www.instagram.com/passionforyeshua/

A NOTE FROM THE AUTHOR

It would be a tremendous blessing for me to hear/read testimonies of how this book has ministered to you and deepened your walk with YHVH. To contact me, please visit my website at www.keyofdavidlove.com. If you were blessed by this book and want to follow more revelations from my times in His Word, please visit my blog at passionforyeshua.wordpress.com

Blessings and Shalom!
Angela Dawn

CPSIA information can be obtained
at www.ICGtesting.com
Printed in the USA
BVHW040248190120
569943BV00005B/107

9 781948 812030